OXFORD practice tests
for the TOEIC® test

with key

TOEIC® IS A REGISTERED TRADEMARK OF EDUCATIONAL TESTING SERVICE (ETS). THIS PUBLICATION (OR PRODUCT) IS NOT ENDORSED OR APPROVED BY ETS OR THE CHAUNCEY GROUP INTERNATIONAL LTD. THE TOEIC® PROGRAM IS ADMINISTERED BY THE CHAUNCEY GROUP INTERNATIONAL LTD., A SUBSIDIARY OF EDUCATIONAL TESTING SERVICE.

OXFORD

2

Oxford University Press, Great Clarendon Street, Oxford OX2 6DP

Oxford New York
Athens Auckland Bangkok Bogotá
Buenos Aires Calcutta Cape Town Chennai
Dar es Salaam Delhi Florence Hong Kong
Istanbul Karachi Kuala Lumpur Madrid
Melbourne Mexico City Mumbai Nairobi
Paris São Paulo Singapore Taipei Tokyo
Toronto Warsaw

and associated companies in
Berlin Ibadan

OXFORD and OXFORD ENGLISH
are trade marks of Oxford University Press

ISBN 0 19 4535304

Printed in Hong Kong

The author and publisher would like to thank Corels for use of royalty-
free images.

Contents

INTRODUCTION

The Test of English for International Communication (TOEIC) was originally designed to test the English proficiency levels of people engaged in international business. However, the TOEIC® test has proven to be such a reliable measure of a test-taker's English language skills that it is now used for academic admissions, for placement purposes, and for measuring achievement. Over 1,500,000 people take the TOEIC test each year.

TOEIC test format

The TOEIC test is divided into two sections. These are Listening Comprehension and Reading. Each section contains 100 questions. You will need approximately 2½ hours to take the test.

Listening Comprehension	**45 minutes**
Part I Photographs	20 questions
Part II Question-response	30 questions
Part III Short conversations	30 questions
Part IV Short talks	20 questions

Reading	**75 minutes**
Part V Incomplete sentences	40 questions
Part VI Error recognition	20 questions
Part VII Reading comprehension	40 questions

Listening Comprehension

Part I Photographs

In this part, you will see a photograph and you will hear four sentences about it. You must choose the sentence that most closely matches what you see. You will hear the sentences once.

You will identify what you see in the photo. This may include people, objects, actions and locations both general and specific. You will also make assumptions; you may not be able to determine if something is actually taking place, but from the clues in the photo, you can assume that it is.

Traps

The three incorrect sentences will contain words that may make them appear correct. A word may have a similar sound to something in the photo (e.g., a *sheep* rather than the *ship* pictured). The sentence may contain a word which has more than one meaning (e.g., a *bottle of port wine* rather than a *ship in port*). There may be a suitable word included which is used inappropriately (e.g., *He is opening the window*. There is a *window* in the photo, but nobody is *opening* it).

Strategies

Scan the picture quickly and try to identify as much as you can. Ask yourself questions: Who (gender, description, occupation) is in the photo? What is happening? Where was the photo taken? When listening, focus on the words that are easier to hear, the stressed words, as they carry the overall meaning.

Part II Question-response

In this part, you will hear a question and three possible responses. You must choose the response that best answers the question. You will hear the question and each response once.

The question may ask about people, location, time, an activity, an event, emotions, reasons, or opinions. In short, the question could be on almost any subject.

Traps

As in Part I, words may sound similar or be used out of context. Words from the question may be repeated in the response, but be used inaccurately. In addition, there is a potential trap with grammar. You will hear different types of questions: *wh-*questions (*who, what, when, where, why,* and *how*), *yes/no* questions and tag questions. When you hear a *yes/no* or a tag question, you may assume that the response will begin with *Yes* or *No*. In the TOEIC test, as in real life, the response may answer the question indirectly instead. For example:

> *Is there any cake left?*
>
> *(A) I ate the last piece.*
> *(B) Yes, the lake is on the left.*
> *(C) No, I left early.*

(A) is the correct option. The respondent doesn't answer with *yes/no* as would be expected. However, we know the answer *is* no, because the respondent ate *the last piece.*

Strategies

You will have to exercise your short-term memory. You must remember the question until you have picked the appropriate response. If you really don't know the answer, then guess. Choose the response that sounds most natural to you, don't leave any questions unanswered.

Part III Short conversations

In this part, you will hear a short dialog. You will read a question and four answer choices in your test booklet. You must choose the option that best answers the question. You will only hear the dialog once.

The question will ask about the general idea of the conversation; usually it will not focus on specific details. You will be asked to identify an activity, an emotion, a relationship, or the location of the speakers. In some instances you may have to do some minor calculations based on measurements in the dialog.

Traps

As in Parts I and II, words may sound similar or be used out of context. Words may be repeated in the options, but be used inaccurately. In addition, listen out for words that can add to or change meaning. Listen carefully for words that indicate time (e.g., *before, until, while, afterwards*, etc.) and words that indicate negation (e.g., *not, hardly, seldom, by no means*, etc.).

The dialog may compare two or more things so listen for words that show degrees of comparisons.

Modals (e.g., *can, could, ought to,* etc.) indicate possibility and advisability. Listen carefully for modals to determine the intent of the speakers.

Word order is also a potential trap. A sentence such as *Never has the weather been so unpredictable* means *The weather is usually predictable*.

Strategies

Try to read the question before you hear the dialog. If you have time, read the answer choices as well. Look at *all* the options, before choosing your answer. As you listen, imagine the speakers and their location.

Part IV Short talks

In this part, you will hear a short monologue about which you will read two or three questions in your test booklet. For each question, you must choose the correct answer from four options. You will only hear the monologue once.

The talks can be in the form of recorded announcements, weather forecasts, special bulletins, etc. The questions will ask you to determine the location, the speaker, the time, the event, or a reason.

Traps

The traps that were set for you in Parts I, II and III are set once again.

Strategies

This is a very difficult section because you have to listen carefully and remember specific details. It is important that you try to read the questions before you hear the talk. If you have time, try to read the answer choices as well. However, you should listen to the whole talk before attempting to answer any of the questions. Timing is crucial in this part. If you cannot read and answer the question in the 8 second pause then don't worry, but move on to the next one. Don't get left behind on the tape.

Reading

Part V Incomplete sentences

In this part, you will read a sentence with one word or phrase missing and four possible choices to fill the blank. You will choose the best word or phrase.

Both your knowledge of vocabulary and your knowledge of grammar are tested. You will have to understand the meaning of the sentence to choose a vocabulary item. You may have to apply your knowledge of phrasal verbs and set expressions. You will, in some instances, have to understand the grammatical function of the *blank* to choose the correct grammatical form of a word. The grammar forms tested most frequently are verb tense, pronouns, prepositions, conjunctions and comparisons with adjectives and adverbs.

Traps

In the items that test grammar, many of the choices are attractive because they seem to complete the meaning of the sentence. However, they may not be grammatically correct. You have to pay close attention to the word endings and make sure you choose the correct grammatical form required.

Strategies

You must develop a quick pace for the Reading section. You have 75 minutes for 100 items. There are 60 items in Parts V and VI. You should save most of your time for the reading passages in Part VII. Try to answer a question in 30 seconds. If the answer is not apparent to you, quickly move on. Return to the unanswered questions after you reach the end of Part VII. Always go back and check your answers at the end if there is time.

Part VI Error recognition

In this part, you will read a sentence with four words or phrases underlined. You must choose the underlined word or phrase which is incorrectly written.

Only grammar is tested. The focus is mainly on errors with subject/verb agreement, pronoun agreement, and word family distinctions. Errors with prepositions are common and occasionally there will be mistakes with verb tense and verb form.

The words that are *not* underlined are always correct.

Traps

A common trap is to insert a word that does not belong. This is usually a pronoun in the subject position e.g., *The workers they are on strike*, or a pronoun which is incorrectly used e.g., *She is going to interview Mr. Robinson itself*.

Strategies

Check each underlined section for an error. If no error is apparent, take each option and see if that word or phrase fits the sentence grammatically. Do not take time to correct an error (even in your head).

Part VII Reading

You will read a passage followed by 2–5 questions. You will have to answer the questions based on the information in the passage. Each question has four options.

You will have to interpret the information in advertisements, forms, reports, correspondence, tables, graphs, announcements, articles, and schedules.

Traps

Many of the answer options repeat information that is found in the passage, but in a different context. Make sure the option you choose directly answers the question.

Strategies

Read over the questions before you read the passage. Don't look at the answer options. Read the passage quickly to get a general idea. Don't worry about words you don't understand. Then read it again more carefully and try to find the answers to the questions as you read. After that, choose from the options. The questions usually match the order information is presented in the passage.

Be familiar with the type of passages that will be presented.

Studying for the TOEIC test

As you take a practice test, pay attention to the way you work through the test. Keep track of your time. Note how long you spend on a part; estimate how long you spend on an item. Ask yourself how you can improve your speed. Try to develop your own test-taking rhythm.

Use the cassette tape to develop your memory. After you take a test, go back to the Listening section and play the tape again. Try to repeat each sentence you hear in your head and hold it in your memory. You can also try this in your own language when you listen to the radio or television. Try to repeat exactly what the announcer says. It is possible to improve your ability to remember. For the TOEIC test, a good memory is a necessity.

Use the explanatory answers in the back of this book. Use them to learn why you made an error and how the test tried to trap you. There will be a lot of new words, phrases and ideas in this book. Taking these practice TOEIC tests will not only help you become comfortable with the test, but will definitely help you improve your English.

Answer sheets and Conversion table

In the exam you will have to put your answers on an Answer sheet, and you can practise doing this by using the Answer sheets provided at the back of the book.

A score conversion table is included on the inside back cover. This converts the scores of the Oxford practice tests and does not correlate with the actual TOEIC tests. The table provides you with an approximation of your total actual score for the practice tests, and can be used to assess your performance as you work through them.

Practice Test One

LISTENING COMPREHENSION

In this section of the test, you will have the chance to show how well you understand spoken English. There are four parts to this section, with special directions for each part.

PART I

Directions: For each question, you will see a picture in your test book and you will hear four short statements. The statements will be spoken just one time. They will not be printed in your test book, so you must listen carefully to understand what the speaker says.

When you hear the four statements, look at the picture in your test book and choose the statement that best describes what you see in the picture. Then, on your answer sheet, find the number of the question and mark your answer. Look at the sample below.

Sample Answer
Ⓐ ● Ⓒ Ⓓ

Now listen to the four statements.

Statement (B), "They're having a meeting," best describes what you see in the picture. Therefore, you should choose answer (B).

GO ON TO THE NEXT PAGE ➤

1.

2.

3.

4.

GO ON TO THE NEXT PAGE ►

5.

6.

7.

8.

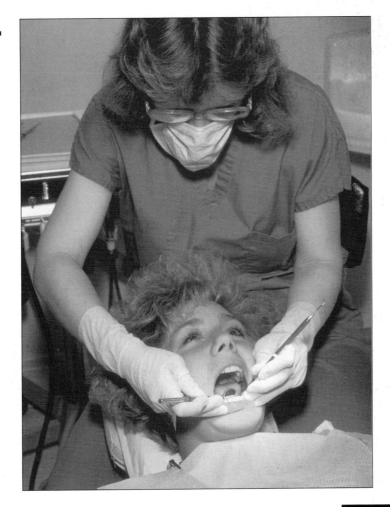

GO ON TO THE NEXT PAGE ▶

9.

10.

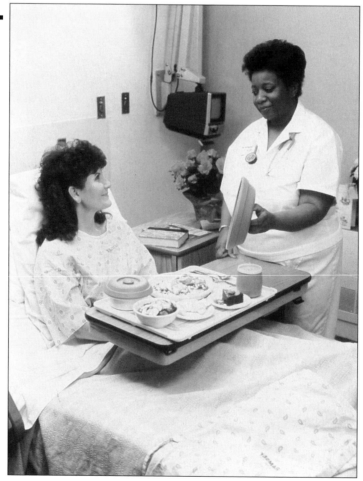

11.

12.

GO ON TO THE NEXT PAGE ▶

13.

14.

15.

16.

GO ON TO THE NEXT PAGE ➤

17.

18.

19.

20.

GO ON TO THE NEXT PAGE ▶

PART II

Directions: In this part of the test, you will hear a question spoken in English, followed by three responses, also spoken in English. The question and the responses will be spoken just one time. They will not be printed in your test book, so you must listen carefully to understand what the speakers say. You are to choose the best response to each question.

Now listen to a sample question.

You will hear:

Sample Answer

You will also hear:

The best response to the question "How are you?" is choice (A), "I am fine, thank you." Therefore, you should choose answer (A).

21. Mark your answer on your answer sheet.

22. Mark your answer on your answer sheet.

23. Mark your answer on your answer sheet.

24. Mark your answer on your answer sheet.

25. Mark your answer on your answer sheet.

26. Mark your answer on your answer sheet.

27. Mark your answer on your answer sheet.

28. Mark your answer on your answer sheet.

29. Mark your answer on your answer sheet.

30. Mark your answer on your answer sheet.

31. Mark your answer on your answer sheet.

32. Mark your answer on your answer sheet.

33. Mark your answer on your answer sheet.

34. Mark your answer on your answer sheet.

35. Mark your answer on your answer sheet.

36. Mark your answer on your answer sheet.

37. Mark your answer on your answer sheet.

38. Mark your answer on your answer sheet.

39. Mark your answer on your answer sheet.

40. Mark your answer on your answer sheet.

41. Mark your answer on your answer sheet.

42. Mark your answer on your answer sheet.

43. Mark your answer on your answer sheet.

44. Mark your answer on your answer sheet.

45. Mark your answer on your answer sheet.

46. Mark your answer on your answer sheet.

47. Mark your answer on your answer sheet.

48. Mark your answer on your answer sheet.

49. Mark your answer on your answer sheet.

50. Mark your answer on your answer sheet.

GO ON TO THE NEXT PAGE

PART III

Directions: In this part of the test, you will hear thirty short conversations between two people. The conversations will not be printed in your test book. You will hear the conversations only once, so you must listen carefully to understand what the speakers say.

In your test book, you will read a question about each conversation. The question will be followed by four answers. You are to choose the best answer to each question and mark it on your answer sheet.

51. What time is the departing flight?

   (A) 8:30
   (B) 11:00
   (C) 12:00
   (D) 12:30

52. Where are they?

   (A) In an office.
   (B) At an airport.
   (C) At a doctor's office.
   (D) In a restaurant.

53. What is being discussed?

   (A) Travel.
   (B) A bus station.
   (C) Rodents.
   (D) Computer training.

54. What is the woman concerned about?

   (A) What time the meeting starts.
   (B) If the chairman will be there.
   (C) If she'll be on time for the match.
   (D) Who won the contest.

55. Who will deliver the paper?

   (A) The mailman.
   (B) The supply clerk.
   (C) The receptionist.
   (D) The company's own service.

56. What is the man concerned about?

   (A) The heat wave.
   (B) Mrs. Kahn's workload.
   (C) The work schedule.
   (D) Dania's health.

57. Whose service is the man upset about?

   (A) The dry cleaner's.
   (B) The tailor's.
   (C) A clothing store's.
   (D) A courier's.

58. What is the man about to do?

   (A) Enter an empty room.
   (B) Enter a waiting room.
   (C) Get into a taxi.
   (D) Get on an aeroplane.

59. Where will the ad be placed?

   (A) On TV.
   (B) In a newspaper.
   (C) On the radio.
   (D) In the Human Resources office.

60. What day is it?

   (A) Wednesday.
   (B) Thursday.
   (C) Friday.
   (D) Saturday.

61. Why weren't there enough binders?

   (A) Mary forgot to order them.
   (B) The supplier misrouted the shipment.
   (C) They were out of stock.
   (D) The wrong number were ordered.

62. What is the company offering?

   (A) Dental care.
   (B) Bridge repairal services.
   (C) Cleaning services.
   (D) Free physicals.

63. What is known about the elevator?

   (A) It can only hold five people.
   (B) It works well going up.
   (C) The doors get stuck in the open position.
   (D) It isn't working at all.

64. Why is the customer going to a different store?

   (A) He doesn't like the printer this store has.
   (B) This store is out of stock.
   (C) This store doesn't have the model he needs.
   (D) The printer in this store isn't working right.

65. What are the secretaries going to do?

   (A) Take up jogging.
   (B) Go on vacation.
   (C) Go for job training.
   (D) Transfer to another branch.

66. What is the problem?

   (A) The driver is late.
   (B) Marie can't get the money for the rentals.
   (C) The rental company needs more notice.
   (D) A bill needs to be paid.

67. Where are the speakers?

   (A) In a key store.
   (B) In a hotel restaurant.
   (C) In a friend's dining room.
   (D) In a liquor store.

68. Who is the man talking to?

   (A) A building manager.
   (B) An office receptionist.
   (C) An answering service.
   (D) A customer service representative.

69. What does the woman need to do?

   (A) Have her house cleaned.
   (B) Dry out her dress.
   (C) Get her skirt ironed.
   (D) Catch an express train.

70. What interested them originally about the brick house?

   (A) The garage.
   (B) The basement.
   (C) The front porch.
   (D) The location.

71. Why is the manager not available?

   (A) He's meeting with his assistant.
   (B) He went to lunch.
   (C) He's speaking with a customer.
   (D) He's out sick today.

72. Where are the speakers now?

   (A) In a hotel room.
   (B) At a drugstore.
   (C) In the reception area.
   (D) At an intersection.

73. Who is the woman talking to?

   (A) A dry cleaning attendant.
   (B) A cleaning company representative.
   (C) A baker.
   (D) A dental receptionist.

74. What are the speakers discussing?

   (A) A CD player.
   (B) A car.
   (C) A cassette player.
   (D) A driveway.

75. What is the current bond program for?

   (A) A building.
   (B) A subway system.
   (C) A bridge.
   (D) A tunnel.

76. Who is the man talking to?

   (A) A car rental agency.
   (B) A travel agent.
   (C) A department store salesperson.
   (D) A camping gear sales representative.

GO ON TO THE NEXT PAGE

77. What is Sonya trying to do?

   (A) Understand the software.
   (B) Read a spreadsheet report.
   (C) Register at a technical school.
   (D) Explain technology.

78. What is John being asked to do?

   (A) Determine the best alarm system.
   (B) Find more office space.
   (C) Interview the research department.
   (D) Work in customer services.

79. How many full-time typists are needed?

   (A) One.
   (B) Two.
   (C) Five.
   (D) Six.

80. Where are they?

   (A) In a book store.
   (B) In a card store.
   (C) In a library.
   (D) In a bank.

PART IV

Directions: In this part of the test, you will hear several short talks. Each will be spoken just one time. They will not be printed in your test book, so you must listen carefully to understand and remember what is said.

In your test book, you will read two or more questions about each short talk. The questions will be followed by four answers. You are to choose the best answer to each question and mark it on your answer sheet.

81. Who is giving this announcement?

    (A) Pet owners.
    (B) The Department of Health.
    (C) The City Town Hall.
    (D) The Animal Rescue League.

82. What is being provided?

    (A) Medical check-ups for pets.
    (B) Free kittens and puppies under five months.
    (C) Rabies vaccinations.
    (D) A seminar on the proper care of house pets.

83. What are participants asked to do?

    (A) Fill out paperwork.
    (B) Volunteer time for screening participants.
    (C) Register their pets at the Department of Health.
    (D) Provide proof of ownership of a pet.

84. What is this report about?

    (A) A traffic accident.
    (B) Power supply problems in Manila.
    (C) Electrical costs in the downtown area.
    (D) A customer rebate program.

85. What were local office building managers asked to do?

    (A) Turn off half of all the office lights.
    (B) Limit the installation of elevators.
    (C) Reduce their electrical consumption voluntarily.
    (D) Assist in cleaning up after the accident.

86. How many substations were affected?

    (A) One.
    (B) Two.
    (C) Three.
    (D) Four.

87. What is Mr. Wiley's new job?

    (A) Hamford district's marketing director.
    (B) Chicago's department head.
    (C) Marlboro district's sales assistant.
    (D) The Federal Highway office manager.

88. What will also be expected of Mr. Wiley?

    (A) To act as a liaison between the Marlboro and Hamford offices.
    (B) To inspect the quality of the used cars.
    (C) To devise a new marketing plan for Hamford.
    (D) To give monthly training sessions.

89. For whom is this notice particularly helpful?

    (A) Anyone planning on moving.
    (B) Long distance callers.
    (C) Moving companies.
    (D) Utilities personnel.

90. What is the purpose of this notice?

    (A) To give a warning.
    (B) To announce a change.
    (C) To provide information.
    (D) To revise a previous notice.

91. What should one remember when contacting the cable company?

    (A) To give them your new address.
    (B) To ask them about extra charges.
    (C) To have them remove the control box.
    (D) To ask how much the deposits are.

92. What is this news story about?

    (A) Oslo Disks new CDs.
    (B) The opening of a CD manufacturing plant.
    (C) Japanese and Norwegian trade relations.
    (D) Improvements in the Hillside District.

GO ON TO THE NEXT PAGE

93. Where does the production technology come from?

(A) Japan.
(B) Norway.
(C) Germany.
(D) Denmark.

94. Who may sell their distribution rights?

(A) Oslo Disks.
(B) World Records.
(C) Wadushi Corporation.
(D) Euro Records.

95. Who is most likely giving this talk?

(A) A manager.
(B) A fellow staff member.
(C) A department head.
(D) A secretary.

96. Why is the speaker addressing the group?

(A) To introduce new employees to the department heads.
(B) To announce a change in office hours.
(C) To let them know when he is available.
(D) To introduce Alex.

97. Where is the speaker's office located?

(A) To the left of the elevator.
(B) To the right of the water fountain.
(C) On the top floor.
(D) On the seventh floor.

98. What is the purpose of the AJGA?

(A) To train professional golfers.
(B) To promote and fund international competitions.
(C) To ensure the growth and development of young golfers.
(D) To act as a public relations arm to the players.

99. Why would a junior golfer join the AJGA?

(A) To have an opportunity to play abroad.
(B) To develop competitive skills.
(C) To gain acceptance into a college.
(D) To get a chance to travel all over the U.S.

100. Who are the people mentioned at the end of the announcement?

(A) Former members of the AJGA.
(B) Founders of the AJGA.
(C) Trainers for the AJGA.
(D) Members of the Board of Directors of the AJGA.

This is the end of the Listening Comprehension portion of Practice Test One. Turn to Part V in your test book.

YOU WILL HAVE ONE HOUR AND FIFTEEN MINUTES TO COMPLETE PARTS V, VI, AND VII OF THE TEST.

READING

In this section of the test, you will have a chance to show how well you understand written English. There are three parts to this section, with special directions for each part.

PART V

Directions: Questions 101–140 are incomplete sentences. Four words or phrases, marked (A), (B), (C), (D) are given beneath each sentence. You are to choose the **one** word or phrase that best completes the sentence. Then, on your answer sheet, find the number of the question and mark your answer.

You will read:

Because the equipment is very delicate, it must be handled with ....

Sample Answer
Ⓐ Ⓑ ● Ⓓ

(A) caring
(B) careful
(C) care
(D) carefully

The sentence should read, "Because the equipment is very delicate, it must be handled with care." Therefore, you should choose answer (C).

Now begin work on the questions.

---

101. The hotel management and the union are at a .... regarding the benefits package.

    (A) stalling
    (B) point
    (C) standstill
    (D) draw

102. The town hopes to collect enough money from the municipal bonds to pay .... the bridge repairs.

    (A) out
    (B) for
    (C) into
    (D) by

103. Jan is working as an .... with Global Printers.

    (A) appellant
    (B) apprentice
    (C) applicant
    (D) appendant

104. I .... it best to look over the competition before deciding to start a consulting business in this town.

    (A) thought
    (B) pondered
    (C) liked
    (D) wondered

105. A car today produces 70% .... pollutants than ten years ago.

    (A) fewer
    (B) less
    (C) lower
    (D) minimal

106. We have two representatives from the Conservative Party who .... invited to speak at the opening ceremonies.

    (A) been
    (B) was
    (C) were
    (D) had

GO ON TO THE NEXT PAGE

107. The lecturer was neither on time .... prepared.

   (A) or
   (B) nor
   (C) and
   (D) but

108. The public utility companies have been forced .... over fifty new personnel to help with all the repairs.

   (A) hired
   (B) hiring
   (C) hire
   (D) to hire

109. Solving environmental problems cannot simply be .... the next generation.

   (A) formulated with
   (B) finished at
   (C) relegated to
   (D) moved over

110. The soybean has provided .... with more than a hundred different products.

   (A) us
   (B) our
   (C) we
   (D) ourselves

111. "If you had examined each factor individually," she argued, "you .... that the error was theirs."

   (A) would have seen
   (B) would have been seeing
   (C) had seen
   (D) saw

112. As a limited ...., she rarely engages in the internal administration of the company.

   (A) partnering
   (B) partnership
   (C) partner
   (D) partners

113. She took the new high speed train .... was advertised on the radio.

   (A) it
   (B) who
   (C) what
   (D) that

114. Her supervisor was very .... in her choice of words when pointing out areas that need improvement.

   (A) discrepant
   (B) discreet
   (C) dissolute
   (D) dissonant

115. A .... of duty motivated him more so than money.

   (A) motion
   (B) sense
   (C) touch
   (D) manner

116. The .... had eroded along the bank.

   (A) soils
   (B) soiling
   (C) soiled
   (D) soil

117. Gloria offered to .... the hall for the celebrations.

   (A) precede
   (B) presume
   (C) predate
   (D) prepare

118. The president of .... Bradford Businessman's Association is hosting the celebration.

   (A) a
   (B) the
   (C) one
   (D) for

119. Certain leathers will .... when treated with oil.

(A) shade
(B) darken
(C) shadow
(D) heighten

120. The company .... the entire staff with an additional two days of vacation.

(A) granted
(B) offered
(C) rewarded
(D) awarded

121. The speeches were given while the guests .... the meal.

(A) enjoyed
(B) enjoying
(C) having enjoyed
(D) enjoyable

122. Professor Haage, as a public speaker, is .... than Professor Doyle.

(A) more entertaining
(B) very entertaining
(C) most entertaining
(D) the more entertaining

123. All departments .... their deadlines will be given a substantial bonus.

(A) meeting
(B) met
(C) will meet
(D) to meet

124. At the time it ...., the contract satisfied all parties.

(A) sign
(B) signed
(C) was signing
(D) was signed

125. Burning tires is .... by law in most states.

(A) prohibited
(B) professed
(C) proclaimed
(D) procured

126. A warm muscle will stretch .... easily than a cold one.

(A) more
(B) some
(C) most
(D) any

127. After she examined the pistons, ... obvious to her that someone had tampered with the speedometer.

(A) they were
(B) she was
(C) it was
(D) those were

128. The Taj Mahal is a must for tourists .... India.

(A) visits
(B) visiting
(C) visit
(D) visited

129. Affordable electric cars will be available .... in the near future.

(A) some
(B) sometime
(C) something
(D) somewhat

130. Our technical department is racing to develop the technology that will give us the competitive edge we'll need .... our profit trend.

(A) to maintain
(B) will maintain
(C) maintain
(D) be maintaining

GO ON TO THE NEXT PAGE

131. The guard gave .... instructions to leave the messages on the phone pad.

    (A) old
    (B) insignificant
    (C) delayed
    (D) explicit

132. Vietnam's first oil refinery .... Dung Quat was a joint venture with French and Malaysian petroleum companies.

    (A) between
    (B) to
    (C) in
    (D) aside

133. The client will reconsider the offer .... you decide to open an office in Taiwan.

    (A) considering
    (B) must
    (C) were
    (D) should

134. Mrs. Corritas always ships her orders out in a .... fashion.

    (A) quickly
    (B) hastily
    (C) timely
    (D) promptly

135. Our family was once a majority shareholder in a company that .... everything during the Depression.

    (A) lose
    (B) was losing
    (C) lost
    (D) to lose

136. Exercise, ... with a sound nutritional plan, is her formula for staying healthy.

    (A) together
    (B) according
    (C) instead
    (D) besides

137. Dr. Klein will be able to meet with us this afternoon .... we can make it.

    (A) if
    (B) which
    (C) under
    (D) how

138. The market crashed right .... he sold most of his stocks.

    (A) since
    (B) after
    (C) at
    (D) yet

139. In this course, you will be learning the most widely used method of taking inventory .... maintaining inventory records.

    (A) to
    (B) because
    (C) and
    (D) with

140. This tax issue is .... our own party.

    (A) dividing
    (B) cutting
    (C) limiting
    (D) distributing

PART VI

Directions: In **Questions 141–160**, each sentence has four words or phrases underlined. The four underlined parts of the sentence are marked (A), (B), (C), (D). You are to identify the **one** underlined word or phrase that should be corrected or rewritten. Then, on your answer sheet, find the number of the question and mark your answer.

Example:

All employee are required to wear their
   A   B

identification badges while at work.
   C   D

Sample Answer
● Ⓑ Ⓒ Ⓓ

The underlined word "employee" is not correct in this sentence. This sentence should read, "All employees are required to wear their identification badges while at work." Therefore, you should choose answer (A).

Now begin work on the questions.

141. The computer training covered everything from
                       A   B
to making a file to creating a database.
   C   D

142. All three towns affected by the earthquake they
        A   B
have applied for federal aid and
    C
other emergency relief.
    D

143. I don't believe there is anyone best suited for
     A   B   C
the job than Mrs. Marellis.
       D

144. Proofreading a technical article is difficulty for
    A   B
most editors, unless they are very familiar with
                          C   D
the subject.

145. Clients still do not avail themselves of
      A   B
up-to-date investment informations,
           C
despite every effort to provide them with it.
      D

146. Library visitors often find that there are too few
            A   B
staff members available to assist them,
especially as funding for libraries have been cut
       C   D
back.

147. The Library of Congress, build to serve
                     A
senators and congressmen who were living in
                         B
D.C., is now open to the
        C
general public free of charge.
      D

148. On our tour of the east coast branch offices,
         A
Zachary, the company's photographer and the
               B
boss's administrative assistant,
         C
will accompanying us.
      D

GO ON TO THE NEXT PAGE

149. Our specific trained engineers have redesigned
    ___A___   ___B___
    the model in accordance with the client's new
             _____C_____ ___D___
    specifications.

150. Today, with highly advanced technology
           _A_
    at their disposal, surgeons are operated with a
    _____B_____   ____C____
    precision undreamed of twenty years ago.
              _____D_____

151. As usual, tourists will be encouraged to try
    _____A_____   _____B_____
    hang glide and mountain climbing
    _____C_____
    when they visit the Appalachians.
    _____D_____

152. I can tell you if your loan has approved just
           __A__   ___B___
    as soon as the credit report arrives.
    ____C____   ___D___

153. The international yacht show, being held in
                                 ____A____
    Florida this year, will attract many
                       ____B____
    boating enthusiasts from around world.
             __C__   ___D___

154. Having been trained in the laws of the host
    _____A_____
    country, I can attest to the fact that it is crucial to
            _____B_____   __C__
    a success export business.
    _____D_____

155. The supervising manager ordered two dozens
        _____A_____   ____B____
    roses for the main table and mixed flowers for
            _____C_____   _____D_____
    the lobby.

156. We looked to hundreds of documents before we
       ___A___   _____B_____
    found what we were looking for.
    __C__   ___D___

157. Counted on the continued expansion of the
    ___A___   _____B_____
    Asian markets, government economists

    are still issuing predictions of no inflation.
    _____C_____   ___D___

158. All South China Sea harbors have been
    _A_   ____B____
    temporarily closed to either commercial and
              __C__   __D__
    private traffic.

159. Fishing permits are normally issued to for
    _____A_____   ____B____
    only one season and for a limited number of
            __C__   _____D_____
    fish.

160. The pressing supplies that are purchased for
        _____A_____   _____B_____
    this project were mistakenly left at the store.
                      ___C___   __D__

PART VII

Directions: Questions 161–200 are based on a selection of reading materials, such as notices, letters, forms, newspaper and magazine articles, and advertisements. You are to choose the **one** best answer (A), (B), (C), or (D) to each question. Then, on your answer sheet, find the number of the question and mark your answer. Answer all questions following each reading selection on the basis of what is **stated** or **implied** in that selection.

Read the following example.

The Museum of Technology is a "hands-on" museum, designed for people to experience science at work. Visitors are encouraged to use, test, and handle the objects on display. Special demonstrations are scheduled for the first and second Wednesdays of each month at 13:30. Open Tuesday–Friday 12:00–16:30, Saturday 10:00–17:30, and Sunday 11:00–16:30.

When during the month can visitors see special demonstrations?

Sample Answer
Ⓐ ● Ⓒ Ⓓ

(A)   Every weekend
(B)   The first two Wednesdays
(C)   One afternoon a week
(D)   Every other Wednesday

The reading selection says that the demonstrations are scheduled for the first and second Wednesdays of the month. Therefore, you should choose answer (B).

Now begin work on the questions.

Questions 161–162 refer to the following article.

A document is the representation of the contract drawn up by the organization delivering service.

There are five categories of documents in the export industry. The first is a document of dispatch. This has to do with the activity of the exporter moving goods inside the country to the point of exit – the docks or the airport.

The second is shipping documents. These cover the movement of goods from one country to another. The third and fourth are customs forms and official invoices, which are special forms required by the importing country. They are prepared, though, by the exporter. The fifth is bank documents. These involve all aspects of the payment process.

161. What is this article about?

(A) The storage and retrieval of documents
(B) The number of export transactions in most organizations
(C) The manner in which export activity is documented
(D) The responsibility of the exporter to the importer

162. Which document would be used to release goods from the originating warehouse?

(A) Bank document
(B) Shipping document
(C) Customs document
(D) Dispatch document

GO ON TO THE NEXT PAGE

MEMORANDUM

To: Comptroller
          Treasurer

From: Jack Sidwell
Date: January 7

The financial section of *The Enteraunt* today reports that many new hotels and restaurants are beginning to falter and that bankruptcies may be on the horizon.

I would like you to take the following actions:
1. Review our credit terms and collection activities and tighten up where necessary.
2. Work out a program whereby we can reduce our average collection period from the current 60 days to 40 days, or better.

Please pay special attention to the hotel in Birmingham. I have reviewed their file and we have been much too lax in our collection efforts. In all cases, follow company policy and report what you are doing to address these issues.

163. Why was this memo written?

(A) As a preventive measure to preclude any nonpayment
(B) To announce a change in credit requirements
(C) To admonish administrators for not following policy
(D) To inform the staff that a hotel had collapsed

164. What specific change has Mr. Sidwell asked for?

(A) That no new hotels be financed
(B) That the time spent on filing reports be reduced
(C) That the collection time be shortened
(D) That more attention be paid to restaurant clients

Questions 165–167 refer to the following news item.

 In Moldavia, the second growing season for grape-laden vines is about to begin. Covered with protective nets and buried in snow, the grapes will be harvested just before they become frozen solid. The grapes are used to make icewine, the most renowned and generally most expensive wine in the area. This unconventional technique produces a fragrant dessert-style wine that, since the early 1980s, has become a staple of Moldavian wine growers. Icewine is also made in smaller quantities in Oregon and New Hampshire states as well as in Bavaria. Icewine is unknown to many wine drinking people largely because it's nearly impossible to produce in areas where the winters aren't harsh.

165. Where is icewine most abundantly produced?

(A) Bavaria
(B) New Hampshire
(C) Moldavia
(D) Oregon

166. What is necessary to grow grapes that will produce icewine?

(A) The grapes must be frozen solid.
(B) It must be severely cold.
(C) The vines must be able to produce a second crop before winter.
(D) The vines must be supported by nets when they are snow-laden.

167. Why is icewine not more widely known?

(A) Because production is limited
(B) Because its pungent fragrance produces a limited market
(C) Because dessert wines are not popular
(D) Because it is very expensive

GO ON TO THE NEXT PAGE

While Vietnam was still under colonial rule in 1912, the Oriental Metropolis Hotel was the center of life in Nha Trang. Visiting dignitaries, artists and celebrities made it their home. Renovated to its original style and charm in 1990, the building has all the flavor of the era in which it was built. Having proudly achieved recognition as the country's first officially accredited five-star hotel, this hotel complex now also houses several banks, multinational corporations and embassies. The Oriental Metropolis Hotel is the only international hotel located in the commercial and tourist heart of Nha Trang, right off Highway 200, adjacent to the Bai Noi Trade Center. Ho Chi Minh City is only a half hour train ride away.

ORIENTAL METROPOLIS HOTEL

168. What is the hotel's biggest accomplishment?

(A) It attracts celebrities and dignitaries.
(B) It is still the center of activity in Nha Trang.
(C) It achieved five-star status.
(D) It purchased a multinational corporation.

169. What happened in 1990?

(A) Colonial rule ended.
(B) The building was restored.
(C) The hotel was officially accredited.
(D) Embassies became part of the complex.

170. What is in walking distance from the hotel?

(A) The Bai Noi Trade Center
(B) The train station
(C) Ho Chi Minh City
(D) The Nha Trang industrial complex

Questions 171–174 refer to the following letter.

May 12, 20—

Taxpayer Identification Number: 3991DS

Form : 1040
Document Locator Number: 0277D

Internal Revenue Service
P.O. Box 987
Industrial Village, NV 37885

Attn: Chief, Taxpayer Review Board

I am writing to propose a payment schedule for my overdue taxes. Because my tax bill was $2,100 more than expected, I would like to pay the balance in monthly installments starting on September 1, as follows:

Payment 1, September 1 $350.00

through

Payment 6, February 1 $350.00
                             $2,100.00

Next month, I will pay whatever interest and penalties have accrued.

$2,600 has already been paid toward my total tax owed of $4,700.

Please let me know if this proposal meets with your approval.

Sincerely,

W.T. Tackst
W.T. Tackst

---

171. Why is the taxpayer's payment late?

(A) Her 1040 arrived late.
(B) Her business had difficulties.
(C) Penalties and interest were too high.
(D) She didn't anticipate such high taxes.

172. What is the taxpayer's purpose in writing the letter?

(A) To explain why payment wasn't made
(B) To prove that an initial payment was made
(C) To inquire as to what penalties will be levied
(D) To request permission for incremental payments

173. How much was the taxpayer able to pay initially?

(A) $350
(B) $2,100
(C) $2,600
(D) $4,700

174. When does the taxpayer propose paying interest due on the taxes?

(A) January
(B) February
(C) June
(D) September

GO ON TO THE NEXT PAGE

As a member of the Electrix team, you know that Electrix is a world leader in the field of electronics. But do you know that we are the leading manufacturer in Spain? Do you know that we have companies in Northern Africa, Europe, and North and South America? Do you know that you are one of over 38,500 employees worldwide?

By reviewing this report of Electrix's operations, you'll learn more about your company. Our very first manufacturing plant, SpanElectrix is still in Madrid and is our European headquarters.

Telecor Ltd. is in Rabat, Morocco, where our capacitors, semiconductor diodes and transistors are manufactured. Electrix in South America, based in Caracas, Venezuela, produces most of our satellite communications equipment as well as office equipment devices like answering machines and all types of telephone equipment. Our sales and distribution outlets stretch from Venezuela to Egypt.

The most recent company to join our ranks is the Softcomp Corporation. This organization designs new software and enhances existing packages. It is based in New York City where the main offices of Electrix in the Americas are located.

175. In what country is Electrix the main producer of electronics?

(A) Egypt
(B) Venezuela
(C) Spain
(D) Morocco

176. Who is this report intended for?

(A) Competing European electronics manufacturers
(B) Software engineers
(C) Business school students
(D) Employees of Electrix

177. Which company in the organization is the newest member?

(A) Softcomp Corporation
(B) Electrix in South America
(C) Telecor
(D) SpanElectrix

178. Where have Electrix companies yet to be established?

(A) South America
(B) North Africa
(C) Asia
(D) Europe

179. Where would an office intercom system be manufactured?

(A) Madrid
(B) Caracas
(C) New York City
(D) Rabat

> *The International Loan Corporation (ILC) will provide $47 million in financing for the construction of the Dhiba Dimond Hotel in the Tabouk region. The $92.5 million hotel is a joint venture between Spain's Gartala Hotel International, Dimond and Blue Orient Hotels. It is to have 400 rooms and 25 serviced apartments. The completion date will be November, 1999. The ILC loan includes $9.5 million from its own account, a $2.5 million subordinate loan by Saudi Finances and a $35 million syndicated loan orchestrated by the Madrid Credit Corporation.*

180. What is the topic of this announcement?

(A) Growth of tourism in Dhiba
(B) A debt
(C) Hotel services
(D) A loan

181. Who is providing the largest part of the loan?

(A) The ILC
(B) Madrid Credit Corporation
(C) Gartala Hotel
(D) Saudi Finances

182. Who is building the hotel?

(A) The ILC
(B) The Madrid Credit Corporation
(C) The Dhiba Dimond hotel
(D) Three hotel chains

GO ON TO THE NEXT PAGE

Attention all passengers! The amount of luggage you are allowed to carry on board is limited by weight, dimensions and number of pieces. You may obtain details from your ticket or reservations office. Carry-on luggage is limited to one piece, which should not exceed 10 x 16 x 20 inches or 66 pounds (30 kilos). If room allows, the one-piece rule may be relaxed according to space and availability in the overhead compartments and the area under the seats. Certain items such as purses and newspapers may be carried on board, over and above the free baggage allowance, if you keep them on your person. It is wise to  **identify your baggage both inside and out and remove any old identifying labels. Combination locks are advisable. Cash, jewelry, medicines and important documents should be carried in your hand luggage.**

183. For whom is this notice intended?

(A) Security personnel
(B) Customs officials
(C) Porters
(D) Travelers

184. What factor does not affect the carry-on allowance?

(A) Space on the plane
(B) Weight of bags
(C) Size of bags
(D) Ticket class

185. What should travelers do with carry-on bags?

(A) Put name tags on them
(B) Check them in at the check-in counter
(C) Identify them for security personnel
(D) Make sure they contain no valuables

186. What should be removed from your luggage?

(A) Out-of-date luggage tags
(B) Combination locks
(C) Personal effects
(D) Combustible items

Questions 187–189 refer to the following form.

HOME TRIAL ORDER FORM

YES! Please accept my order for the products indicated. I agree to pay for my selection under the payment terms listed in the Payment Terms page of this catalog and in the agreement which accompanies the displayed products, or return it at my expense by the end of my 30-day free trial and owe nothing. The Free Gifts I was sent are, in any event, mine to keep. This order is subject to credit approval.

Please sign your name here _____

Home Phone: Area Code __ __ __ / __ __ __ - __ __ __ __

Product Code: __ __ __ __ Page # ____ Quantity _____ Color ____ Size _____

Product Code: __ __ __ __ Page # ____ Quantity _____ Color ____ Size _____

Surprise Gift with this order ($35.00 value). Check here [   ] for express delivery.
This order is non-transferable.

187. What is known about this order form?

(A) The customer has credit approval.
(B) Only the recipient can place an order on it.
(C) It clearly states the payment terms.
(D) Returned items will not be refunded.

188. What should a dissatisfied customer do?

(A) Apply for credit according to the payment terms
(B) Send back the free gift
(C) Send the goods back within 30 days
(D) Request a refund

189. Which information must the customer provide?

(A) Billing address
(B) Credit approval number
(C) A reason for the return
(D) Catalog page number

GO ON TO THE NEXT PAGE

PENSION TRUSTS for employees of Southern Pacific Railroad

Operating Statement	Year 2 (in millions)	Year 1
Total Assets – January 1	$923.5	$836.1
Plus: Company contributions	62.0	53.3
Employee contributions	5.5	20.7
Investment income	37.6	35.6
Less: Pensions paid	24.8	22.2
Total assets – December 31	$1,003.8	$923.5

===

Financial Position – December 31

Investments	$982.8	$902.7
Cash	1.6	2.9
Other assets	19.4	17.9
Total assets	$1,003.8	$923.5
Liability to pensioners	$191.4	$174.6
Reserve for pensions to participants not yet retired	812.4	748.9
Liabilities and reserves	$1,003.8	$923.5

===

190. How much money did Southern Pacific pay out to its retirees in Year 2?

(A) $5.5 million
(B) $24.8 million
(C) $62.0 million
(D) $191.4 million

191. How much was set aside in Year 1 for future retirees?

(A) $20.7 million
(B) $174.6 million
(C) $748.9 million
(D) $923.5 million

192. How much did the workers put towards their retirement in Year 2?

(A) $5.5 million
(B) $19.4 million
(C) $24.8 million
(D) $191.4 million

CORCORAN MANUFACTURING COMPANY
665 NORTH TOBIL STREET
HIGHLANDS, NV 34619

MEMORANDUM

To: Mr. William Corcoran, General Director
From: Joseph Bradigan, Sales Director
Subject: Sales by District for Month Ending February 28, 2000

Here are the sales figures by district for the month of February, which you requested in our telephone conversation yesterday.

District	February Sales	February Sales last year
Carrington	$ 11,564	$ 13,274
Marlboro	$ 16,892	$ 31,463
West Grammit	$ 26,387	$ 26,057
Abidole	$ 19,095	$ 19,374

Sales dropped by about 50% in the Marlboro district and about 20% in Carrington. The other two districts have managed to hold their own. Part of the drop may be explained, in my opinion, by the fact that there is a new sales supervisor in the Marlboro area and half of his salesforce is inexperienced. On the other hand, the drop may have nothing at all to do with that. I have already dispatched Jerry Baldwin that he should immediately troubleshoot the area to find out the actual cause. In the meantime, I would like to see the new staff be given a chance to prove themselves and I shall see what I can do to help them.

By the way, while over at the plant, I heard that the electrical components and the housing assemblies, which have been held up in Mali, are finally on their way and should be here in about a week.

---

193. What is the purpose of this memo?

(A) To criticize the new sales force
(B) To inform Mr. Corcoran of a drop in sales
(C) To give details of a situation in Marlboro
(D) To explain sales figures for the month

194. Which district improved sales slightly?

(A) Carrington
(B) Marlboro
(C) West Grammit
(D) Abidole

195. What might be influencing the slump in sales?

(A) Fifty percent of the market has been won over by the competition.
(B) The sales supervisor is new.
(C) The area has only half its usual sales force.
(D) The staff hasn't been given enough help.

196. What is Jerry Baldwin's job?

(A) To train the sales people
(B) To assist the sales supervisor
(C) To expedite the shipment from Mali
(D) To find the reason for the drop in sales

GO ON TO THE NEXT PAGE

Questions 197–200 refer to the following news article.

 The Train 'n Wheels program, an Environmental Defense Fund project, has finally arrived in southeast Los Angeles where it is assisting low-income communities with a gas-fueled shuttle service. The shuttle consists of eight vehicles that transport people from home or work to the nearest train stations. The service has several benefits. It allows the citizens more mobility, eases congestion, reduces air pollution, and increases job retention by easing the commute for low-income workers.

According to economic analyst Michael Cameron, many of the low-income residents are not able to get to certain jobs because they cannot afford to own a car. Train 'n Wheels gives these people access to jobs that were hitherto out of their reach.

The EDF had two goals in mind when it created the shuttle plan: to pool commuters, thereby reducing pollution and the use of resources, and to provide transportation improvements that would not increase cost to low-income commuters. By determining where most of the shuttle riders would come from, the EDF is, in fact, helping the primary sponsor, the Southeast Community Development Corporation, find the sources that will financially back up this community outreach program.

197. What is the main point of this article?

- (A) Gas-powered vehicles are gaining in popularity
- (B) Air quality in Los Angeles is improving
- (C) The EDF is providing real assistance to southeast Los Angeles
- (D) The ride-share program is lessening traffic congestion

198. Why was the shuttle program started?

- (A) To test the efficiency of the gas-powered engines
- (B) To promote commuting by train
- (C) To offer second jobs to low-income workers
- (D) To give workers access to the train stations

199. Who is Michael Cameron?

- (A) The Train 'n Wheels director
- (B) An economist
- (C) A systems analyst
- (D) An employment specialist

200. What is the Southeast Community Development Corporation?

- (A) The main source of money for the shuttle project
- (B) A partner of the Environmental Defense Fund
- (C) An organization that studies the effects of pollution on Los Angeles
- (D) An employment resource center

Stop! This is the end of the test. If you finish before one hour and fifteen minutes have passed, you may go back to Parts V, VI, and VII and check your work.

Practice Test Two

LISTENING COMPREHENSION

In this section of the test, you will have the chance to show how well you understand spoken English. There are four parts to this section, with special directions for each part.

PART I

Directions: For each question, you will see a picture in your test book and you will hear four short statements. The statements will be spoken just one time. They will not be printed in your test book, so you must listen carefully to understand what the speaker says.

When you hear the four statements, look at the picture in your test book and choose the statement that best describes what you see in the picture. Then, on your answer sheet, find the number of the question and mark your answer. Look at the sample below.

Sample Answer
Ⓐ ● Ⓒ Ⓓ

Now listen to the four statements.

Statement (B), "They're having a meeting," best describes what you see in the picture. Therefore, you should choose answer (B).

GO ON TO THE NEXT PAGE

1.

2.

3.

4.

GO ON TO THE NEXT PAGE ▶

5.

6.

7.

8.

GO ON TO THE NEXT PAGE

9.

10.

11.

12.

GO ON TO THE NEXT PAGE ▶

13.

14.

15.

16.

GO ON TO THE NEXT PAGE ▶

17.

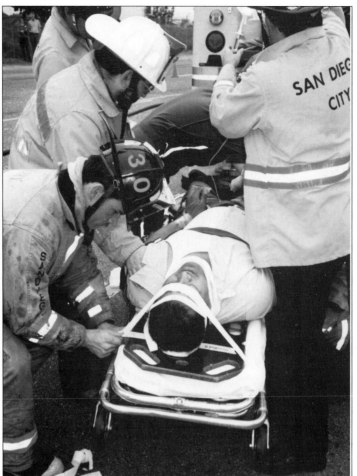

18.

19.

20.

Directions: In this part of the test, you will hear a question spoken in English, followed by three responses, also spoken in English. The question and the responses will be spoken just one time. They will not be printed in your test book, so you must listen carefully to understand what the speakers say. You are to choose the best response to each question.

Now listen to a sample question.

You will hear:

Sample Answer

You will also hear:

The best response to the question "How are you?" is choice (A), "I am fine, thank you." Therefore, you should choose answer (A).

21. Mark your answer on your answer sheet.

22. Mark your answer on your answer sheet.

23. Mark your answer on your answer sheet.

24. Mark your answer on your answer sheet.

25. Mark your answer on your answer sheet.

26. Mark your answer on your answer sheet.

27. Mark your answer on your answer sheet.

28. Mark your answer on your answer sheet.

29. Mark your answer on your answer sheet.

30. Mark your answer on your answer sheet.

31. Mark your answer on your answer sheet.

32. Mark your answer on your answer sheet.

33. Mark your answer on your answer sheet.

34. Mark your answer on your answer sheet.

35. Mark your answer on your answer sheet.

36. Mark your answer on your answer sheet.

37. Mark your answer on your answer sheet.

38. Mark your answer on your answer sheet.

39. Mark your answer on your answer sheet.

40. Mark your answer on your answer sheet.

41. Mark your answer on your answer sheet.

42. Mark your answer on your answer sheet.

43. Mark your answer on your answer sheet.

44. Mark your answer on your answer sheet.

45. Mark your answer on your answer sheet.

46. Mark your answer on your answer sheet.

47. Mark your answer on your answer sheet.

48. Mark your answer on your answer sheet.

49. Mark your answer on your answer sheet.

50. Mark your answer on your answer sheet.

GO ON TO THE NEXT PAGE ▶

Directions: In this part of the test, you will hear thirty short conversations between two people. The conversations will not be printed in your test book. You will hear the conversations only once, so you must listen carefully to understand what the speakers say.

In your test book, you will read a question about each conversation. The question will be followed by four answers. You are to choose the best answer to each question and mark it on your answer sheet.

51. What is the debate about?

    (A) A pipeline.
    (B) Traffic.
    (C) The town's boundaries.
    (D) An oil spill.

52. What are they discussing?

    (A) Placing an overseas call.
    (B) Getting facts straight.
    (C) Sending a fax.
    (D) Someone entering the house.

53. What are they talking about?

    (A) Directions to a store.
    (B) The parking problem.
    (C) A bump in the road.
    (D) A new apartment building.

54. What kind of establishment is being referred to?

    (A) A restaurant.
    (B) A furniture manufacturer.
    (C) A hotel.
    (D) A cleaning company.

55. What does the man want to do?

    (A) Make a certain color paint.
    (B) Hang a picture.
    (C) Find a key.
    (D) Buy some office supplies.

56. What is the repairman going to fix?

    (A) The boiler.
    (B) An air-conditioner.
    (C) A fan.
    (D) The heater.

57. What will John be asked to do?

    (A) Buy a new computer.
    (B) Attend a sales seminar.
    (C) Help meet the sales goal.
    (D) Set a new sales record.

58. What is the woman testing?

    (A) A CD player.
    (B) A computer.
    (C) A car.
    (D) A truck.

59. What does the woman offer to do?

    (A) Loan Paul her computer.
    (B) Sell him the adapter.
    (C) Ask a friend to help.
    (D) Send him to a store.

60. What are they talking about?

    (A) Baked goods.
    (B) A building.
    (C) A restaurant.
    (D) The price of food.

61. What is being explained?

    (A) An alarm system.
    (B) A calculator.
    (C) A radio.
    (D) A fax machine.

62. What does the man want to do?

    (A) Get to the train station.
    (B) Get out of the heat.
    (C) Leave town.
    (D) Compare transportation.

63. What has been improved?

   (A) Train safety.
   (B) The cleanliness of the house.
   (C) How the car is running.
   (D) The public transport system.

64. What does Tom suspect?

   (A) The bill is incorrect.
   (B) The computers need repair.
   (C) Wasteful use of the air-conditioner.
   (D) The electrical wiring is faulty.

65. How many copies of each form are there?

   (A) One.
   (B) Two.
   (C) Three.
   (D) Four.

66. How will the group travel to the seminar?

   (A) By car.
   (B) By bus.
   (C) By plane.
   (D) By train.

67. What is Barbara's job?

   (A) A mechanic.
   (B) An inspector.
   (C) A chauffeur.
   (D) A bus driver.

68. Where are the reports now?

   (A) On the boss's desk.
   (B) In Hong Kong.
   (C) With Susan.
   (D) In the mail.

69. What are they discussing?

   (A) A train schedule.
   (B) A watch.
   (C) A work schedule.
   (D) A light.

70. What does Mr. Tam want to do?

   (A) See Mr. Braun.
   (B) Avoid city traffic.
   (C) Change offices.
   (D) Have lunch.

71. What is the man's problem?

   (A) He has poor vision.
   (B) The newspapers have sold out.
   (C) Both New York and overseas flights are sold out.
   (D) There are no English language magazines.

72. What kind of company do they have?

   (A) A furniture company.
   (B) A construction company.
   (C) A finance company.
   (D) A real estate company.

73. What are they discussing?

   (A) Management.
   (B) Finances.
   (C) The vice president.
   (D) A phone conference.

74. What is the man's occupation?

   (A) Broker.
   (B) Real estate agent.
   (C) Boat salesman.
   (D) Banker.

75. What does the man suggest?

   (A) Charging the phone.
   (B) Returning it.
   (C) Checking the phone.
   (D) Calling the Better Business Bureau.

76. When is the sale?

   (A) This week.
   (B) This weekend.
   (C) This Friday.
   (D) Monday through Friday.

GO ON TO THE NEXT PAGE

77. What are they discussing?

    (A) Accounting procedures.
    (B) Money market funds.
    (C) A new office design.
    (D) Business expenditure.

78. What does the woman want to do?

    (A) Get a job as a temp.
    (B) Buy a new computer.
    (C) Verify some data.
    (D) Put addresses in a computer.

79. Where is Cathy?

    (A) At the banquet.
    (B) At the hospital.
    (C) At the card store.
    (D) At the bank.

80. Why is the man going to Tokyo?

    (A) To work.
    (B) To open a shop.
    (C) To interview the local people.
    (D) To photograph the city.

PART IV

Directions: In this part of the test, you will hear several short talks. Each will be spoken just one time. They will not be printed in your test book, so you must listen carefully to understand and remember what is said.

In your test book, you will read two or more questions about each short talk. The questions will be followed by four answers. You are to choose the best answer to each question and mark it on your answer sheet.

81. Who may receive a library borrower's card?

    (A) Anyone attending school in New York City.
    (B) Anyone who pays sales tax in New York City.
    (C) Anyone who regularly studies in the library.
    (D) Anyone with a legitimate need for the services.

82. What is the longest time a book may be borrowed?

    (A) 10 days.
    (B) 14 days.
    (C) 28 days.
    (D) 38 days.

83. Which equipment is available for library patrons?

    (A) Portable cassette players.
    (B) Photocopying machines.
    (C) Radios.
    (D) Cell phones.

84. What is the key factor in keeping food safe?

    (A) Avoiding mayonnaise in lunch foods.
    (B) Serving meat and poultry whole.
    (C) Maintaining appropriate temperature.
    (D) Washing hands to kill bacteria.

85. Which food is more likely to cause illness?

    (A) Mayonnaise.
    (B) Chicken.
    (C) Vegetables.
    (D) Hot foods.

86. What raises the chance of bacterial problems?

    (A) The use of mayonnaise.
    (B) Using vegetable dips.
    (C) Chopped meats.
    (D) Using fruit fillings.

87. Who would this most likely interest?

    (A) Vacationers.
    (B) Entrepreneurs.
    (C) College students.
    (D) Chefs.

88. What is the topic of the talk?

    (A) Renting a room at Jeanne and Tom's.
    (B) Running a successful B&B.
    (C) Traveling in Maine.
    (D) Starting an adventure.

89. Who is this notice directed to?

    (A) Fishermen.
    (B) Fund-raisers.
    (C) Beach officials.
    (D) Vacationers.

90. Where can you get registration materials?

    (A) The beach.
    (B) The Town Hall.
    (C) Cape Troll.
    (D) Tackle shops.

91. Who is sponsoring the Mallory Beach event?

    (A) Mallory Beach Chamber of Commerce.
    (B) Myrtle Beach Town Hall.
    (C) The New York Fishermen's Association.
    (D) Cape Troll residents.

92. What is this story about?

    (A) The growth of Parisian Intercontinental Hotels.
    (B) The curriculum of elementary schools.
    (C) A donation of books.
    (D) The financial condition of regional libraries.

GO ON TO THE NEXT PAGE

93. How were book numbers determined?

   (A) By hotel employees.
   (B) By six elementary schools.
   (C) By the Parisian Literacy Crusade.
   (D) By the number of hotel guests.

94. What has the Parisian Literacy Crusade agreed to do?

   (A) Donate more books.
   (B) Help bring in and set up the books.
   (C) Promote the Intercontinental Hotels.
   (D) Offer free tutoring at the elementary schools.

95. What is being discussed?

   (A) The possible purchase of air-conditioners.
   (B) The difference between central air and single units.
   (C) Noise in the offices.
   (D) Technical data.

96. Who is most likely being addressed?

   (A) Kitchen staff.
   (B) Building engineers.
   (C) Dining room personnel.
   (D) Office workers.

97. What information is being asked for?

   (A) Opinions on the menu.
   (B) How many units should be purchased.
   (C) Information that could help educate decision-makers.
   (D) How best to finance the purchase.

98. What is being advertised?

   (A) Golf courses in Scotland.
   (B) Training in archery.
   (C) Scottish antiques.
   (D) Tours of Scotland.

99. What happened in 1457?

   (A) Archery reached its peak in popularity.
   (B) James II forbade golfing.
   (C) Aristocrats developed the rules of golf.
   (D) James II became an outlaw.

100. What is known about St. Andrew's Old Course?

   (A) It is hundreds of years old.
   (B) It is an excellent course.
   (C) It is for preferred players.
   (D) There are dozens of tours of it.

This is the end of the Listening Comprehension portion of Practice Test Two. Turn to Part V in your test book.

YOU WILL HAVE ONE HOUR AND FIFTEEN MINUTES TO COMPLETE PARTS V, VI, AND VII OF THE TEST.

READING

In this section of the test, you will have a chance to show how well you understand written English. There are three parts to this section, with special directions for each part.

PART V

Directions: Questions 101–140 are incomplete sentences. Four words or phrases, marked (A), (B), (C), (D) are given beneath each sentence. You are to choose the **one** word or phrase that best completes the sentence. Then, on your answer sheet, find the number of the question and mark your answer.

You will read:

Because the equipment is very delicate, it must be handled with ....

(A) caring
(B) careful
(C) care
(D) carefully

Sample Answer
Ⓐ Ⓑ ● Ⓓ

The sentence should read, "Because the equipment is very delicate, it must be handled with care." Therefore, you should choose answer (C).

Now begin work on the questions.

---

101. The board of directors convinced him to .... action against the other firm.

    (A) take
    (B) do
    (C) give
    (D) make

102. Tooth enamel is one of the .... substances in the world.

    (A) hardly
    (B) hardest
    (C) harder
    (D) hard

103. The secretary told me that a new .... was being mailed to all interested investors.

    (A) prospectus
    (B) prosecution
    (C) prosthesis
    (D) prosperity

104. The publisher will .... need the report by week's end.

    (A) maybe
    (B) probably
    (C) possible
    (D) eventually

105. The judge made it clear that those facts were not ....

    (A) admission
    (B) admit
    (C) admissible
    (D) admittance

106. Ever since they discovered that little resort off the coast of Spain, they .... anywhere else for vacation.

    (A) didn't go
    (B) weren't going
    (C) went
    (D) haven't gone

GO ON TO THE NEXT PAGE

107. The financial statement would have reflected our difficulties if we .... our accounting year.

(A) had not changed
(B) have not changed
(C) have not been changing
(D) had not been changing

108. The fundraisers located themselves next to the entrance to take advantage of all the people .... through.

(A) passed
(B) passing
(C) passes
(D) pass

109. His discoveries, which were heavily promoted in the *Explorer's Club Journal*, ... also given considerable attention by the media.

(A) was
(B) it was
(C) had
(D) were

110. Most electrical wiring is installed behind walls .... it is not visible.

(A) because
(B) for that
(C) to
(D) so

111. Bondholders are generally .... more conservative than stockholders.

(A) consider
(B) considering
(C) considerable
(D) considered

112. Professor Zagrov praised Mr. Modello for his literary contribution before presenting him with what .... money the group had gathered.

(A) little
(B) few
(C) small
(D) less

113. Electric cars today are able .... three times longer than those of just five years ago.

(A) running
(B) to run
(C) be run
(D) run

114. I don't understand .... of these is to be included in the shipment.

(A) which
(B) that
(C) some
(D) what

115. We cannot print .... the financial report until the computer is working.

(A) with
(B) on
(C) forth
(D) out

116. The elevator door didn't .... at the sound of the bell.

(A) closed
(B) be closed
(C) close
(D) to close

117. Ms. Yen's contribution to the company has been ....

(A) industrial
(B) indigenous
(C) invaluable
(D) inclement

118. Customer Service, on the fifth floor, will have .... your application before I can process it.

(A) approve
(B) been approved
(C) approving
(D) to approve

119. I would like to .... the conference call until both analysts have sent us their conclusions.

(A) postpone
(B) move
(C) hinder
(D) detain

120. The hotel manager would have offered us a 25% discount if we .... a party of ten or more.

(A) had been
(B) were
(C) are
(D) been

121. We weren't able to get any gas there because the pumps were ....

(A) empty
(B) used
(C) order
(D) repaired

122. They said my qualifications were .... varied than those of any other applicant.

(A) most
(B) best
(C) more
(D) very

123. Municipal bonds are issued by state and local governments to pay for keeping roads and bridges in good ....

(A) state
(B) repair
(C) quality
(D) manner

124. She wanted to wander .... Lisbon by herself.

(A) among
(B) around
(C) the
(D) out

125. Mrs. Stein, the chairwoman and founder of Women's World, ... to an enthusiastic audience at the fashion show.

(A) who spoke
(B) was spoken
(C) that she spoke
(D) spoke

126. Opinions based on personal inspection .... much more substantial than those based on conjecture.

(A) is
(B) are
(C) they are
(D) have

127. She wanted to find out for .... what the Norwegian fjords were like.

(A) himself
(B) itself
(C) themselves
(D) herself

128. Manhattan residents usually prefer less .... areas when they go on vacation.

(A) population
(B) populations
(C) populate
(D) populous

129. The court made it obvious that illegal parking would no longer be ....

(A) tolerated
(B) tolerate
(C) tolerant
(D) tolerance

130. Our department is neither prepared .... willing to fund this research.

(A) or
(B) nor
(C) but
(D) also

GO ON TO THE NEXT PAGE

131. Lawmakers were about to end their summer session, but not before they passed a proposal giving .... a pay raise.

(A) himself
(B) themselves
(C) herself
(D) yourselves

132. The curator of the national museum of art is .... ready to issue a statement regarding last night's theft.

(A) though
(B) how
(C) yet
(D) not

133. In .... rising health care costs, many companies are streamlining their benefits program.

(A) to light
(B) light of
(C) lights on
(D) lighted

134. Calendar years and fiscal years don't .... coincide.

(A) almost
(B) already
(C) always
(D) also

135. The shares had been .... for quite some time.

(A) undernourished
(B) undervalued
(C) undercharged
(D) underdeveloped

136. The bank laid down several policies designed .... simplify the collection process.

(A) to
(B) so
(C) that
(D) what

137. .... the managers enhanced the training program for new employees, absenteeism has been declining.

(A) Before
(B) When
(C) Since
(D) During

138. Mr. Bagglio's definition of "professional" unfortunately doesn't include "being .... ".

(A) friendly
(B) politely
(C) courteously
(D) respectfully

139. The building, for .... a purchasing fund had been set aside, was severely damaged in the hurricane.

(A) that
(B) which
(C) whom
(D) this

140. These tires are highly .... because of their durability.

(A) recollected
(B) recommended
(C) recompensed
(D) reconciled

PART VI

Directions: In **Questions 141–160**, each sentence has four words or phrases underlined. The four underlined parts of the sentence are marked (A), (B), (C), (D). You are to identify the **one** underlined word or phrase that should be corrected or rewritten. Then, on your answer sheet, find the number of the question and mark your answer.

Example:

All employee are required to wear their
   A   B

identification badges while at work.
      C   D

Sample Answer
● Ⓑ Ⓒ Ⓓ

The underlined word "employee" is not correct in this sentence. This sentence should read, "All employees are required to wear their identification badges while at work." Therefore, you should choose answer (A).

Now begin work on the questions.

---

141. In larger cities, crime is becoming
       A
lesser and lesser of a problem because
    B
education has been given priority over
           C   D
punishment.

142. The merger of Whitehurst and Brown
      A
are causing a stir in the business community
    B   C
and in the media.
        D

143. These days, the only way to deal with tax
        A   B
issues revolving around real estate is in a
            C
conservatively fashion.
      D

144. I would feel better if we had all the logistical
     A   B   C
worked out before we left.
        D

145. One of a manager's much valuable assets
    A   B   C
may be his ability to say 'no'.
        D

146. The diverse of languages throughout the
      A   B
many Indonesian islands adds to their color.
      C   D

147. The Vietnamese automobile industry
is growing, but agricultural will always be its
        A   B   C
economic mainstay.
      D

148. I asked if we could have just a little
       A   B
more times to prepare for the meeting.
      C   D

GO ON TO THE NEXT PAGE ➤

149. This year alone, over three thousand
    _A_ _____B_____
    inventors from all over the country
    _____C_____
    are application for patent rights.
    _____D_____

150. Some increase at all in income taxes
    _____A_____
    will be met with stiff resistance from all sides.
    ___B___   ___C___   _____D_____

151. To celebrate the grand opening, the
    ___A___
    supermarket is selling red roses at five
    ____B____   ___C___
    dollars dozen.
    ___D___

152. He was able to buy the new car on a
    ____A____   _B_
    thirty-six months installment plan with no
    _____C_____   _D_
    down payment.

153. Due to an increase in the minimum wage,
    _A_   _B_
    the pay scales for the waitstaff will have to be
    ___C___
    recalculate.
    ___D___

154. The chairman is being briefed on the events
    ____A____   _B_
    scheduled for the next many days.
    ___C___   ___D___

155. Although one would not expect it, ice cream
    _A_   _____B_____
    sales are highest in the winter season or
    ____C____   _D_
    lowest in the summer.

156. The data should be transferred to the hard
    _____A_____
    drive where they can be safely stored until
    _____B_____   ___C___
    we need it.
    ___D___

157. It is better to write down appointments
    ___A___   ___B___
    as they come up as one may have forgotten
    _____C_____   _____D_____
    to do so later.

158. It came as no surprise when consultants
    _____A_____
    discovered that the corporation had lost
    ___B___
    nearly every its profits in the year prior to the
    _____C_____   ___D___
    lawsuit.

159. Hiring a well-mannered and articulate
    _A_
    receptionist is no different from investing
    _____B_____
    thousands dollars in a good
    _____C_____
    public relations campaign.
    _____D_____

160. By the time we read the paper,
    ___A___
    the news are old, since we've already heard
    ___B___   _____C_____
    on television what's happening in the world.
    _____D_____

PART VII

Directions: Questions 161–200 are based on a selection of reading materials, such as notices, letters, forms, newspaper and magazine articles, and advertisements. You are to choose the **one** best answer (A), (B), (C), or (D) to each question. Then, on your answer sheet, find the number of the question and mark your answer. Answer all questions following each reading selection on the basis of what is **stated** or **implied** in that selection.

Read the following example.

> The Museum of Technology is a "hands-on" museum, designed for people to experience science at work. Visitors are encouraged to use, test, and handle the objects on display. Special demonstrations are scheduled for the first and second Wednesdays of each month at 13:30. Open Tuesday–Friday 12:00–16:30, Saturday 10:00–17:30, and Sunday 11:00–16:30.
>
> When during the month can visitors see special demonstrations?
>
> *Sample Answer*
> Ⓐ ● Ⓒ Ⓓ
>
> (A)   Every weekend
> (B)   The first two Wednesdays
> (C)   One afternoon a week
> (D)   Every other Wednesday

The reading selection says that the demonstrations are scheduled for the first and second Wednesdays of the month. Therefore, you should choose answer (B).

Now begin work on the questions.

Questions 161–162 refer to the following article.

> **SINGAPORE AIRLINES** is extending its "Free Dinner for Two" (FDT) campaign due to popular demand. The campaign, which will now run until June 30, is open to all holders of economy and first class round trip tickets for flights from North or South America to Kuala Lumpur or beyond.
>
> Participating restaurants in Kuala Lumpur include: Asian Delights, The Silver Terrace, Little Flower, and many more. A complete listing is available through your ticket agency.

161. What is Indonesian Airlines offering?

(A) Two complimentary meals
(B) Free tours of Kuala Lumpur
(C) A list of preferred dining locations
(D) Discounts at popular hotels

162. How can one participate?

(A) By visiting a travel agency
(B) By patronizing any participating hotel
(C) By purchasing particular airline tickets
(D) By flying round trip on Singapore Airlines

GO ON TO THE NEXT PAGE ▶

MEMORANDUM

To: John Stevens, Factory Operations

From: Hans Pomanz

Date: August 5

Subject: Inspection of Technical Area

For: [**X**] Decision   [ ] Action   [ ] Information

On the basis of a report that one of the aisles was blocked and therefore presented a safety hazard, I did an inspection in the technical area. The reported blockage was not located.

Outside the cutting room, though, several pallets of lumber have been stored in the aisle. Although this is not a serious issue (but definitely an annoyance), it could easily be resolved by allocating about 150 square feet of storage to the technical department.

I have already talked with Jeremy, the storage manager, and he assured me the space could be arranged.

---

163. Why was an inspection done?

(A) Because of complaints from cutting room workers
(B) To determine if more pallets were needed
(C) Because of technical difficulties
(D) In response to a report of blockage

164. What is Hans suggesting?

(A) That safety inspections should be taken more seriously
(B) That the wood could be moved to storage
(C) That nothing should be left outside the cutting room
(D) That John Stevens meet with Jeremy

A subsidiary of the Russian PB Group, PB Cable and Machinery, Ltd., has completed construction of a power-cable plant in Istanbul. The $27 million plant is 47% owned by local partner Buyuk Power and Water Machine Co., 48% owned by PB Cable and Chorny Electrical, and 5% by PB Group. The plant has an annual production capacity of 5,500 tons of cable. It will produce power cables with a capacity from 220 volts to 40KV. PB Group officials say they expect domestic cable sales to reach $25 million by 1999.

165. What is being produced?

(A) Heavy machinery
(B) Water filtration devices
(C) Electrical power
(D) Power cables

166. Who is the biggest investor?

(A) Buyuk Power & Water Machine Company
(B) PB Cable and Chorny Electrical
(C) PB Group
(D) PB Cable and Machinery, Ltd.

167. What is the purpose of the news item?

(A) To protest foreign ownership
(B) To hold investors accountable
(C) To announce a new factory
(D) To explain Russian–Turkish business relations

GO ON TO THE NEXT PAGE

WHAT IN THE WORLD DO YOU HAVE TO DO TO GET GOOD RETURNS?

WORLDWIDE
WATCHERS

To begin with, you could wade through piles of financial publications from all over the world. Then, you could develop a software system that tracks the performance of the companies you selected. And to further tighten things down, you could hire a team of researchers who could study the data and then identify the ones showing strong, sustainable growth. Finally, you could invest a little more time visiting each of the best-looking companies. On the other hand, you could just call Worldwide Watchers. We save you time and money. Our records prove our merit. In the rocky waters of international investing, we maximize your profits while minimizing risk from currency fluctuations.

168. What is the purpose of the ad?

(A) To highlight the benefits of using Worldwide Watchers
(B) To sell financial newsletters
(C) To explain overseas investments
(D) To promote investment in software companies

169. Who is this promotion targeted at?

(A) Computer programmers
(B) Financial analysts
(C) Investors
(D) Research analysts

170. What risk is involved?

(A) High costs
(B) Unpredictable tides
(C) Changing investment patterns
(D) Shifting exchange rates

January 13, 2000

Dr. Raul Garcia
3062 Wilshire Blvd.
Los Angeles, CA 90037

Dear Dr. Garcia,

I am writing to you about the bill I received from your office.

First, I would like to tell you that the results of the surgery have been very positive. I am very pleased with the results, particularly my arm's increased range of motion.

Regarding my bill, you will recall that when we scheduled the operation, my insurance company assured me that the entire procedure, to include any follow-up care, would be 100% covered by my plan. To my dismay, I have since been informed that the insurance will only cover 70% of the cost, leaving me with an unpaid charge of $950.

Although I am recovering most satisfactorily, I will not be working again until next Monday. Additionally, our finances are at an all-time low from the holidays. I would like to suggest a monthly installment plan of one hundred dollars starting February 1. I will mail you fifty dollars for this month. I hope this plan will meet with your satisfaction. If not, please let me know what would.

Sincerely,

Juan Veron

Juan Veron

---

171. What is Juan's main purpose in writing?

(A) To request more insurance coverage
(B) To propose a payment plan
(C) To report on his post-surgery progress
(D) To have the bill reviewed

172. Why is payment for the surgery changing?

(A) Follow-up care was unexpectedly expensive.
(B) Juan thought he would only be responsible for 30% of the cost.
(C) Juan had incorrect information about his coverage.
(D) The type of surgery performed is not included in the plan.

173. What did Juan experience after surgery?

(A) A more positive outlook
(B) Ability to work
(C) He could enjoy the holidays
(D) More flexibility in his arm

174. When will Dr. Garcia start to receive money from Juan?

(A) December
(B) January
(C) February
(D) March

GO ON TO THE NEXT PAGE ▶

Questions 175–179 refer to the following report.

Here are some statistics that may heighten your interest in the Pacific Basin. Half of the world's wealth and over half of its population live in the 34 countries and 23 island states that embrace the Basin, which itself consists of 70 million square miles. Ninety-five percent of the world's natural silk can be found there as well as 88 percent of its natural rubber, 22 percent of its oil resources, and 64 percent of its cotton. Well over a thousand languages are spoken in the area, and it is the source of some of the richest religious and cultural traditions in the world.

The most rapidly expanding economy in the region is Taiwan, with South Korea expected to be amongst the richest countries in the world in the twenty-first century. Not enough can be said about the market potential of China. As these countries continue to develop, their manufacturing capabilities will become increasingly complex and their market for advanced technology will expand. The telecommunications industry, for instance, will soon take off.

It is the educated labor force as well as the work ethic that accounts for the growing manufacturing power of the Pacific nations. Lying on the trade routes to both East and West, this area has a unique advantage, something that few businesses can ignore.

175. Who is this report most likely intended for?

(A) Companies wanting to expand their market reach
(B) Translators for the Pacific region languages
(C) Natural rubber manufacturers
(D) The Department of Labor

176. Only five percent of what product can be found outside the Pacific Basin?

(A) Oil
(B) Natural rubber
(C) Natural silk
(D) Cotton

177. How should readers of this report view the Pacific Basin?

(A) As an overly populated region with little buying power
(B) As a growing market
(C) As a forbidding competitor
(D) As a powerful opponent

178. Which industry is likely to excel in the Pacific Basin in the near future?

(A) Mobile phone manufacturers
(B) Rubber tire manufacturers
(C) Oil refineries
(D) Clothing manufacturers

179. Why is the Pacific Basin becoming the focus of the business community?

(A) The cost of labor is considerably less.
(B) It is well poised for great economic expansion.
(C) The area has superior educational standards.
(D) There are few trade restrictions in the countries there.

Over the last few weeks, twenty thousand dollars' worth of audio-visual equipment has been stolen from these premises, including several computer terminals and printers from the training center. An expensive camera was also taken from the conference room. Most of the thefts have occurred during normal working hours (9 to 5).

Due to these incidents of theft, we have adopted specific increased security measures. From now on, the entire staff, including the managing director, is to wear an ID tag with a photo. Visitors will also be issued name tags with a code indicating which department they will be visiting. Visiting hours will now be from 9 to 11 in the morning and from 2 to 5 in the afternoon. The IDs must be worn and be visible at all times. To further assist the staff, video phones have been installed at each entrance.

180. What is the purpose of the announcement?

(A) To explain how new IDs can be obtained
(B) To inform staff of heightened security measures
(C) To describe stolen goods
(D) To blame faulty security steps for the thefts

181. During what time frame were things stolen?

(A) 9 to 11
(B) 11 to 2
(C) 2 to 5
(D) 9 to 5

182. What will be required of visitors?

(A) To use the video phone when entering
(B) To wear a photo ID at all times
(C) To wear ID that shows destination
(D) To submit a visitor's form to their department

GO ON TO THE NEXT PAGE

The European Film Festival (EFF) box office is located in the Victory Building at the Brandenburg Plaza. It is open 5:00 p.m. to 9:00 p.m. on weekdays when films are scheduled. It is open 1:00 p.m. to 9:00 p.m. Saturday and Sunday. On days for which there are no scheduled screenings, the box office is not open. For a pre-recorded program, please call 365-8000; to hear 60-second reviews call 365-7786.

The EFF accepts American Express, Visa and Mastercard. Phone orders can be made by calling 221-8937 during box office hours. Members may also reserve tickets by phone five days in advance. These reservations are held until 20 minutes before showtime. A current membership card is required for all member transactions. There is a limit of two member-price tickets per show. Parking at the Brandenburg Plaza is free from 3:00 p.m. to 5:00 p.m. with theater validation.

183. Who would be interested in this notice?

(A) Victory Building office workers
(B) Actors and actresses
(C) Job applicants
(D) Show goers

184. What number gives a listing of shows?

(A) 365-8000
(B) 221-8937
(C) 365-7786
(D) 800-EFF-SHOWS

185. What is a benefit of membership in the EFF?

(A) Free tickets
(B) Scheduled pre-screenings
(C) Advance ticket reservations
(D) Free parking

186. What event would you be likely to see at the Brandenburg Plaza?

(A) A play
(B) A movie
(C) A boxing match
(D) A car race

REGISTERED NO.

To be filled out by mailing agency:
Reg. Fee $ _____ Handling Charge $ _____ Postage $ _____
Special Delivery $ _____ Return Receipt $ _____ Received by _____

To be filled out by Customer:
Please complete your address legibly. This will be used to notify you of the receipt of your registered letter.

Customer must declare full value of all shipped goods to receive insurance on items valued over $20,000. All items under $20,000 are automatically insured and are covered by the registration fee. Rates for items over $20,000 are listed on reverse of this document. International liability is limited.

Value: _____

FROM: _____
_____

TO: _____
_____

This is an official receipt for registered mail.
Customer copy

---

187. What is this form used for?

(A) To get a refund for missent packages
(B) As a substitute for postage
(C) To register a shipment
(D) To ensure mail is returned if undeliverable

188. In order for goods valued at over $20,000 to be insured, the customer must

(A) Declare the value
(B) Get the recipient's signature
(C) Notify the recipient
(D) Cancel other insurance

189. How must the form be completed?

(A) Clearly
(B) With a pen
(C) In duplicate
(D) Illegibly

GO ON TO THE NEXT PAGE

Dear Tenant,

This letter will serve as an official warning. I have reasonable cause to believe that there has been cigarette smoking in your unit. For the past week, I have cleaned up cigarette butts and ashes from below your balcony. Initially, the downstairs neighbors complained, and that is what caused me to check the area. Since this time, I have smelled smoke when walking by your front door.

As stated in your lease, this is a non-smoking building. Violation of this, or any other terms of your lease, makes the year-long agreement void. Three months ago, I had tenants living in 404B who smoked in their apartment. They chose to ignore their warning and were given thirty days' notice immediately. I want you to know that I take this seriously.

I have run Mr. Sheldon's building for over ten years. People like living here because it is clean, healthy and safe. I try to pick all renters carefully. I hope that I have done so in your case.

Sincerely,

Lydia Thornton
Lydia Thornton

190. Who is Lydia Thornton?

(A) A neighbor
(B) A building manager
(C) A landlord
(D) A past tenant

191. What was Lydia's first clue of smoking in the apartment?

(A) She found cigarette butts and ashes below the balcony.
(B) Three months ago, other neighbors smoked in an apartment.
(C) There was a complaint by fellow neighbors.
(D) She smelled smoke when walking by.

192. What happened to the other tenants who smoked?

(A) They moved to apartment 404B.
(B) They heeded the warning.
(C) They took the situation seriously.
(D) They were evicted.

MEMORANDUM

To: Constance Lubitsch
From: Richard Eckert

Subject: Popularity of Booklet

About 2,800 requests have come in over the last few months asking for our booklet, *This Is How the Stock Exchange Works*, which we issued for our twentieth anniversary. I would like your views on whether or not we should have it reprinted.

Mr. Studie has reported the following facts:
1. The cost of reprinting 6,000 copies is approximately $2,500.
2. A breakdown of the requests shows that 1,521 came from college and high school students, 387 from private industries, and 911 from individuals.
3. Our previous printing of 12,000 copies was distributed among shareholders, employees, and educational leaders in the area.
4. Pages 10 and 11 should be revised to reflect the current sales figures and a more accurate understanding of the costs.

FYI: I am sending this request to all middle managers and I would greatly appreciate it if you would answer the questions I have provided below so that we can tabulate answers more easily.

1. Would a reprinting of 6,000 copies be enough?
2. What is the message of this booklet?
3. Could it be improved upon so as to get our message across more clearly?

Please respond by June 1.

---

193. What is the purpose of the memo?

(A) To propose a better booklet
(B) To survey opinions on reprinting
(C) To request permission to reprint 6,000 copies
(D) To suggest a meeting of managers

194. Why was the booklet originally distributed?

(A) To offer opportunities to employees
(B) To educate high school students
(C) To tap into the college student market
(D) To celebrate an anniversary

195. Who received the last printing?

(A) Other industries
(B) Leaders in education
(C) Private individuals
(D) High school students

196. Who will receive this memo?

(A) The company's shareholders
(B) Community leaders
(C) Middle management
(D) Employees

GO ON TO THE NEXT PAGE

New power plants and power lines are filling up the utility vacuum in South America. An agreement, for instance, has been reached between Germany's Energie-Versorgung Schwaben (EVS) and the Nova-Lima Power Company. Under this agreement Nova Lima Power will sell EVS a 40% share of a power plant venture. Brazil's Nova Lima Lignite Company, which owns Nova Lima Power, is constructing a one billion dollar power plant in Peru that will supply electricity to Brazil.

According to an EVS representative, the company paid over $60 million for its share in the project. Three hundred million dollars in working capital is already on hand. The Export–Import Bank of Brazil, Belo Horizonte Bank, and Santo Bank PCL, are also lining up as possible shareholders. Percy Zahar, Nova Lima Power's executive director of finance, has hinted at offering them a 20% stake.

Electricity of Argentina is planning a second 500 kilovolt power line from Rio de Janeiro to Sao Paulo. The expected cost, between $130 million and $140 million, will be borne 60% by the World Bank. The line will transmit 500–700 megawatts of power per year from the Iguape Hydroelectric Power Plant. If the work proceeds as scheduled, construction will begin in February of 1998 and be completed before the opening of the Iguape plant in the year 2000.

197. What is the main point of this article?

(A) That South America is expanding its power production
(B) That Brazil and Argentina are sharing power resources
(C) That Germany is entering a joint venture with Brazil
(D) That almost half of Brazil's power company is foreign owned

198. How much money is currently available for the Nova Lima Lignite project?

(A) $60 million
(B) $130 million
(C) $140 million
(D) $300 million

199. What percentage of Nova Lima Power is currently under consideration for sale?

(A) 20%
(B) 40%
(C) 60%
(D) 80%

200. Where will the Argentinean 500 kilovolt power line draw its power from?

(A) Sao Paulo
(B) The Iguape power plant
(C) Electricity of Brazil
(D) Nova Lima Lignite

Stop! This is the end of the test. If you finish before one hour and fifteen minutes have passed, you may go back to Parts V, VI, and VII and check your work.

Practice Test Three

LISTENING COMPREHENSION

In this section of the test, you will have the chance to show how well you understand spoken English. There are four parts to this section, with special directions for each part.

PART I

Directions: For each question, you will see a picture in your test book and you will hear four short statements. The statements will be spoken just one time. They will not be printed in your test book, so you must listen carefully to understand what the speaker says.

When you hear the four statements, look at the picture in your test book and choose the statement that best describes what you see in the picture. Then, on your answer sheet, find the number of the question and mark your answer. Look at the sample below.

Sample Answer
Ⓐ ● Ⓒ Ⓓ

Now listen to the four statements.

Statement (B), "They're having a meeting," best describes what you see in the picture. Therefore, you should choose answer (B).

GO ON TO THE NEXT PAGE

1.

2.

3.

4.

GO ON TO THE NEXT PAGE

5.

6.

7.

8.

GO ON TO THE NEXT PAGE ►

9.

10.

11.

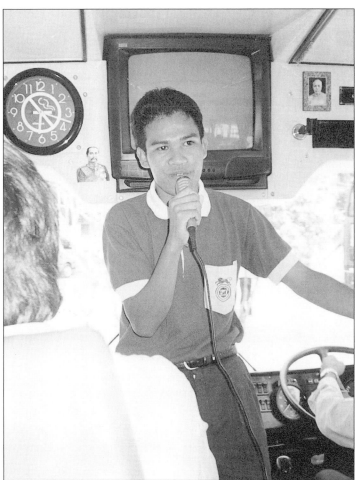

12.

GO ON TO THE NEXT PAGE

13.

14.

15.

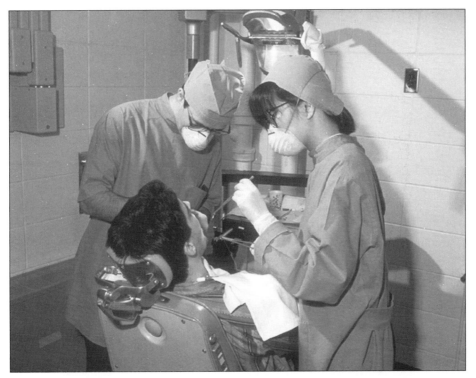

16.

GO ON TO THE NEXT PAGE ►

17.

18.

19.

20.

GO ON TO THE NEXT PAGE ▶

PART II

Directions: In this part of the test, you will hear a question spoken in English, followed by three responses, also spoken in English. The question and the responses will be spoken just one time. They will not be printed in your test book, so you must listen carefully to understand what the speakers say. You are to choose the best response to each question.

Now listen to a sample question.

You will hear:

Sample Answer

You will also hear:

The best response to the question "How are you?" is choice (A), "I am fine, thank you." Therefore, you should choose answer (A).

21.   Mark your answer on your answer sheet.

22.   Mark your answer on your answer sheet.

23.   Mark your answer on your answer sheet.

24.   Mark your answer on your answer sheet.

25.   Mark your answer on your answer sheet.

26.   Mark your answer on your answer sheet.

27.   Mark your answer on your answer sheet.

28.   Mark your answer on your answer sheet.

29.   Mark your answer on your answer sheet.

30.   Mark your answer on your answer sheet.

31.   Mark your answer on your answer sheet.

32.   Mark your answer on your answer sheet.

33.   Mark your answer on your answer sheet.

34.   Mark your answer on your answer sheet.

35. Mark your answer on your answer sheet.

36. Mark your answer on your answer sheet.

37. Mark your answer on your answer sheet.

38. Mark your answer on your answer sheet.

39. Mark your answer on your answer sheet.

40. Mark your answer on your answer sheet.

41. Mark your answer on your answer sheet.

42. Mark your answer on your answer sheet.

43. Mark your answer on your answer sheet.

44. Mark your answer on your answer sheet.

45. Mark your answer on your answer sheet.

46. Mark your answer on your answer sheet.

47. Mark your answer on your answer sheet.

48. Mark your answer on your answer sheet.

49. Mark your answer on your answer sheet.

50. Mark your answer on your answer sheet.

GO ON TO THE NEXT PAGE ▶

Directions: In this part of the test, you will hear thirty short conversations between two people. The conversations will not be printed in your test book. You will hear the conversations only once, so you must listen carefully to understand what the speakers say.

In your test book, you will read a question about each conversation. The question will be followed by four answers. You are to choose the best answer to each question and mark it on your answer sheet.

---

51. What is Mr. Barasso going to do?

  (A) Visit the doctor.
  (B) Get out of the car.
  (C) Have the brakes fixed.
  (D) Pick up a friend at five o'clock.

52. On what does their meeting depend?

  (A) Ahmet leaving at twelve o'clock.
  (B) Ahmet leaving Cairo early.
  (C) Ahmet taking an early flight to Cairo.
  (D) Ahmet leaving Cairo by noon.

53. What have the women done?

  (A) Written a series of ads.
  (B) Increased their credit line.
  (C) Thanked their boss.
  (D) Created an appealing advertisement.

54. What time is the meeting?

  (A) Three o'clock.
  (B) Four o'clock.
  (C) Five o'clock.
  (D) Six o'clock.

55. Where are they?

  (A) In a car.
  (B) In a train.
  (C) In a gas station.
  (D) In an empty place.

56. What time of day is it?

  (A) In the morning.
  (B) In the early afternoon.
  (C) In the late afternoon.
  (D) In the evening.

57. What does Jeanie offer to do?

  (A) Call a taxi.
  (B) Make a reservation.
  (C) Carry the luggage.
  (D) Drive to the airport.

58. What is the problem?

  (A) There are no available rooms at the conference.
  (B) The hotel is fully booked.
  (C) Mrs. Blair forgot to make reservations.
  (D) The secretary can't remember the name of the hotel.

59. Where is the theater?

  (A) On First Avenue.
  (B) On Second Avenue.
  (C) On Third Avenue.
  (D) On Fourth Avenue.

60. What is known about the man?

  (A) He is over 65.
  (B) He likes county fairs.
  (C) He takes public transportation to work.
  (D) He reads a monthly journal.

61. What is George's job?

  (A) Secretary.
  (B) Telephone operator.
  (C) Real estate agent.
  (D) Estate manager.

62. What is being talked about?

  (A) A door.
  (B) Glassware.
  (C) Eye glasses.
  (D) A machine.

63. Why doesn't the man go on vacation?

   (A) His company needs him at work.
   (B) He wants to spend his vacation at home.
   (C) He'd find it too expensive.
   (D) He doesn't have vacation time left this year.

64. What does the customer decide to do?

   (A) Get a different model.
   (B) Place several orders.
   (C) Try another branch.
   (D) Buy more stock.

65. What is the man considering?

   (A) Talking to the vice president.
   (B) Taking a new position elsewhere.
   (C) Opening a company himself.
   (D) Continuing his education.

66. What was wrong with the restaurant?

   (A) The food was bad.
   (B) The manager was frequently absent.
   (C) There weren't enough customers.
   (D) They couldn't get enough help.

67. What is being sold?

   (A) A computer.
   (B) A car.
   (C) A telephone.
   (D) A stereo.

68. Where is this taking place?

   (A) At a bank.
   (B) At an auto checkpoint.
   (C) At a motor vehicle office.
   (D) At a police station.

69. Who is having an open house?

   (A) A drug company.
   (B) The college.
   (C) The high school.
   (D) A nautical club.

70. What took a long time?

   (A) The train ride.
   (B) The walk.
   (C) The taxi ride.
   (D) The car ride.

71. What does Nathan want the woman to do?

   (A) Work in the shipping department.
   (B) Help out more at work.
   (C) Play softball.
   (D) Coach the team.

72. What does the man want?

   (A) Stationery.
   (B) A map of the city.
   (C) A particular book.
   (D) Directions to the city.

73. What is the woman's profession?

   (A) Actress.
   (B) Baker.
   (C) Scientist.
   (D) Sound technician.

74. What is the man buying?

   (A) Cufflinks.
   (B) Silverware.
   (C) Hats.
   (D) Shoes.

75. What day is it?

   (A) Monday.
   (B) Tuesday.
   (C) Wednesday.
   (D) Friday.

76. What does Joan offer to do?

   (A) Make some art work.
   (B) Schedule a dental appointment.
   (C) Buy some art supplies.
   (D) Post some signs.

GO ON TO THE NEXT PAGE ▶

77. What is the man talking about?

    (A) His wife's birthday.
    (B) His anniversary.
    (C) His promotion.
    (D) His birthday.

78. How much was the customer charged?

    (A) $14.00
    (B) $14.75
    (C) $17.00
    (D) $17.35

79. What is bothering the man?

    (A) He has to switch his working hours.
    (B) The light is going on and off.
    (C) He doesn't like fluorescent lights.
    (D) The electrician didn't show up.

80. What is the man's problem?

    (A) He can't find Calvert Street.
    (B) Nobody answers at the number he has.
    (C) The event was moved across the street.
    (D) He can't find an address.

Directions: In this part of the test, you will hear several short talks. Each will be spoken just one time. They will not be printed in your test book, so you must listen carefully to understand and remember what is said.

In your test book, you will read two or more questions about each short talk. The questions will be followed by four answers. You are to choose the best answer to each question and mark it on your answer sheet.

81. Who will be raising the funds for the project?

(A) The Home Builders.
(B) Oklahoma City National Bank.
(C) The Macomb Club.
(D) The Neighborhood Corps, Incorporated.

82. Where is the work being done?

(A) In Woodside.
(B) In Bedford.
(C) In Oklahoma City.
(D) In Marlboro.

83. Who makes up the Neighborhood Corps, Incorporated?

(A) Construction workers.
(B) Volunteers.
(C) Low-income families.
(D) Architects.

84. What is being looked for?

(A) Reports from radiation victims.
(B) The cause of the accident.
(C) The exact amount of fall-out.
(D) Long-term effects of radiation.

85. What effect did the exposure have on humans?

(A) Many passed on defects to their offspring.
(B) The number of their offspring has declined.
(C) Their genes were damaged.
(D) They became whiter.

86. What is known about the birds near the accident?

(A) They had areas of white feathers.
(B) They were unusually weak.
(C) They had blotches on them.
(D) They had not reached breeding age.

87. Who is probably listening to this introduction?

(A) Students of Chinese.
(B) Public relations personnel.
(C) Business people.
(D) Bankers.

88. What is known about Mr. Yan?

(A) He was a customs agent.
(B) He instructs others in protocol.
(C) He is managing this year's trade convention.
(D) He gives bank management seminars.

89. What is this notice about?

(A) Applying for credit.
(B) Keeping good credit.
(C) Correcting bad credit.
(D) Accessing your credit history.

90. How does the Fair Credit Reporting Act serve consumers?

(A) It ensures that credit bureaus will stay in business.
(B) It ensures that all credit checks will be reported.
(C) It helps consumers pay their debts.
(D) It gives consumers information.

91. What may a credit bureau be asked to do if they deny someone credit?

(A) Refund the agency for the report.
(B) Review the data in the credit history.
(C) Send the consumer a written report of the credit history.
(D) Provide credit within thirty days.

GO ON TO THE NEXT PAGE

92. Where are water treatment facilities going to be built this year?

    (A) Japan.
    (B) Sweden.
    (C) Port Pacifica.
    (D) Brazil.

93. In what country was the method of treatment developed?

    (A) Brazil.
    (B) Vietnam.
    (C) Japan.
    (D) Sweden.

94. What kind of company is Vinacon?

    (A) A waste disposal company.
    (B) A water treatment company.
    (C) A construction company.
    (D) An investment company.

95. Who is this speaker talking to?

    (A) Dignitaries.
    (B) Actors.
    (C) Audience members.
    (D) Electronic manufacturers.

96. What is the main point of this talk?

    (A) The cast members are all professionals.
    (B) The theater needs donations.
    (C) The theater is new.
    (D) The show is disrupted by noise.

97. What can you buy at intermission?

    (A) Tickets and T-shirts.
    (B) Sweets and beverages.
    (C) Pagers and beepers.
    (D) Proceeds and benefits.

98. Where would you be likely to hear this announcement?

    (A) On your TV.
    (B) At a sports event.
    (C) In a theater.
    (D) On the radio.

99. Who is this broadcast directed at?

    (A) Drivers.
    (B) Athletes.
    (C) Music-lovers.
    (D) Police officers.

100. How might someone feel who was listening to this message?

    (A) Worldly.
    (B) Frustrated.
    (C) Encouraged.
    (D) Manipulated.

This is the end of the Listening Comprehension portion of Practice Test Three. Turn to Part V in your test book.

YOU WILL HAVE ONE HOUR AND FIFTEEN MINUTES TO COMPLETE PARTS V, VI, AND VII OF THE TEST.

READING

In this section of the test, you will have a chance to show how well you understand written English. There are three parts to this section, with special directions for each part.

PART V

Directions: Questions 101–140 are incomplete sentences. Four words or phrases, marked (A), (B), (C), (D) are given beneath each sentence. You are to choose the **one** word or phrase that best completes the sentence. Then, on your answer sheet, find the number of the question and mark your answer.

You will read:

Because the equipment is very delicate, it must be handled with ....

(A) caring
(B) careful
(C) care
(D) carefully

Sample Answer

Ⓐ Ⓑ ● Ⓓ

The sentence should read, "Because the equipment is very delicate, it must be handled with care." Therefore, you should choose answer (C).

Now begin work on the questions.

---

101. Ursula was the vice president of .... for the East Coast last year.

    (A) marketings
    (B) marketing
    (C) markets
    (D) marketed

102. Professor Mintz has been invited .... his observations in the research article.

    (A) include
    (B) for inclusion
    (C) including
    (D) to include

103. If it weren't for venture capital, the American business machine .... collapse.

    (A) would
    (B) will
    (C) was
    (D) were

104. He asked us not to .... our opinions on hearsay only.

    (A) base
    (B) think
    (C) have
    (D) give

105. The volume of paperwork that needs to be filled out to buy a home can .... it seem insurmountable.

    (A) make
    (B) cause
    (C) put
    (D) appear

106. Our chemists will .... the results of the test.

    (A) empathize
    (B) catalyze
    (C) symbolize
    (D) analyze

GO ON TO THE NEXT PAGE ➤

107. If inflation gets too high, it steadily .... the buying power of people with a fixed income.

(A) would erode
(B) erodes
(C) eroded
(D) will be eroding

108. Although improving, the unemployment problem still ....

(A) persistence
(B) persists
(C) persisting
(D) persistently

109. Enabling consumers to make educated .... was the purpose of enacting the Truth in Lending Act.

(A) decisive
(B) deciding
(C) decides
(D) decisions

110. An estimated 35 million tax dollars is lost every year .... the black economy.

(A) in
(B) for
(C) at
(D) over

111. Albrecht Dürer's house was bought by the townspeople, who .... it to its original condition.

(A) reconstituted
(B) restructured
(C) restored
(D) redone

112. He .... pyramiding as simply using the profits of one investment to make another.

(A) explaining
(B) are being explained
(C) had been explained
(D) explained

113. Arthur Morris created the first .... loan in 1916 despite all advice to the contrary.

(A) increment
(B) installment
(C) internment
(D) involvement

114. The receptionist informed customers that there would be a two-week delay in deliveries .... the current stock had been exhausted.

(A) ever since
(B) as
(C) whenever
(D) until

115. Fiber optic technology is allowing .... companies to offer a remarkably improved picture.

(A) cables
(B) cabling
(C) cable
(D) cabled

116. The new employee found it difficult to work .... such stressful conditions.

(A) beneath
(B) besides
(C) under
(D) over

117. His insurance premiums are lower .... mine because he is a non-smoker.

(A) than
(B) until
(C) besides
(D) from

118. .... amount of money was going to stop her from blowing the whistle on the company's policy regarding waste disposal.

(A) None
(B) Not
(C) Such
(D) No

119. The field staff was .... articulate in expressing its dissatisfaction with the company's restructuring.

   (A) greatly
   (B) keenly
   (C) moreover
   (D) quite

120. City officials are predicting that the new subway system will .... the city traffic by 45%.

   (A) lessen
   (B) to lessen
   (C) be lessened
   (D) lessening

121. We were told that the expense budget was being trimmed .... the company was considering the purchase of a larger warehouse.

   (A) because
   (B) so
   (C) neither
   (D) or

122. Inflation is eating .... at our hard-earned savings.

   (A) down
   (B) on
   (C) through
   (D) away

123. The desert .... cool at night.

   (A) it is
   (B) is
   (C) unless it is
   (D) and is

124. She is, in .... respect, an ideal candidate for the position.

   (A) every
   (B) all
   (C) individual
   (D) other

125. Because of a stable economic growth rate, the president can probably look .... to another term.

   (A) up
   (B) forward
   (C) over
   (D) above

126. Arteries lead blood away from the heart, ... veins guide it back.

   (A) whereas
   (B) because
   (C) in case
   (D) should

127. The buying and selling of stocks and bonds is .... I would like to learn more about.

   (A) something
   (B) somewhere
   (C) somehow
   (D) somewhat

128. The findings of the investigation confirmed that there was no .... amongst the local police force.

   (A) interruption
   (B) corruption
   (C) eruption
   (D) disruption

129. The Concerned Businessmen's Association will have its annual meeting in the ballroom .... the Bombay Lux Hotel.

   (A) with
   (B) to
   (C) on
   (D) of

130. Most investment brochures carry the following caveat: "Past performance cannot .... future results."

   (A) guarantor
   (B) guaranty
   (C) guaranteed
   (D) guarantee

GO ON TO THE NEXT PAGE

131. .... software appears to be much more useful than we had anticipated.

    (A) A
    (B) The
    (C) These
    (D) Those

132. The retail merchants knew that a price .... was inevitable.

    (A) enlargement
    (B) increase
    (C) progress
    (D) growth

133. Bond activity increased .... our intense marketing efforts.

    (A) with respect to
    (B) in regard to
    (C) in light of
    (D) as a result of

134. A farmer can .... a contract with a mill to lock in a certain price for six months in order to be protected against falling prices.

    (A) draw out
    (B) draw up
    (C) draw in
    (D) draw on

135. On behalf of the Historical Society, I would like to thank you all for your most generous contribution toward the .... of the original railroad station.

    (A) fabrication
    (B) renovation
    (C) manifestation
    (D) calculation

136. A good way to avoid misunderstandings in business is to .... all agreements in writing.

    (A) put off
    (B) put away
    (C) put
    (D) put up with

137. The backup system .... turned on by that time.

    (A) will
    (B) should
    (C) is being
    (D) will have been

138. The electrician would .... repaired the transformer late last night if it weren't for the wind.

    (A) have
    (B) done
    (C) had
    (D) did

139. To avoid paying overtime, the company allowed the employees to work up to five o'clock, but .... could not work any later.

    (A) them
    (B) he
    (C) they
    (D) those

140. Please bring my wife and .... up-to-date on the portfolio changes that you have been working on.

    (A) she
    (B) us
    (C) I
    (D) me

PART VI

Directions: In **Questions 141–160**, each sentence has four words or phrases underlined. The four underlined parts of the sentence are marked (A), (B), (C), (D). You are to identify the **one** underlined word or phrase that should be corrected or rewritten. Then, on your answer sheet, find the number of the question and mark your answer.

Example:

Sample Answer
● Ⓑ Ⓒ Ⓓ

All <u>employee</u> are required <u>to wear</u> their
    A   B

<u>identification</u> badges <u>while</u> at work.
    C   D

The underlined word "employee" is not correct in this sentence. This sentence should read, "All employees are required to wear their identification badges while at work." Therefore, you should choose answer (A).

Now begin work on the questions.

141. <u>Several delegates</u> flew from Calcutta
       A
<u>to greeting</u> the <u>ambassador</u> and her family
    B   C
<u>before the concert.</u>
    D

142. The new accountant had <u>erroneously</u> filed
                 A
all of the <u>taxes reports</u> with the
        B
<u>wrong agency</u>, causing a series of problems
    C
<u>over</u> the weeks that followed.
  D

143. The committee treasurer <u>simply</u> requested
              A
<u>that the results</u> of the budget meeting <u>be</u>
    B   C
typed <u>for.</u>
    D

144. By the time the <u>debt is paid off</u>, the country
     A   B
<u>it will have paid</u> over two million dollars
    C
<u>in interest alone.</u>
    D

145. We needed <u>thousands of pencils</u> for the
             A
convention, <u>so we bought</u> the <u>less</u> expensive
         B   C
<u>ones</u> we could find.
  D

146. The Turkish <u>work force</u> is now an <u>integral</u>
         A   B
<u>part</u> of the German <u>economics.</u>
  C   D

147. Many retailers have <u>been regained</u> the
               A
<u>ground they lost</u> as a result of <u>last year's</u>
    B   C
nationwide <u>economic slump.</u>
    D

148. Labor negotiators <u>worked through the night</u>
             A
<u>in an effort</u> to avoid a <u>nationwide</u> strike and
    B   C
the <u>accompaniment media attention.</u>
    D

GO ON TO THE NEXT PAGE ▶

149. With the carefully devised marketing plan
         A
    that Tara put together, we were able to
              B   C
    recover back our market share.
         D

150. Solar technology is being development
         A   B
    around the world to keep pace with the
                         C
    energy needs of developing countries.
                       D

151. At about half the cost, we enjoyed a
              A
    memorable trip to Norway on the Majestic
         B   C
    Cruise Liner this passing summer.
                 D

152. Credit cards are usually issued to these with a
                       A   B
    good history of paying their bills on time.
                  C   D

153. The travel agent works out a vacation
                      A
    package that would take us into the very
            B   C
    heart of China.
         D

154. Activity in the commodities market is doubled
      A   B
    this past year due to an intense marketing
                   C
    effort to erase its risky, unpredictable image.
                    D

155. What are taxable and how much one pays is
          A   B   C
    determined by a government agency.
               D

156. According to this author, dining etiquette are
      A   B
    different from country to country and even
              C   D
    within countries.

157. Because of the flood, all the wood
      A
    had warped, the nails had begun to rust, and
         B   C
    the entire floors had to be replaced.
        D

158. If you are at all dissatisfied with the product,
              A   B
    your money will be refunded and paid back to
                        C
    you upon request.
         D

159. Feared inflation, investors are not as willing
      A   B
    to make the bold moves
    that have characterized the last six months of
              C   D
    stock market activity.

160. Not only did the new cashier call in sick, and
      A   B   C
    she also asked how much vacation time
    was due her.
        D

PART VII

Directions: Questions 161–200 are based on a selection of reading materials, such as notices, letters, forms, newspaper and magazine articles, and advertisements. You are to choose the **one** best answer (A), (B), (C), or (D) to each question. Then, on your answer sheet, find the number of the question and mark your answer. Answer all questions following each reading selection on the basis of what is **stated** or **implied** in that selection.

Read the following example.

> The Museum of Technology is a "hands-on" museum, designed for people to experience science at work. Visitors are encouraged to use, test, and handle the objects on display. Special demonstrations are scheduled for the first and second Wednesdays of each month at 13:30. Open Tuesday–Friday 12:00–16:30, Saturday 10:00–17:30, and Sunday 11:00–16:30.

> When during the month can visitors see special demonstrations?

Sample Answer
Ⓐ ● Ⓒ Ⓓ

> (A)   Every weekend
> (B)   The first two Wednesdays
> (C)   One afternoon a week
> (D)   Every other Wednesday

The reading selection says that the demonstrations are scheduled for the first and second Wednesdays of the month. Therefore, you should choose answer (B).

Now begin work on the questions.

Questions 161–162 refer to the following article.

The Environmental Safety Bureau has announced that it will pay farmers anywhere in the continental U.S. to set up grass or tree buffers to filter sediment, herbicides and fertilizer running off crop lands into streams and wetlands. It has been established that rainwater running off farm fields contributes more pollution to the nation's lakes and streams than any other single source. The farmers will be entitled to an annual payment of 125% of the rental value of the land each year for 20 years. The ESB has been advocating buffers for some time now because vegetated areas near streams can filter out up to 85% of pollutants.

161. What is this article about?

   (A) The need to protect waterways
   (B) Farmers problems in preventing run-off
   (C) The proposed solution to agricultural pollution
   (D) The effectiveness of water filters

162. What incentive is given to farmers?

   (A) Financial compensation
   (B) More land to use
   (C) Guaranteed renters
   (D) New crops

GO ON TO THE NEXT PAGE ➤

MEMORANDUM

To: Jay D. Moran, Office Manager   Date: April 2, 1995

From: Detlef Glanz   CC: Mark Roberts
Mildred Beir
Po Wang
Barry Thomas

Subject: Need for smoke detectors

About three years ago, an insurance agent named Briggs did an inspection of the warehouse to determine our need for fire insurance.

I have just been notified we are being charged an additional $18,500 yearly because of inadequate fire protection.

Have there been any changes in the layout since Briggs did his inspection? It is obvious that something has to change.

Didn't Briggs quote us a figure of about $200 for smoke detectors, maybe $300 with one-time installation cost. We can surely do better than $18,500 a year. Please dig out Briggs' report and prepare a cost-analysis of our various options for smoke detectors and/or sprinkler systems.

163. Why was this memo written?

(A) To investigate cost-saving measures
(B) To find out who did the last inspection
(C) To stress the need for safety
(D) To locate a new insurance agent

164. What did Briggs do?

(A) Issued a warning on warehouse safety
(B) Increased the fire insurance coverage
(C) Inspected smoke detectors
(D) Submitted a cost estimate for smoke detectors

Questions 165–167 refer to the following news item.

The New York Baseball Club, an investor group led by the computer chip executive Henry B. Lawson, paid the New York Baseball Stadium Authority well over $500,000 last week in return for a one-year extension of its exclusive status with the state agency. This would mean that the only one able to negotiate a lease for a stadium facility would be Lawson's New York Baseball Club.

Lawson hopes to buy a major league baseball team that would play in a 50,000-seat stadium to be built by the state. He would get the major league team by either winning an expansion franchise or by moving an existing team to New York.

The agreement, approved by the authority last week, would give Lawson's group the right to receive extensions for as many as five years, in return for additional payments that would total $4.1 million over that period. The investor group would receive over half the payments if a stadium is built.

165. Why did Lawson pay $500,000?

(A) To buy a major league team
(B) To block off any competition
(C) To help build the new stadium
(D) To lease the stadium for another year

166. Who is funding this activity?

(A) A computer company
(B) The state
(C) A group of investors
(D) The New York Baseball Club

167. Who would be responsible for building the stadium?

(A) New York State
(B) The New York Baseball Club
(C) The stadium authority
(D) A major league team

GO ON TO THE NEXT PAGE

 IRC, INFORMATION RETRIEVAL CORPORATION, is a multinational computer manufacturer based in Australia and Indonesia. The main office is in Brisbane, Australia, with other offices in Kuchino, Malaysia, Bonn, Germany, Pusan, South Korea, Tokyo, Japan and in Atlanta, Georgia in the U.S. IRC is one of the fastest growing computer companies in the world. It is a leader in the field of laptop computers. It also enjoys a considerable market for its software products, which are serviced by a battery of customer service representatives in every major country. With manufacturing plants in Seoul, Himmelstadt and Topeka, it is planning on expanding manufacturing capacity over the next three years. Of its 15,000 employees worldwide, 6,000 are technical staff, 2,000 software, 2,500 administration and 4,500 sales and marketing.

168. Where does IRC build its computers?

(A) Pusan
(B) Atlanta
(C) Seoul
(D) Bonn

169. What is known about IRC?

(A) Their customer service is the best in the industry.
(B) It is enjoying a threefold expansion in software production.
(C) The central office is in Malaysia.
(D) It leads the way in laptop computers.

170. What area uses the least manpower?

(A) Sales and marketing
(B) Manufacturing
(C) Software
(D) Clerical and financial

September 29, 1993

Paul Bergstein, President
Stone & Brick Contractors
423 Ridgewell Road
Burbank, CA 91345

Dear Mr. Bergstein,

Because I have not been able to reach you by phone, I am resorting to registered mail. On May 2 of this year, I signed a contract with your Mr. Alan Stevenson for a five-foot high stone wall. It had an arched entrance with fittings for a particular black swinging metal gate. Completion was scheduled for September 15 and the agreed-upon price was $5,500. Enclosed is a copy of the contract.

Although the work began and ended as scheduled and the wall itself is a constant source of compliments from the neighbors, it turns out that the fittings for the gate were incorrectly placed. Not only that, but the bill was $400 over the quoted price.

I was not concerned about the overcharge of $400 until I found out about repair costs. The wall has to be opened up in eight separate spots where the old fittings are so that they can be rearranged to accommodate the new gate. That adjustment alone will cost me $500.

I, therefore, respectfully request that you refund at least $400 as soon as possible. As I had such difficulty in trying to reach you by phone, I am somewhat concerned about your willingness to account for this error. While I would prefer not to, I will not hesitate to refer this matter to my attorney if I don't hear from you in the coming week.

Sincerely,

Ingrid Baum

Ingrid Baum

171. What is Ingrid's main purpose in writing the letter?

(A) To request a refund
(B) To inquire about the additional charge of $400
(C) To give the dimensions for the gate she wants installed
(D) To compliment the workers on their work

172. How did Ingrid initially try to reach Mr. Bergstein?

(A) Through her lawyer
(B) By phone
(C) By e-mail
(D) Through registered mail

173. How much did Ingrid pay for the building of the wall?

(A) $4,000
(B) $5,500
(C) $5,900
(D) $6,000

174. How will the gate be repaired?

(A) By rearranging the fittings
(B) By buying a new gate
(C) By paying $400 more
(D) By taking down part of the stone wall

GO ON TO THE NEXT PAGE

Construction Outlook for the Haiphong District

This report is concerned primarily with construction of homes in the Haiphong area in the next decade. There are many factors which influence the construction of houses in the area, and part of the report is devoted to an analysis of these factors: population growth and the increased need for housing, economic activity, and current housing facilities. The information used in the preparation of this report was gathered from the Haiphong Chamber of Commerce, census tracts, government reports and books relating to housing.

Last year, the estimated population of corporate Haiphong was 724,000, an increase of eleven percent over the Vietnam Census figure. The population of metropolitan Haiphong was 922,000. The considerable growth of metropolitan Haiphong is reflected in expansion of the city's living area by roughly thirteen percent. Haiphong covers an area of 295.5 square miles, of which 197 square miles is land. There is more than enough room for expansion, especially in the Gingh Bo, Quan To and Shangti areas.

Although there may appear to be adequate housing facilities for the population, twenty-five percent of those units are dilapidated. In general, the economic conditions in Haiphong seem extremely favorable for a continued increase in new housing construction and housing improvements. The introduction of the new Hunddei automobile manufacturing plant will further develop the economy of the metropolitan area. Income, in general, will continue to rise as the industrial activity in the area picks up.

One could conclude that home construction in the future will be at least as high as it was last year, with a good chance of a five to ten percent increase.

---

175. What is the purpose of this report?

(A) To explain the rate of success of previous construction efforts
(B) To criticize the housing conditions in Haiphong
(C) To estimate the prospects for home building in Haiphong
(D) To detail proposed industrial activity for the area

176. Which factor would NOT have an impact on the building of homes in the area?

(A) The availability of public transportation
(B) The level of industrial activity in the area
(C) How fast the population was growing
(D) How many living quarters are currently available

177. What was the estimated population of Haiphong's business center last year?

(A) 724,000
(B) 922,000
(C) 1,646,000
(D) 198,000

178. What percentage of Haiphong's housing needs repair or replacement?

(A) 10%
(B) 11%
(C) 13%
(D) 25%

179. What effect will the Hunddei plant have on the area?

(A) It will raise the price of homes in the area.
(B) Wages, in general, should go up five to ten percent.
(C) It will boost the local economy.
(D) The company will help subsidize the repair of dilapidated homes.

BULK TRASH PICK-UP

In June, July and August, the Department of Public Works will once again be accepting requests for pick-up of bulk trash from residences that are serviced by the city for regular pick-ups. If you need bulk trash picked up, you can call (517) 453-8967 to make an appointment. Bulk trash is anything over sixty pounds. Items such as doors, broken chairs or pieces of machinery are permissible.

Please remember to remove all doors from things like refrigerators, freezers and ovens, so that a child cannot get trapped inside. Do not place items outside for pick-up before 6 p.m. the previous evening or after 6 a.m. the day of the pick-up. Combustibles and items like paint or solvents cannot be picked up. They must be disposed of at the Fort Thornton Station at 436 Wattes Road N.W. The station's Environmental Safety Section accepts drop-offs on weekdays from 8 a.m. to 4 p.m.

180. Who may put out their bulk trash for pick-up?

(A) Only regular city sanitation customers
(B) Only residents whose written application has been accepted
(C) Only people wishing to dispose of kitchen appliances
(D) Anyone with non-combustible bulk trash

181. Which items would have to be brought to the Fort Thornton Station?

(A) Turpentine
(B) Metal fence poles
(C) Transmission parts
(D) Doors

182. What time does bulk trash have to be put out the day before pick-up?

(A) Before 4 p.m.
(B) Before 6 p.m.
(C) After 6 p.m.
(D) After 8 a.m.

GO ON TO THE NEXT PAGE

Questions 183–186 refer to the following notice.

PLEASE BE ADVISED of the following changes in international travel to and from Montreal. Check your airline ticket carefully or ask your ticket agent if you are returning to Montreal on or after September 20. Starting September 20, several airlines that offer scheduled international flights will start operating their services out of Dorval airport. All charter flights, both overseas and to the United States, will leave from Dorval airport. So, if you are already booked for a flight during that period, it is possible that you will be leaving from Dorval and returning to Mirabel – or vice versa. On your airline ticket, the code "VRV" designates Mirabel and "TMT" designates Dorval. If your return flight is landing at a different airport from your departing, it would be better to use public transportation rather than drive yourself. You might find yourself at one airport and your car parked at another. A convenient shuttle bus connects Dorval and Mirabel and the city center with regular service from 4 a.m. to midnight, seven days a week.

183. Why was this notice issued?

(A) Because of construction work at Dorval airport
(B) Because of a change in international flight paths
(C) Because of the additional services being offered
(D) Because of a change in the bus schedules

184. What are customers being asked to do?

(A) To try to book flights before September 20
(B) To take chartered flights when possible
(C) To use parking near the airport
(D) To review their tickets carefully

185. How can a customer know which airport he/she is landing in?

(A) Arrivals are at the same airport as departures.
(B) Tickets indicate destination airport.
(C) Charter flight customers land in Dorval, others in Mirabel.
(D) Airport ticket agents will provide updated reports.

186. What advice is given regarding transportation to and from the airports?

(A) To wait for arriving passengers at the airport of departure
(B) To take advantage of the shuttle bus service
(C) To leave the car at the airport you depart from
(D) To park only in designated areas

Questions 187–189 refer to the following form.

Yes. I want all of my credit, debit and ATM cards protected by *The Watchguard.*

Check one: SEND NO MONEY
____ One year only $18.00   ____ Three years only $41.00 *(You save $13.00)*

_____

Name
_____

Address   City
_____

State   Zip

Credit Card Account Number: _____ - _____ - _____ - _____

X _____

Sign here   Date

Please bill my credit card for the amount I have chosen. I understand that my account will automatically be billed as long as I am a credit card member or unless I cancel the service. I understand that this protection is not required to maintain my credit account. An explanation of terms and benefits, as stated in the Membership Kit I will be sent, will provide complete details.

---

187. Why would someone send in this form?

   (A) To extend the length of the card's validity
   (B) To subscribe to *The Watchguard*
   (C) To have one's credit cards protected
   (D) To apply for additional debit cards

188. If a person wants to participate, how much will it cost for the longest protection?

   (A) Nothing
   (B) $13.00
   (C) $18.00
   (D) $41.00

189. What will the buyers receive?

   (A) A membership account number
   (B) A bill
   (C) A membership kit
   (D) A duplicate credit card

GO ON TO THE NEXT PAGE ▶

Questions 190–192 refer to the following chart.

```
CURRENT ANNUAL COST OF ADDRESSING BILLS BY HAND:

Wages: 48 days at $15 per day                    $720.00
   (12 months. at 4 working days a month)
Second mailings: 25 mailings per month
   at $.10 each for 12 months                     $30.00
Total                                            $750.00

For 20 years: 20 x $750                       $15,000.00


CURRENT ANNUAL COST OF ADDRESSING BILLS WITH A PRINTER:

Cost of printer: $500 (initial cost) amortized
   over 20 years ($500 divided by 20)            $25.00
Cost of printing head: $150 amortized
   over 20 years ($150 divided by 20)             $7.50
Cost of address changes: 25 changes
   a month at $.10 each for 12 months            $30.00
Total                                            $62.50

For 20 years: 20 x $62.50                     $1,250.00
```

190. What is the purpose of showing both tables?

   (A) To illustrate how much is being spent on wages
   (B) To indicate the cost difference
   (C) To show how many more days are spent doing it by hand
   (D) To show the additional step if a printer is used

191. How many address corrections are there monthly?

   (A) 10
   (B) 15
   (C) 20
   (D) 25

192. How much does each mailing cost if done by hand?

   (A) $.10
   (B) $.12
   (C) $.15
   (D) $.25

MEMORANDUM

To: Nathaniel Foley   Date: June 3

From: Jeanne Eckhardt

Subject: Adherence to company policy

It has long been the policy of this company to pay one-half the membership fees for our employees whose membership in certain organizations would be of practical benefit to the company. So that all departments process these requests in a uniform fashion, we request that all department heads follow these instructions:

1. Any employee wishing to renew a membership or to join such an organization must request permission from his or her department head, in writing.
2. Once the employee has obtained a signature indicating approval, he or she may make arrangements to join, paying the membership in full and obtaining a receipt showing the amount and the length of membership.
3. Using Form 33R5, he or she will prepare a reimbursement voucher for one-half the amount of the fees.
4. Once the department head has signed the voucher, he or she can go to the cashier's office to receive a check for reimbursement.

If there are any questions regarding this policy, please address them to Mr. Faulkner in our communications department.

---

193. Why was this memo written?

(A) To encourage membership in professional organizations
(B) To survey department heads on the use of uniforms
(C) To request compliance with established procedures
(D) To issue new company policy

194. How is the company helping its employees?

(A) By streamlining its reimbursement process
(B) By increasing employee benefits
(C) By allowing applicants to cash their paychecks at the cashier's office
(D) By subsidizing membership in certain organizations

195. What should department heads do?

(A) Approve and sign Form 33R5
(B) Make sure membership fees are reasonable
(C) Process the paperwork for the cashier's office
(D) Act as a liaison between the company and these organizations

196. When should Form 33R5 be used?

(A) When one is asking to be recompensed
(B) When one is applying for membership
(C) When one is requesting department approval
(D) When one is requesting certain fees be waived

GO ON TO THE NEXT PAGE

The Association of Southeast Asian Nations (ASEAN) has decided to admit Myanmar, Laos and Cambodia to that region's association. This took place despite counter-efforts by the European Union, the U.S., and the opponents of the SLORC party. This decision is considered a turning point in the development of these countries, which for for years have struggled with poverty, civil war and political unrest.

The inclusion of these countries is expected to boost their status on the world stage as well as to provide them assistance and cooperation from other members of ASEAN. All members of ASEAN will reap the benefits of the ASEAN Free Trade Area (AFTA) agreement, which comes into effect in 1998. Also, a maximum tariff of five percent will be levied on exports from Laos, Cambodia and Myanmar to ASEAN countries, according to the Common Effective Preferential Tariff (CEPT) scheme. In the meantime, these three countries will be given a ten year grace period in which to lower their tariffs to AFTA's satisfaction.

It has been a long-term goal of ASEAN to have all nations of Southeast Asia as part of its organization. With these three countries now on board, the total membership is ten. A

ceremony formally admitting the new members into the ASEAN will take place in Kuala Lumpur on July 24 and 25 during the annual ASEAN convention.

197. What is the main point of the article?

(A) Myanmar is experiencing civil unrest
(B) SLORC's position is weakened
(C) ASEAN membership is growing
(D) ASEAN tariffs have changed

198. How will membership in ASEAN affect Cambodia?

(A) It will enhance trade with the European Union.
(B) It strikes a blow at the SLORC party.
(C) It will raise export tariffs.
(D) It will open its doors to economic cooperation.

199. What is AFTA expecting the new member countries to do?

(A) To relinquish all trade barriers between themselves
(B) To propose any needed changes to the CEPT
(C) To decrease their tariff rate
(D) To take action by 1998

200. What has ASEAN been seeking to do?

(A) To embrace all Southeast Asian countries
(B) To move their headquarters to Kuala Lumpur
(C) To add ten member countries
(D) To gain recognition from the European Union

Stop! This is the end of the test. If you finish before one hour and fifteen minutes have passed, you may go back to Parts V, VI, and VII and check your work.

Practice Test Four

LISTENING COMPREHENSION

In this section of the test, you will have the chance to show how well you understand spoken English. There are four parts to this section, with special directions for each part.

PART I

Directions: For each question, you will see a picture in your test book and you will hear four short statements. The statements will be spoken just one time. They will not be printed in your test book, so you must listen carefully to understand what the speaker says.

When you hear the four statements, look at the picture in your test book and choose the statement that best describes what you see in the picture. Then, on your answer sheet, find the number of the question and mark your answer. Look at the sample below.

Sample Answer
Ⓐ ● Ⓒ Ⓓ

Now listen to the four statements.

Statement (B), "They're having a meeting," best describes what you see in the picture. Therefore, you should choose answer (B).

GO ON TO THE NEXT PAGE

1.

2.

3.

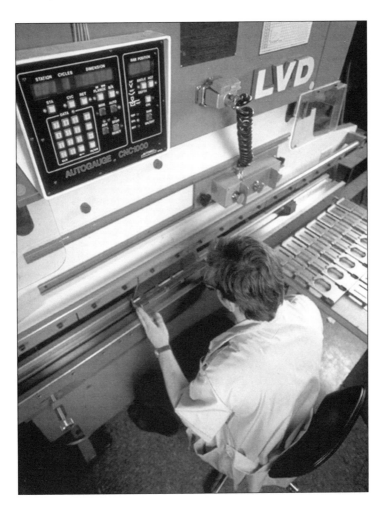

4.

GO ON TO THE NEXT PAGE ▶

5.

6.

7.

8.

GO ON TO THE NEXT PAGE

9.

10.

11.

12.

GO ON TO THE NEXT PAGE ➤

13.

14.

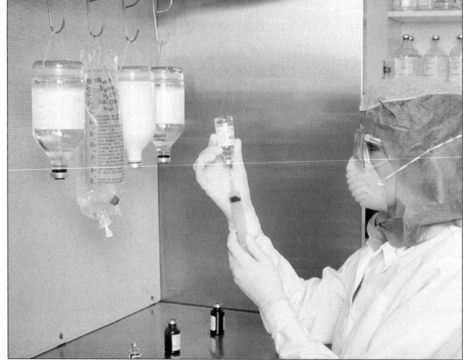

15.

16.

GO ON TO THE NEXT PAGE ➤

17.

18.

19.

20.

GO ON TO THE NEXT PAGE ▶

21.   Mark your answer on your answer sheet.

22.   Mark your answer on your answer sheet.

23.   Mark your answer on your answer sheet.

24.   Mark your answer on your answer sheet.

25.   Mark your answer on your answer sheet.

26.   Mark your answer on your answer sheet.

27.   Mark your answer on your answer sheet.

28.   Mark your answer on your answer sheet.

29.   Mark your answer on your answer sheet.

30.   Mark your answer on your answer sheet.

31.   Mark your answer on your answer sheet.

32.   Mark your answer on your answer sheet.

33.   Mark your answer on your answer sheet.

34.   Mark your answer on your answer sheet.

35. Mark your answer on your answer sheet.

36. Mark your answer on your answer sheet.

37. Mark your answer on your answer sheet.

38. Mark your answer on your answer sheet.

39. Mark your answer on your answer sheet.

40. Mark your answer on your answer sheet.

41. Mark your answer on your answer sheet.

42. Mark your answer on your answer sheet.

43. Mark your answer on your answer sheet.

44. Mark your answer on your answer sheet.

45. Mark your answer on your answer sheet.

46. Mark your answer on your answer sheet.

47. Mark your answer on your answer sheet.

48. Mark your answer on your answer sheet.

49. Mark your answer on your answer sheet.

50. Mark your answer on your answer sheet.

GO ON TO THE NEXT PAGE

Directions: In this part of the test, you will hear thirty short conversations between two people. The conversations will not be printed in your test book. You will hear the conversations only once, so you must listen carefully to understand what the speakers say.

In your test book, you will read a question about each conversation. The question will be followed by four answers. You are to choose the best answer to each question and mark it on your answer sheet.

51. What are the speakers discussing?

   (A) Buying a new bicycle.
   (B) Going to the doctor.
   (C) A broken down automobile.
   (D) When the store opens.

52. Why can't the man get a dog?

   (A) He wants to buy bagels.
   (B) Because of his wife.
   (C) It's on the shelf.
   (D) He already has one.

53. What has closed down?

   (A) The street.
   (B) The hardware store.
   (C) The supermarket.
   (D) The grocery store.

54. What furniture is new?

   (A) The coffee table.
   (B) The sofa.
   (C) The desk.
   (D) The bed.

55. What is John doing now?

   (A) He has a new job.
   (B) He's in school.
   (C) He still works at his old job.
   (D) He's between jobs.

56. How did the man lose weight?

   (A) He went on a diet.
   (B) He got sick.
   (C) He started exercising.
   (D) He doesn't know.

57. Where does this conversation take place?

   (A) In a school.
   (B) In a restaurant.
   (C) In France.
   (D) In a bank.

58. What does Betty suggest?

   (A) He uses a ballpoint.
   (B) He takes the weekend off.
   (C) The suit is dry cleaned.
   (D) The meeting is cancelled.

59. What does the man want to do?

   (A) Use a pencil.
   (B) Write a check.
   (C) Run an errand.
   (D) Borrow a pen.

60. How long was the woman in Beijing?

   (A) A week.
   (B) Two weeks.
   (C) Six weeks.
   (D) Two months.

61. Where is Susan's aunt?

   (A) In the room.
   (B) In the shower.
   (C) On the telephone.
   (D) On television.

62. What's the problem?

   (A) The computer is broken.
   (B) The report is late.
   (C) It's hard to tell the cables apart.
   (D) The phone and fax are mixed up.

63. When might the woman go to Boston?

   (A) Next week.
   (B) This year.
   (C) In the Fall.
   (D) Next year.

64. Who got the job?

   (A) Mrs. Dupont.
   (B) Carol.
   (C) Mr. Dupont.
   (D) The woman.

65. Where does this conversation take place?

   (A) At the computer lab.
   (B) In the library.
   (C) In the cafeteria.
   (D) At the office.

66. What kind of store are they in?

   (A) A kitchen shop.
   (B) A home improvement store.
   (C) A paint store.
   (D) A plumbing store.

67. Why won't the man buy the sweater?

   (A) He doesn't like the color.
   (B) It doesn't fit.
   (C) It's poor quality.
   (D) It's too expensive.

68. Why are the speakers playing tennis again?

   (A) Because nobody won the game.
   (B) Because Michelle won.
   (C) Because it rained the first time.
   (D) Because they only played for three hours.

69. What are they waiting for?

   (A) A drink.
   (B) A taxi.
   (C) A meal.
   (D) A flight.

70. What does the man want to do?

   (A) Change neighborhoods.
   (B) Start a business.
   (C) Build a garage.
   (D) Make space.

71. Where does this conversation take place?

   (A) In an elevator.
   (B) In the cafeteria.
   (C) In a golf club.
   (D) In court.

72. What are the speakers talking about?

   (A) A play.
   (B) A new set.
   (C) A TV show.
   (D) A computer game.

73. How will the woman help the man?

   (A) By wiping the counter.
   (B) By cleaning the bathroom.
   (C) By putting away the dishes.
   (D) By clearing the table.

74. What is the woman expecting?

   (A) A new job.
   (B) A promotion.
   (C) An office on a higher floor.
   (D) A meeting with the boss.

75. Who is talking?

   (A) Designers.
   (B) Teachers.
   (C) Scientists.
   (D) Students.

76. What has the woman realized?

   (A) That some of the reports are missing.
   (B) That the company's finances are in bad shape.
   (C) That she should go back right away.
   (D) That the bank is suing them.

GO ON TO THE NEXT PAGE

77. What are the speakers discussing?

    (A) A watch.
    (B) The radio.
    (C) The TV.
    (D) A local fair.

78. What are the speakers discussing?

    (A) A goodbye party.
    (B) A birthday party.
    (C) A retirement party.
    (D) An anniversary party.

79. What are the speakers discussing?

    (A) A TV show.
    (B) A movie star.
    (C) A play.
    (D) A rock group.

80. What is the woman going to do?

    (A) Eat breakfast.
    (B) Clean the refrigerator.
    (C) Go shopping.
    (D) Say what she needs.

PART IV

Directions: In this part of the test, you will hear several short talks. Each will be spoken just one time. They will not be printed in your test book, so you must listen carefully to understand and remember what is said.

In your test book, you will read two or more questions about each short talk. The questions will be followed by four answers. You are to choose the best answer to each question and mark it on your answer sheet.

81. What is happening at the time of the announcement?

    (A) The monthly reports are being printed out.
    (B) The offices are preparing to close.
    (C) The staff is in the middle of a long meeting.
    (D) The treasurer is making copies of all the expense receipts.

82. Where is this announcement taking place?

    (A) A TV station.
    (B) A financial company.
    (C) A newspaper office.
    (D) An ad agency.

83. What will be expected next week?

    (A) The TVs will be repaired.
    (B) The client will want the newspapers.
    (C) Some staff will work long hours.
    (D) The magazines will be ready for print.

84. What does the report mainly concern?

    (A) How to detect high blood pressure.
    (B) The relationship between a certain drug and cancer.
    (C) A new treatment for heart disease.
    (D) The nutritional need for calcium.

85. What advice is being given?

    (A) To take the drug twice a week.
    (B) To take an alternative drug if over 65.
    (C) To continue with the medication.
    (D) To increase one's calcium intake.

86. What did they find out about the users of the drug?

    (A) Their risk of breast cancer was doubled.
    (B) Their blood pressure increased.
    (C) They put on extra weight.
    (D) They reported increased levels of stress.

87. Why is Mr. Gupta late?

    (A) There were take-off problems in New Delhi.
    (B) He spoke at an earlier engagement which ran late.
    (C) His plane was delayed in Paris.
    (D) He was held up at a huge fair.

88. What is Mr. Gupta's message?

    (A) He believes the court's decision was fair.
    (B) India's economy is not healthy.
    (C) Leaders of industrialized nations must unite behind India.
    (D) India is a prominent industrial country.

89. What will soon be finished?

    (A) Plans for redevelopment of the city.
    (B) The town council's report.
    (C) Repair work on the turnpike.
    (D) Construction of the park.

90. Who is making plans for the park?

    (A) The town council.
    (B) Park officials.
    (C) A volunteer commission.
    (D) Highway authorities.

91. What kind of recreational park will be built?

    (A) A botanical garden.
    (B) A car park.
    (C) A zoological park.
    (D) A water theme park.

GO ON TO THE NEXT PAGE

92. What happened in March of last year?

(A) Comptor opened an office in Spain.
(B) A computer chip manufacturing plant opened in Barcelona.
(C) A representative from Comptor met with the Spanish Trade Council.
(D) Comptor became the world's largest computer chip manufacturer.

93. What is Comserve?

(A) A computer training institute.
(B) A Spanish Comptor partner.
(C) A Comptor distributor.
(D) An educational research corporation.

94. Where may future production be done?

(A) Madrid.
(B) Barcelona.
(C) Milan.
(D) Rome.

95. Who is most likely being addressed?

(A) Real estate agents.
(B) Company employees.
(C) Apartment managers.
(D) Entrepreneurs.

96. What advice is being offered?

(A) To place an ad in the newspaper.
(B) To live near friends or business associates.
(C) To call real estate agencies for their listings.
(D) To move to the outskirts of Kansas City.

97. Why is this talk being given?

(A) To promote car sales.
(B) To offer assistance.
(C) To sell real estate.
(D) To explain classified ads.

98. What is being advertised?

(A) A Russian sporting event.
(B) Russian massage therapy.
(C) A new pharmaceutical drug.
(D) Educational techniques in Russia.

99. How has the focus of the Russian medical field differed from the world at large?

(A) The Russians have promoted natural healing.
(B) Russian medical doctors have had to be trained in massage.
(C) The Russians have directed their efforts to outpatient clinics.
(D) Russian physicians have done more research in physical therapy.

100. What is not affected by the Russian Sports Massage?

(A) Anxiety levels.
(B) Lymph activity.
(C) Stress hormones.
(D) Depression.

This is the end of the Listening Comprehension portion of Practice Test Four. Turn to Part V in your test book.

YOU WILL HAVE ONE HOUR AND FIFTEEN MINUTES TO COMPLETE PARTS V, VI, AND VII OF THE TEST.

READING

In this section of the test, you will have a chance to show how well you understand written English. There are three parts to this section, with special directions for each part.

PART V

Directions: Questions 101–140 are incomplete sentences. Four words or phrases, marked (A), (B), (C), (D) are given beneath each sentence. You are to choose the **one** word or phrase that best completes the sentence. Then, on your answer sheet, find the number of the question and mark your answer.

You will read:

Because the equipment is very delicate, it must be handled with ....

(A) caring
(B) careful
(C) care
(D) carefully

Sample Answer

Ⓐ Ⓑ ● Ⓓ

The sentence should read, "Because the equipment is very delicate, it must be handled with care." Therefore, you should choose answer (C).

Now begin work on the questions.

---

101. I felt that we had finally .... some headway on these tax issues.

(A) made
(B) took
(C) had
(D) went

102. After looking at all his .... he resigned himself to another two years of schooling.

(A) options
(B) opts
(C) optional
(D) opting

103. With the holidays coming, department stores are gearing up for their busy ....

(A) era
(B) epoch
(C) course
(D) season

104. He avoided any technical jargon .... the sake of clarity.

(A) in
(B) for
(C) to
(D) at

105. Although profit is one indicator of success, it need not be the .... one.

(A) alone
(B) single
(C) lonely
(D) only

106. The warm reception to the Bauhaus style .... that people were looking for a change from the baroque.

(A) states
(B) tells
(C) suggests
(D) advises

GO ON TO THE NEXT PAGE

107. The American Indians guarded the buffalo because it was a valuable resource for
....

(A) their
(B) them
(C) they
(D) theirs

108. The letter from the attorney .... nothing about the lease amendments.

(A) mentions
(B) mentioning
(C) has been mentioned
(D) is being mentioned

109. Our original .... was very reliable and always delivered on time.

(A) supplicant
(B) supporter
(C) suppressor
(D) supplier

110. He was able to rise .... his fears and enter the competition.

(A) over
(B) up
(C) above
(D) on

111. The form of a computer command is so precise that any alteration of it is .... to the computer.

(A) unintelligibly
(B) unintelligibility
(C) unintelligent
(D) unintelligible

112. .... fruits are now in season in the south.

(A) Much
(B) Many
(C) Any
(D) Less

113. The entire industry .... out of the need to conserve energy.

(A) evolution
(B) are evolving
(C) has evolved
(D) have evolved

114. The inspector noticed that not everyone .... their safety gear.

(A) was being worn
(B) will have worn
(C) was wearing
(D) wearing

115. The lease states that you must .... the apartment in good condition.

(A) vacate
(B) move in
(C) escape from
(D) go out

116. The mail sorting machine is out of .... again.

(A) operation
(B) performance
(C) order
(D) function

117. According to the findings of the investigative committee, the company is not .... for the damages.

(A) liable
(B) guilty
(C) obligated
(D) susceptible

118. I prefer to buy engine parts at Auto World .... they always have every conceivable part on hand.

(A) so
(B) which
(C) because
(D) but

119. My colleague has always had luck .... his investments.

(A) throughout
(B) among
(C) with
(D) on behalf of

120. Sonya & Company settled the matter out of .... to avoid the pending lawsuit.

(A) courthouse
(B) courting
(C) courts
(D) court

121. .... opening her bed and breakfast, Mrs. Miller had managed a small restaurant.

(A) Ahead of
(B) Beforehand
(C) Prior to
(D) Previously

122. After the improvements the value of our home jumped .... $95,000 to $145,000.

(A) from
(B) to
(C) for
(D) out

123. The fringe benefits .... him to accept the position.

(A) enticed
(B) teased
(C) illustrated
(D) attracted

124. The trainees helped .... out during the seminar.

(A) another
(B) the other
(C) each other
(D) other

125. The decision to hire her rests ultimately with the director of human ....

(A) resource
(B) resources
(C) resourcing
(D) resourceful

126. .... time was the most difficult part of the plane ride to Calcutta.

(A) Passes
(B) Passing
(C) Pass
(D) Passed

127. During the inspection of the production process, the consultant paid particular .... to the assembly line workers.

(A) observation
(B) notice
(C) time
(D) attention

128. The comptroller asked the treasurer for a breakdown of the .... in his report.

(A) information
(B) informations
(C) informative
(D) inform

129. Properly conducted business ventures would .... more for strengthening international relations than anything else.

(A) done
(B) able to do
(C) do
(D) doing

130. As a result of our trip to Lima, we were able to forge a partnership with one of our .... competitors.

(A) precedent
(B) former
(C) last
(D) sooner

GO ON TO THE NEXT PAGE

131. .... he not become emotionally involved, I think he could have been instrumental in averting the strike.

(A) Had
(B) Since
(C) Should
(D) Were

132. Our division is responsible for making and .... frozen foods.

(A) delivered
(B) delivers
(C) deliverer
(D) delivering

133. The ship tossed and turned as it crashed .... the waves.

(A) with
(B) against
(C) away
(D) behind

134. .... of the downtown shopping district was done to attract more business.

(A) Reinforcement
(B) Fabrication
(C) Restoration
(D) Furbishing

135. The transport strike is becoming a .... for small businesses.

(A) disgust
(B) discord
(C) disaster
(D) disclosure

136. There was a definite .... of expectation in the room when the general manager brought up the topic of wages.

(A) air
(B) stillness
(C) moment
(D) scent

137. In many Eastern homes, ... off your shoes is mandatory before entering a house.

(A) the take
(B) taken
(C) take
(D) taking

138. The marketing department chalked .... the high sales to their new ad campaign.

(A) out
(B) up
(C) on
(D) for

139. Both parties were at an .... because nothing was written down at the time of the negotiations.

(A) impairment
(B) impedance
(C) impasse
(D) implosion

140. The company had scarcely gotten back on its feet when it was .... completely by the fire.

(A) ravage
(B) ravaging
(C) ravaged
(D) ravages

PART VI

Directions: In **Questions 141–160**, each sentence has four words or phrases underlined. The four underlined parts of the sentence are marked (A), (B), (C), (D). You are to identify the **one** underlined word or phrase that should be corrected or rewritten. Then, on your answer sheet, find the number of the question and mark your answer.

Example:

All <u>employee</u> are required <u>to wear</u> their
    A   B

<u>identification</u> badges <u>while</u> at work.
    C   D

Sample Answer
● Ⓑ Ⓒ Ⓓ

The underlined word "employee" is not correct in this sentence. This sentence should read, "All employees are required to wear their identification badges while at work." Therefore, you should choose answer (A).

Now begin work on the questions.

---

141. <u>Even</u> she had <u>never seen</u> him before, she
   A   B
immediately <u>identified</u> him when he stepped
         C
<u>off the plane.</u>
   D

142. For seventeen <u>uninterrupted years</u>, the
  A   B
shareholders <u>they have received</u> <u>quarterly</u>
           C   D
dividend checks.

143. We <u>tested</u> several printers at the trade show,
   A
and the new Cordax 3500 <u>seemed to be</u> the
                 B
<u>good</u> one <u>for our purposes.</u>
  C   D

144. The Office of Economic Indicators
<u>reported</u> that retail sales <u>declining</u> <u>before</u>
   A   B   C
the national sales tax <u>was reduced.</u>
                D

145. Our trainees <u>found</u> the product
         A
demonstration at this meeting <u>difficult</u> to
       B   C
understand than in <u>previous years.</u>
             D

146. The new computer program
was <u>user-friendly</u> that <u>the employees were</u>
      A   B
able to <u>master it</u> in <u>a matter of days.</u>
     C   D

147. The memo <u>was written</u> to the members of
        A
the committee to <u>reminding</u> them <u>to bring</u> the
          B   C
progress reports to the <u>negotiating table.</u>
               D

148. The contract looks fine <u>to me</u>, but my
         A
attorney <u>would like</u> to <u>review</u> it before
       B   C
<u>it will be signed.</u>
   D

149. A study <u>is being done</u> to see <u>how the many</u>
               A   B
Indonesian dialects <u>relation</u> to Malay and
                         C
<u>how they've evolved.</u>
             D

150. <u>As a sponsor</u> of the Baywaer Symphony
           A
Orchestra, she was able to get discounted

<u>balcony</u> tickets to the <u>more unusual</u> and
           B   C
<u>interested</u> performances.
           D

151. Earlier this year we <u>went to</u> an African safari
                 A   B
that <u>was exciting</u> and adventurous,
              C
<u>to say the least.</u>
         D

152. Generally, a credit check <u>required</u> before you
          A   B
<u>can open</u> an account like <u>this one</u> at Northern
         C   D
Savings.

153. <u>Not understanding</u> how <u>many glue</u> would
             A   B
be necessary to mend the broken pot, he

<u>applied</u> an <u>extraordinary amount</u> to each
         C   D
piece.

154. The <u>noticeable decline</u> in tourism <u>has drove</u>
                A   B
the city <u>to renovate</u> the <u>entire</u> downtown
             C   D
area.

155. <u>Even though we asked</u> politely, the corner
               A
store <u>was</u> not <u>able to cash</u> our twenty <u>dollars</u>
          B   C   D
bill.

156. <u>Not understood</u> the risks <u>involved,</u> she
          A   B
invested her <u>entire</u> inheritance <u>in the stock</u>
                 C   D
market.

157. The real estate agent tried to <u>convince us</u>
                                   A
that the house <u>had</u> a <u>certain</u> charm <u>of it.</u>
                B   C   D

158. <u>Faced</u> growing dissatisfaction <u>with the tax</u>
         A   B
code, the <u>legislative body</u> has appointed a
                 C
committee to <u>formulate</u> a solution.
                 D

159. The agent <u>not only</u> overcharged <u>them</u> for the
               A   B
flight, <u>then also</u> forgot <u>to give</u> them first-class
             C   D
tickets.

160. <u>Despite the clear</u> instructions from their
             A
lawyers, the publishers <u>forget</u> to add the
                        B
copyright symbol <u>when</u> they made the cover
                   C
<u>for</u> the book.
        D

PART VII

Directions: Questions 161–200 are based on a selection of reading materials, such as notices, letters, forms, newspaper and magazine articles, and advertisements. You are to choose the **one** best answer (A), (B), (C), or (D) to each question. Then, on your answer sheet, find the number of the question and mark your answer. Answer all questions following each reading selection on the basis of what is **stated** or **implied** in that selection.

Read the following example.

The Museum of Technology is a "hands-on" museum, designed for people to experience science at work. Visitors are encouraged to use, test, and handle the objects on display. Special demonstrations are scheduled for the first and second Wednesdays of each month at 13:30. Open Tuesday–Friday 12:00–16:30, Saturday 10:00–17:30, and Sunday 11:00–16:30.

When during the month can visitors see special demonstrations?

Sample Answer
Ⓐ ● Ⓒ Ⓓ

(A)   Every weekend
(B)   The first two Wednesdays
(C)   One afternoon a week
(D)   Every other Wednesday

The reading selection says that the demonstrations are scheduled for the first and second Wednesdays of the month. Therefore, you should choose answer (B).

Now begin work on the questions.

Questions 161–162 refer to the following magazine article.

Cattle play a major role in modern society. Broadly speaking, there are four major categories for the use of cattle: food, work, commercial products and sports. Over fifty percent of the meat we eat is beef or veal, and more than ninety-five percent of the world's milk supply is from cattle.

In developing countries like Ethiopia, cattle play a role in agriculture by pulling plows and carts. In countries like Sudan and Chad, cattle are often used as a pack animal. Additionally, many commercial products are derived from cattle. Glue, for instance, is made from their bones, leather goods such as bags and shoes, from their hides. Certain types of carpets and blankets, and even brushes, are made from cow hair.

If that isn't enough, one popular spectator sport in Oklahoma in the United States is the rodeo, where cattle play an important role. In Spain and Mexico, their task is grueling as they provide entertainment for the bullfighters.

161. What is this article about?

(A) The number of cattle in various countries
(B) The use of cattle in developed countries
(C) The role of cattle in agriculture
(D) The use of cattle in today's world

162. Where do cattle assist farmers?

(A) Sudan
(B) Oklahoma
(C) Spain
(D) Ethiopia

GO ON TO THE NEXT PAGE ▶

MEMORANDUM

To: George Belcher

From: Jenny Lang

Date: September 13

Subject: November Sales Conference

I just received the deadline for the materials we'll need for the sales conference presentations: October first. I would appreciate it if you could have your staff start putting together what author photos they have. We're going to do the same thing we did last year. We'll present the book cover along with a photo of the author.

I know that we have quite a few photographs on file, but please have one of your staff go over them, as I'm sure not all of them are in usable condition. New authors will send in their shots, which have to meet certain size, print and paper quality requirements. This point needs to be made very clear to new authors. It often happens that authors send in a perfectly good photo of themselves, but because it doesn't meet our technical requirements for the projector, we lose valuable time in trying to replace it.

Any other materials that you think would be of help, please send along.

---

163. Why was this memo written?

(A) As notification of requirements for the upcoming deadline
(B) To invite authors to a conference
(C) As a request for postponement of the presentation
(D) To announce changes in photo specifications

164. What is being asked of the authors?

(A) They should send in their book covers.
(B) They should limit their use of technical terminology.
(C) They should send in pictures that meet certain requirements.
(D) They should come in to have their pictures taken.

165. What is a common problem with new authors' photographs?

(A) They are poor quality.
(B) They are not in black and white.
(C) They don't meet certain specifications.
(D) They take a long time to get.

Questions 166–168 refer to the following newspaper article.

> **A**ccording to documents submitted to the Kuala Lumpur stock exchange, capital for a $10 million joint venture between Timber Master Industries of Malaysia, Laos Lumber, and Myanmar's May Flower Trading Company, Ltd., will be raised over a five-year period. The venture will deal with timber and timber-related production in Myanmar. This news comes in the wake of a ban on all wood exports from Vietnam in an effort to salvage what forest land is left there. Timber Master has stated that it will contribute 65% of the capital for the venture, with May Flower Trading covering the balance.

166. Why was the joint venture formed?

(A) Because capital was available
(B) Because the period was extended to five years
(C) Because the three companies have excellent relations
(D) Because nearby forests have been depleted

167. Which country has curtailed their wood exports?

(A) Myanmar
(B) Vietnam
(C) Laos
(D) Malaysia

168. Who will provide the most financial backing for the venture?

(A) The May Flower Trading Company
(B) The Kuala Lumpur government
(C) Timber Master Industries
(D) Laos Lumber

GO ON TO THE NEXT PAGE

THE EDINBURGH PLEXIGLAS CORPORATION, which has been operating a successful plastics processing plant in Edinburgh has transferred its manufacturing facility to an industrial park just outside of Tampico, Mexico. The company cited "global competition" as among its reasons for reducing operating costs.

The ideally situated plant in Edinburgh is now being used as an administrative headquarters as well as a research and development facility. The company is considering a joint venture with a German manufacturer in developing and fabricating new products at the Edinburgh plant.

169. What will happen in Mexico?

(A) Research and development
(B) Production
(C) Administration
(D) Organization of a joint venture

170. Why is the plant moving?

(A) The old factory was run down.
(B) The Edinburgh factory is being converted.
(C) Research and development is ending.
(D) Costs need to be reduced.

Winfried Vonneilich
884 Shennecossett Road
6080 Bremerhaven
Germany

May 12, 2000

Ramona Garcia
12202 Melton Road
Bristol, Connecticut 06011
U.S.A.

Dear Ramona,

This is to confirm Thursday's telephone conversation about the purchase of the Intex 5000 computer and to thank you again for the invitation to take part in the Pusan Project in New Delhi. I appreciate your thinking of me.

I found out today that I will be in East Grinstead on Monday, June fourth. If it works for you, I could meet you in London either on the morning of the third or the fifth. It would be an excellent opportunity to work out the details of the ad campaign in Brunei. I'll be staying at the Intercontinental on Fulbright Street until the sixth.

I'm hoping that Julie Stein will be able to join us. Did you know that she won the competition for the "Most Successful Ad" this year? Her experience would be invaluable for the Pusan Project.

I look forward to working with you again.

Sincerely,

Winfried Vonneilich

Winfried Vonneilich

171. What is the purpose of the letter?

(A) To express appreciation and to confirm a call
(B) To invite Ramona to take part in the Pusan Project
(C) To pass on preliminary ideas for the ad campaign
(D) To sell an Intex 5000

172. What does Winfried most likely do for a living?

(A) He is an office manager.
(B) He is a computer technician.
(C) He is a marketing executive.
(D) He is an ambassador.

173. Where might their meeting take place?

(A) East Grinstead
(B) Bristol
(C) Brunei
(D) London

174. How could Julie Stein be of assistance?

(A) She could advise on the Intex 5000 computer.
(B) She is familiar with the competitors.
(C) She could contribute ideas to the Pusan Project.
(D) She could work out the travel itinerary.

GO ON TO THE NEXT PAGE

Questions 175–179 refer to the following report.

The main topic of last week's meeting was suggestion boxes. All departments in the factory are to have conspicuously labeled suggestion boxes. At the meeting, it was obvious that the employees' suggestions would not only save the company money, but would do much to lift morale and streamline production. To further this process, the suggestion box idea was adopted.

Forms for the suggestions are to be kept inside the box. When employees fill out a form, they should clearly state which situation they are trying to improve, list all pertinent data, and then offer a solution, stating how the company would benefit. Forms will then be collected each month by the department heads, who will then pass them on to the plant manager. Where necessary, the plant manager will consult with the respective departments to gather any relevant data. If applicable, the matter will then be passed on to the finance department for approval.

A bonus will be paid to employees for any suggestions that are adopted. The amount of the bonus will be commensurate with the savings to the company.

175. What is the topic of the report?

(A) A meeting
(B) Morale
(C) Production
(D) A new system

176. Why has the company decided to use suggestion boxes?

(A) To take advantage of the employees' ideas
(B) To minimize complaints
(C) To take some of the burden off department heads
(D) To appease the finance department

177. How do the employees get the suggestion slips?

(A) By requesting them from department heads
(B) By applying to the plant manager
(C) By looking in the suggestion box itself
(D) By asking the director of finance

178. What is the plant manager supposed to do?

(A) Review each suggestion with the employee
(B) Issue bonus checks
(C) Route all suggestions through the finance department
(D) Compile data from other areas

179. What, specifically, should employees include in their suggestions?

(A) The names of troublesome coworkers
(B) The duration of the problem
(C) What they would consider to be an appropriate bonus
(D) A description of the point they are trying to remedy

Questions 180–182 refer to the following announcement.

 Part of the water treatment facilities on the Yangtze River will be undergoing modernization. This will not affect the potability of your water, but you may notice a slight rust discoloration. There is no need for alarm. This is simply a result of minute amounts of residue in the pipes. In addition, you may notice that the water pressure is diminished. This is a result of shutting down half of the facility. This was necessary for the installation of the latest, state-of-the-art equipment, which will filter out 99% of all foreign and toxic substances.

The new system will increase filtration threefold and produce the cleanest water of any city in Asia. Installation should be complete within two weeks time. Should you have any questions or concerns, please feel free to contact the Yushu Water Department. Brochures explaining the process and the new technology being applied are available to all citizens affected by the change. We thank you for your patience.

180. What is happening at the water treatment facility?

(A) Water is getting polluted.
(B) Equipment is being updated.
(C) A dam is being built.
(D) A new alarm system is being installed.

181. What changes will customers notice in this two-week period?

(A) There will be intermittent changes in water pressure.
(B) The water will have a rusty taste.
(C) The color will change.
(D) The odor will diminish.

182. How is the Yushu Water Department helping?

(A) It is undertaking an educational program.
(B) Its crew is working overtime to shorten installation time.
(C) It is providing free potable water until the work is complete.
(D) It is conducting tours to show off the new technology.

GO ON TO THE NEXT PAGE

THE T-SHIRT RUN FOR ALZHEIMER'S is for the entire family. From young to old, runners at any ability level are encouraged to join. By collecting pledges, runners and walkers are able to raise funds for the Alzheimer's Foundation for the fight against one of the nation's most debilitating diseases.

Early registration is only $15. It includes a running pack and a one-of-a-kind T-shirt. After December first, registration is $20. Children under 12 can register for only $5 straight through to race day. All participants will receive an information pack, a pledge kit, and tips on raising funds for research and finding a cure for ALZHEIMER'S.

183. Who may participate in the run?

(A) Anyone whose family member has Alzheimer's
(B) Anyone who has already raised money for the cause
(C) Anyone who has purchased a T-shirt
(D) Anyone who is willing to take part

184. How are funds raised for the run?

(A) Participants ask people to promise donations.
(B) Each participate donates $25.
(C) T-shirts are sold to the spectators.
(D) The Alzheimer's Foundation contributes funds.

185. How much would an eleven-year-old have to pay to register on the day of the race?

(A) $0
(B) $5
(C) $15
(D) $20

186. What do participants receive when they register?

(A) Running gear
(B) A special T-shirt
(C) Research findings on Alzheimer's
(D) Enrollment in the Alzheimer's Foundation

Questions 187–189 refer to the following form.

TRY AIR MILES RISK-FREE

Send for your free trial issue and start your subscription today. If not 100% satisfied, you can cancel your subscription and receive full refund on all unmailed issues. The trial issue is yours no matter what you decide. You'll also be awarded 1,000 Air Miles. They will be credited to your account upon receipt of full payment.

Name _____

Address _____

City _____ State _____ Zip _____

Signature _____ Phone _____

Your subscription will be automatically renewed and billed annually at the current subscription price until you decide to cancel.
This offer is valid for new subscribers only.

187. What happens if you want to cancel the subscription?

(A) You are expected to return the trial issue.
(B) Simply return any unwanted issues.
(C) You will not receive Air Miles.
(D) The unused portion of your payment will be refunded.

188. Who is this ad intended for?

(A) First-time subscribers
(B) Pilots
(C) Lawyers
(D) Credit card users

189. How do you get the 1,000 Air Miles?

(A) By paying the subscription in full
(B) By accepting the trial issue
(C) By being a new subscriber
(D) By accepting a subscription renewal

GO ON TO THE NEXT PAGE

Questions 190–192 refer to the following table.

TRAVEL ITINERARY

Date	From	To	Via	Hotel Accommodations
3/8/00	Atlanta (5:00 pm)	L.A. (8:30 pm)	Amtrak Rail	Intercontinental 3/8/00 to 3/11/00
3/11/00	L.A. (8:00am)	Hawaii (2:00 pm)	US Air Flight 101	Pacific Breeze 3/11/00 to 3/13/00
3/13/00	Hawaii (10:30 am)	Hong Kong (4:45 pm)	Pacific Air* Flight 885	Hong Kong Heights 3/13/00 to 3/17/00
- open -	Hong Kong	Atlanta	Pacific Air	

*Limousine service at airport

190. How many nights will the person spend in Hawaii?

   (A) One
   (B) Two
   (C) Four
   (D) Six

191. Where does the trip originate?

   (A) Atlanta
   (B) L.A.
   (C) Hawaii
   (D) Hong Kong

192. What is known about the traveler?

   (A) He uses a limo service in Atlanta.
   (B) He doesn't always travel by plane.
   (C) He prefers arriving in the morning hours.
   (D) He always travels third-class.

MEMORANDUM

To: Shirley Griffin

From: John Rankine

Subject: Personnel Turnover

In response to your concern over Metro Food Store's personnel turnover, I've already had Judy review the wage and working conditions. These have both been ruled out because they were found to be comparable to those of competitors. Could personnel possibly be hiring the wrong people? If this is the problem, what factors should we look into? The testing questionnaire, the application, the interviewer? Also, are there any specific factors such as interests, education, or experience that indicate who is more likely to stay with us? You may want to coordinate your efforts with Judy and with personnel as they have already begun the problem-solving work.

193. Why has John Rankine sent a memo to Shirley Griffin?

(A) To inquire about the wage increase at Metro Food
(B) To explain Judy's role
(C) To ask about hiring practices
(D) To speak out about the working conditions

194. What is known about the employees at Metro Food?

(A) They don't stay very long.
(B) They are paid less than their counterparts in other stores.
(C) They work overtime every week.
(D) They are dissatisfied with their working conditions.

195. What does John Rankine think the problem might be?

(A) Hiring practices
(B) Health benefits
(C) Management
(D) New business

196. What is Shirley's concern?

(A) Wages
(B) Employees quitting
(C) Competition
(D) Promotions

GO ON TO THE NEXT PAGE

We know who owns the islands of Indonesia or the land masses of North America, but who owns Antarctica? It is the fifth largest continent and the most remote, and although seven nations have laid claim to her, it is still questionable who should be called "owner".

Oddly enough, this is one continent that was truly "discovered," as no one lived there when the adventurers arrived. And even though Antarctica contains ten percent of the earth's entire land surface, it has never had a native or permanent population. With its steep mountain ranges, two active volcanoes, and a reputation for being the coldest, windiest, and driest continent on earth, it is not a popular place.

Captain James Cook is reputed to be the first to approach the continent. It is possible that Polynesian navigators reached Antarctica earlier, but Cook, an English explorer, claims the first recorded approach.

 An American whaling captain, Nathaniel Palmer, and a Russian expedition led by Fabian Gottieb von Bellinghausen, were the first to actually reach the mainland in 1820. Since 1950, the following nations have staked claims to the mineral wealth and oil reserves on this continent (although exploitation of these resources is not allowed): Australia, New Zealand, France, Norway, Chile, South Africa, the United States, Russia, Japan, Belgium, China, India and Brazil.

197. What is the article mainly about?

(A) The conditions in Antarctica
(B) Land claimants of Antarctica
(C) Ownership settlements between seven nations
(D) The discovery of the South Pole

198. Who may have been the very first to reach Antarctica?

(A) A Polynesian
(B) An American
(C) A Russian
(D) An Englishman

199. How was von Bellinghausen's expedition distinguished?

(A) He befriended the native population there.
(B) He traveled with an American.
(C) He found a gold vein.
(D) He landed on the mainland itself.

200. What is known about Antarctica?

(A) The native population has disappeared.
(B) Ten percent of its land is arable.
(C) It has a considerable whale population.
(D) Its fossil fuels and minerals cannot be extracted.

Stop! This is the end of the test. If you finish before one hour and fifteen minutes have passed, you may go back to Parts V, VI, and VII and check your work.

Tapescripts

Tapescript Practice Test One

PART I

Sample question:

(A) They're looking out the window.
(B) They're having a meeting.
(C) They're eating in a restaurant.
(D) They're moving the furniture.

1. (A) The shops are full of flowers.
   (B) The cars are passing in the street.
   (C) The pedestrians are gathering at the fountain.
   (D) The stores are on both sides of the walkway.

2. (A) The people are on the deck.
   (B) The sailors are docking the boat.
   (C) The passengers are disembarking.
   (D) The sails blow in the wind.

3. (A) He's putting the instrument in the case.
   (B) He's playing the saxophone.
   (C) He's holding the fax.
   (D) He's honking the horn.

4. (A) They're handing over the business.
   (B) They're giving the customers tips.
   (C) The conductor is calling the passengers.
   (D) Both men are wearing glasses.

5. (A) The grocery store is open.
   (B) The vegetables are frozen.
   (C) The market is outside.
   (D) The meat is in the basket.

6. (A) They're enjoying the ride.
   (B) The ship is at the dock.
   (C) They're loading the cars onto the ship.
   (D) The canoe is in the ocean.

7. (A) They're standing in line to see a movie.
   (B) The beverage is on the bar.
   (C) The caps are above the bar.
   (D) They're purchasing something to drink.

8. (A) The dentist is checking her teeth.
   (B) The doctor is operating.
   (C) The hygienist is washing her hands.
   (D) The receptionist is making an appointment.

9. (A) The flight attendant is serving drinks.
   (B) The passengers are sleeping.
   (C) They're eating in the car.
   (D) She's selling goods.

10. (A) The waiter is serving the meal.
    (B) The nurse is uncovering the food.
    (C) The patient is getting out of bed.
    (D) The technician is adjusting the tray.

11. (A) The man isn't able to see.
    (B) The men are looking over her shoulders.
    (C) The woman isn't sitting.
    (D) The group is presenting the report.

12. (A) The tricycle is on the floor.
    (B) The motorcycle is stored in the garage.
    (C) The bike is stationary.
    (D) The bicycle has fifteen gears.

13. (A) She's waiting in line at the bank.
    (B) She's depositing her check at the store.
    (C) She's filling her bag with bills.
    (D) She's taking money out at the machine.

14. (A) The lawnmowers are on display.
    (B) The tractors are in the warehouse.
    (C) The trailers carry the farm equipment.
    (D) The engines are above the machines.

15. (A) The construction worker is looking at plans.
    (B) The architect is taking measurements.
    (C) The foreman is looking for more space.
    (D) The interior designer is finishing his work.

16. (A) The fortress is by the ocean.
    (B) The building is in the desert.
    (C) The castle is across the river.
    (D) The palace is in the forest.

17. (A) The waiter is serving the stew.
    (B) The sailor is cleaning the pot.
    (C) The worker is wrapping the soap.
    (D) The cook is stirring the soup.

18. (A) She's searching for the table.
    (B) She's taping something.
    (C) She's typing her notes.
    (D) She's sipping her coffee.

19. (A) The participants are having a conversation.
    (B) The orchestra is playing to a full house.
    (C) The people are attending a conference.
    (D) The dancers are presenting their new show.

20. (A) He's holding the receiver with his shoulder.
    (B) The wire connects the computers.
    (C) His phone is in his hand.
    (D) The bone is resting on the counter.

PART II

Sample question:

Good morning, John. How are you?
(A) I am fine, thank you.
(B) I am in the living room.
(C) My name is John.

21. What do you think should be done with the funds?
(A) You should learn the fundamentals.
(B) They should be set aside for emergencies.
(C) We had fun last night.

22. How much snow are they expecting?
(A) There's no way to get there from here.
(B) We're expecting it to snow.
(C) The forecast said several feet.

23. Would you prefer to travel first class?
(A) I would, but only on the return trip.
(B) The class was hard for me.
(C) They referred me to this agency.

24. Your package arrived, didn't it?
(A) I'll drive to the package store.
(B) Not that I know of.
(C) I left my luggage at the house.

25. Why not ask the waiter for a fresh napkin?
(A) I'd like some fresh coffee.
(B) I think I will.
(C) It's all right I'll just wait here.

26. How do you get tickets for the concert?
(A) Just use this 1-800 number.
(B) She's certain that she saw her.
(C) There are no bigots here.

27. You were going over the blueprints, weren't you?
(A) No, I painted it blue.
(B) Yes, I think they're excellent.
(C) I couldn't find any footprints.

28. What do you think is causing the delays?
(A) The long days tired her.
(B) I went because I was curious.
(C) There's an accident on the bridge.

29. Do you conduct a lot of business overseas?
(A) We saw several Japanese businessmen.
(B) The conductor is from Austria.
(C) Not as much as I would like to.

30. Where does the gas line appear to be leaking?
(A) I think it's right at the joint.
(B) I got in line about ten minutes ago.
(C) The gas pumps are locked.

31. Have you ever participated in the negotiations?
(A) As a consultant I have.
(B) This is part of the negation.
(C) The classifications were too general.

32. Can't you change the height if you need to?
(A) I have to check with the architect first.
(B) Her height changes every month.
(C) There's no need to fight.

33. She's getting her raise, isn't she?
(A) The president praised her for her work.
(B) She can't raise it any higher.
(C) That's what she was promised.

34. Why did you decide on a merger with National Gas?
(A) I can't decide which way to go.
(B) Their management is remarkably efficient.
(C) We lost it because of a power surge.

35. Why should construction be halted because of the rain?
(A) The train stops here.
(B) New vaults are being constructed.
(C) Dangerously high winds are being forecast as well.

36. Will Mr. Tan be attending the seminar?
(A) He's very punctual.
(B) The whole department has to be there.
(C) They tend to be late.

37. This is the approval code, isn't it?
(A) He'll never approve it.
(B) It looks like it, but I'll check.
(C) We have a new dress code.

38. What did he give for an explanation?
(A) He said he lost his job.
(B) I asked for some clarification.
(C) His explorations made him famous.

39. Would you rather I fax it or mail it?
(A) We looked at all the facts.
(B) The mail box was moved.
(C) I'll just pick it up when I come today.

40. When can we expect to see an improvement?
(A) We're making home improvements.
(B) It will take several days.
(C) You can see her tonight.

41. Where in Saudi Arabia do you live?
(A) We have a home in the north.
(B) They wear light clothes there.
(C) About seven years ago.

42. How often does the ink pen need refilling?
(A) I don't use the pencil often.
(B) I think it's a pin.
(C) It usually lasts a good month.

43. Can I get you anything to drink?
(A) Iced tea would be nice.
(B) I didn't take anything.
(C) No, she doesn't drink.

44. Who's preparing the final draft?
(A) No one is ready yet.
(B) This is the last raft.
(C) I asked Jennifer to.

45. How far south is your warehouse?
    (A) It's just over the border.
    (B) It's too hot down there.
    (C) It's a big house.

46. Don't you send out promotional mail?
    (A) I sent you a letter.
    (B) Normally we do.
    (C) We promoted him.

47. He's signing the lease today, isn't he?
    (A) He hasn't found the leash yet.
    (B) After he puts down a deposit.
    (C) The sign is going up immediately.

48. How much did we earn last year?
    (A) We learned how to sail.
    (B) Over eighty thousand dollars.
    (C) Two years in a row.

49. How many times has that reporter called here?
    (A) She has ten reports to deliver.
    (B) I'd like to meet them.
    (C) At least a dozen times.

50. You're buying a new computer, aren't you?
    (A) I was thinking about it.
    (B) We're primarily in sales.
    (C) Magazines keep me updated on technology.

PART III

51.
Woman   Would you have an earlier flight? I'm trying to get to Manila before noon.
Man   There is an 8:30 flight that will get you there by 11:00.
Woman   8:30 is perfect – then I can easily make the 12:30 meeting.

52.
Woman A   Let's go have some coffee. Boarding time isn't for another hour.
Woman B   We could drink it in the waiting area overlooking the runway.
Woman A   Good, that'll give us time to go over these files.

53.
Man   Did you find the training helpful?
Woman   To a degree. Words like 'terminal' and 'mouse pad' aren't strange sounding anymore.
Man   Well, that's good. The more you use them the easier it will be.

54.
Woman   The meeting will be over by five, right?
Man   It should be, but you know how the chairman likes to talk.
Woman   I know. I just hope he knows the bowling championship is tonight.

55.
Woman   The supply clerk ordered the fax paper over a week ago. Have you seen it?
Man   The mailman delivered several boxes this morning. Let me check with the receptionist.
Woman   No, the company has its own delivery service.

56.
Man   Mrs. Kahn, Dania hasn't been to work for several days now.
Woman   You know, I think she worked too hard during that heat wave last week.
Man   I'm going to call and see if she's all right.

57.
Man   I don't think I'll use them anymore.
Woman   Why, too much starch again?
Man   No, they lost one of my suits and my trousers had double creases in them.

58.
Man   Sorry to keep you waiting. Do you have enough room for all our luggage?
Woman   Yes, the trunk is empty and there's also room on the roof rack.
Man   Great. We'd like to make it to the airport for a ten o'clock flight.

59.
Man   If TV and stereo sales keep going like this, we're going to need more help.
Woman   Well, let's run a Help Wanted Ad in the classifieds.
Man   OK. I'll call personnel and find out how much ads usually cost.

60.
Man   Jennifer, we're going to the hockey game this weekend. Why don't you join us?
Woman   That would be fun, but I have a big presentation to do first thing Monday morning.
Man   Come on, it's only Wednesday – you've still got Thursday and Friday to prepare.

61.
Woman   We're short six binders for the meeting, but I know Mary ordered enough.
Man   She did. The supplier faxed us that the six are backordered.
Woman   He should never have taken the order if he knew he didn't have them in stock.

62.
Man   Now that the company has included dental care in the health care package, I'm going for a check-up and a cleaning.
Woman   I'm going too. I need to have some bridge work looked at.
Man   Who do you go to?

63.
Man   The elevator goes up fine but sometimes gets stuck going down.
Woman   Did it stop at the fifth floor like the last time?
Man   Yes. At least we didn't have to climb up the stairs.

64.

Man	I like the quality of this printer. Does it work with the Computer 500 series?
Woman	Not this particular one, sir. Only with the 600 series and above. I'm afraid we don't stock the 500.
Man	What a shame. Do you know which store might carry the kind I have?

65.

Man	Will we be able to send the staff to the west coast for these computer classes?
Woman	Well, things are really tight, but the secretaries do need to have this training for their jobs.
Man	You're right. Even if we have to dip into our advertising dollars, it will be worth it in the long run.

66.

Man	Marie, we're going to need about one hundred rental chairs for the seminar on Wednesday. Can you call the rental company?
Woman	I can Jack, but we still owe four hundred dollars from the last event.
Man	Well, I'll just send a messenger over with a check before you call them.

67.

Man	Joan, will you order for me? I left my wallet upstairs in my room.
Woman	Here's the key. Do you want to start with a glass of wine?
Man	Yes, thanks. I'll be right down.

68.

Man	We just had service transferred to our new offices, but the calls aren't getting through.
Woman	It will take another day before everything is back to normal because your new building had to be rewired.
Man	Nobody told us about this. You must have some kind of answering service that you can provide for the day.

69.

Woman	I need to have this skirt pressed. Is there a dry cleaner nearby?
Man	Yes, it's two blocks over on your right.
Woman	Thanks, I sure hope they have an express service.

70.

Man	We're thinking of buying a house.
Woman	Is it the brick one with the large front porch that you liked so much?
Man	No, the entry was nice, but we found out the garage and basement needed a lot of work. And commuting would have been too much.

71.

Man	Could I please speak to the manager?
Woman	He just stepped out but will be back after lunch, or would you like to speak with his assistant?
Man	That's fine, I'll just come back later.

72.

Man	We left in such a hurry, I forgot to pack my comb.
Woman	I noticed there was a drugstore on the corner.
Man	I'll run down there after I've finished unpacking, or maybe the front desk can help me.

73.

Woman	I didn't get much sleep last night. Do you think I could reschedule?
Man	Let me check the appointments. It's just a cleaning, right?
Woman	Yes, but I'd also like her to look at a loose filling.

74.

Man	Is the battery dead, Carla?
Woman	Yes, and I was just about to go to the music store.
Man	Well, at least it broke down here in the driveway. Let's try pushing it.

75.

Man	When will the city start construction of the new subway system?
Woman	Once they've raised enough money from the bond sales.
Man	Well, if they could do it for that mountain tunnel that is being built, they can do it for a subway.

76.

Man	I'm looking for men's umbrellas.
Woman	Do you want the full-size or the compact?
Man	I travel a lot, so I guess the compact would be best.

77.

Man	Sonya, are you familiar with this new spreadsheet software?
Woman	Not yet. I'm reading up on it, but all this technical terminology slows me down.
Man	I'm hoping you can figure it out so you can explain it to me.

78.

Woman	John, could you do a little research on alarm systems? We're going to need one for the new office building.
Man	I've looked over the ratings from several consumer reports, and it seems the Motion Detector is best.
Woman	Well, then, it's just a matter of finding the best buy.

79.

Man	Do you know there are dozens of applicants out there for those typist positions?
Woman	But there are only two full-time positions vacant.
Man	That's fine, there are about five or six part-time positions opening up.

80.

Man	You can take out up to ten books.
Woman	Here's my borrower's card.
Man	These are due back in thirty days.

PART IV

Questions 81 through 83 refer to the following announcement.

The Animal Rescue League's second annual free rabies clinic is Saturday from 1 p.m. to 5 p.m. at the League's medical center on 225 Litchfield Road. It's located right next to the new Department of Health building. The vaccine will protect dogs and cats from rabies for four years. All animals taking part in the clinic must be at least five months old and in good health. You'll need time for filling out paperwork and a five-minute screening. You need proof of City residency from the Town Hall and of any previous vaccinations.

Questions 84 through 86 refer to the following report.

The Manila Electric Power Company customers in twelve square blocks of downtown Manila were asked to cut back power consumption yesterday after a maintenance operation and an accident halved the power supplied by a substation on Pacific Street. Managers of office and commercial buildings in the affected areas were asked to take voluntary steps, such as turning off decorative lighting and shutting down elevators, to avoid triggering a blackout. All three of the Pacific Street substation's transformers are expected to be back to normal tomorrow.

Questions 87 and 88 refer to the following introduction.

Before we start this meeting, I would like to introduce Mr. John Wiley, who has just recently joined our company as the Hamford district's director of marketing. Mr. Wiley was the department head and marketing assistant at our dealership in Chicago for twelve years. There he won the Marlboro district's Salesman of the Year Award four years in a row. I have also asked him to run a monthly training seminar for those of you working in our used car center on Federal Highway.

Questions 89 through 91 refer to the following notice.

When you move, call your local phone company a week before you go to get your new phone numbers. Then have your long distance calling plans and services transferred to the new number. With electricity and other utilities, have the service turned off at your old address the day after you move out. Ask that any deposits be returned. If you have cable, call the cable company to have the service disconnected at the old address. Make sure they take the control box with them or you will be charged extra to have it picked up later.

Questions 92 through 94 refer to the following news story.

Oslo Disks, in a joint-venture with Euro Records, has opened Norway's first compact disk factory. The factory is located in an upscale section of the Hillside District. The plant uses a CD manufacturing system purchased from Japan's Wadushi Corporation. The production line itself costs over $2.5 million, but can produce up to 30,000 audio or video CDs per day. Oslo Disks has also been negotiating with Germany's World Records for the right to distribute World Record products in Norway and Denmark and for possible manufacturing of World Record CDs at the Hillside factory.

Questions 95 through 97 refer to the following talk.

Before you all meet with your new department heads, I would just like you to know that I'm available to see any staff member on Monday and Wednesday mornings between 10:00 and 11:30 in my office. And if those times don't work for you, just give my secretary a call. Alex can set up an appointment. My office is suite 700 on the seventh floor. When you come out of the elevator, just go straight ahead until you pass the water fountain. My office is right after it.

Questions 98 through 100 refer to the following advertisement.

The American Junior Golf Association is dedicated to the overall growth and development of aspiring junior golfers. The purpose of the AJGA is to provide positive life experiences through competitive golf, while setting high standards to preserve the integrity of the game. With a membership representing all fifty states and more than ten foreign countries, the AJGA provides junior golfers with the opportunity to develop and showcase their competitive skills while gaining exposure for college golf scholarships. AJGA alumni include Phil Mickelson, Tiger Woods, Davis Love III, and Brandie Burton. These illustrious past members set an example for our young golfers to follow.

Tapescript Practice Test Two

PART I

Sample question:

(A) They're looking out the window.
(B) They're having a meeting.
(C) They're eating in a restaurant.
(D) They're moving the furniture.

1. (A) She's resting on the stool.
   (B) She's sitting in the trench.
   (C) She's opening the cream.
   (D) She's removing the lid.

2. (A) The manual control is on his left.
   (B) The screens are side by side.
   (C) The desk is long and straight.
   (D) The fan is above the monitor.

3. (A) They're selling goods at the market.
   (B) They're hurrying to catch the bus.
   (C) They're waiting on the corner.
   (D) They're pushing through the crowd.

4. (A) His watch is on the table.
   (B) His hand is on the notebook.
   (C) The man's suit hangs in the closet.
   (D) The shorts are striped.

5. (A) The engineers are drilling for oil.
   (B) The work crew is installing the tires.
   (C) The laborers are working together.
   (D) The boss is holding the line.

6. (A) The naval officer is on deck.
   (B) The pilot is flying the plane.
   (C) The doctor is reaching for some medicine.
   (D) The pharmacist is filling the boxes.

7. (A) She's not sitting at the desk.
   (B) She's riding the horse.
   (C) She's not wearing glasses.
   (D) She's studying in a library.

8. (A) They're at a passenger lounge.
   (B) They're at an admissions office.
   (C) They're at a train station.
   (D) They're at a self-serve restaurant.

9. (A) The author is explaining her experiences.
   (B) The chemist is examining the flask.
   (C) The engineer is weighing the glass.
   (D) The cook is measuring food for the recipe.

10. (A) The floor is dirty.
    (B) The carpet is rolled up.
    (C) The chairs are stacked in piles.
    (D) The door is being cleaned.

11. (A) The restaurant is full.
    (B) The handle is on the table.
    (C) The candle isn't lit.
    (D) The glass isn't in the woman's hand.

12. (A) The women are assisting the man.
    (B) The women are executives.
    (C) The man is checking through his baggage.
    (D) The pub has information on the table.

13. (A) The painting is at the rear of the building.
    (B) The drawing of the winner is next week.
    (C) The brush is in the paint.
    (D) The trees appear in the work.

14. (A) They're selling the boats.
    (B) The boats are racing.
    (C) The sails are coming down.
    (D) They're paddling the kayaks.

15. (A) He's not wearing a belt.
    (B) The metal is sold in sheets.
    (C) He's working on the motor.
    (D) The engine is under the hood.

16. (A) The places are set.
    (B) The customers sit at the first table.
    (C) The water glasses are full.
    (D) The curtains are drawn.

17. (A) They're fighting a fire.
    (B) The man's shirt is striped.
    (C) The man is strapped down.
    (D) They're operating in a hospital.

18. (A) The fax machine is dialing.
    (B) The receivers are hanging on the hooks.
    (C) She's talking in her home.
    (D) They are phoning next to each other.

19. (A) The crowd is fighting.
    (B) The supporters are waving flags.
    (C) The fans are moving their hands.
    (D) The entertainers are cheering on the crowd.

20. (A) No-one can enter the room.
    (B) The area is restricted.
    (C) The passport is stamped.
    (D) All movement is to the left.

PART II

Sample question:

Good morning, John. How are you?
(A) I am fine, thank you.
(B) I am in the living room.
(C) My name is John.

21. He's the captain of the ship, isn't he?
(A) He's on the ship.
(B) He's got ten seats.
(C) Yes, I talked with him earlier.

22. How many employees do you have now?
(A) We employ men and women.
(B) We'll have seventy-five by the end of the year.
(C) My employer has the report.

23. Why not add an extra car for the rush hour?
(A) We already have.
(B) Because of his rash.
(C) There's no need to rush.

24. Could I see the new features you talked about?
(A) There'll be another demonstration shortly.
(B) We talked for hours.
(C) Everyone talked about her facial features.

25. When will electrical services be restored?
(A) The service here is very prompt.
(B) The store doesn't have any electricity.
(C) Probably not until morning.

26. Are you interested in studying financial planning?
(A) Yes, we have a financial plan.
(B) Possibly, I'd like to know more about it.
(C) I subscribe to the *Financial Times*.

27. How will the department finance this purchase?
(A) She'll buy both of them.
(B) The apartment is for sale.
(C) The funds have already been set aside.

28. Do you have any experience in data entry?
(A) There's no entry here.
(B) I'm missing some data.
(C) That's what I do in my job.

29. Do you find the revised contract too lengthy?
(A) I like the title.
(B) No, but too complicated.
(C) She re-typed it.

30. What about hiring temporary staff for the event?
(A) I'd rather pay our people overtime.
(B) It will be over shortly.
(C) Four people were fired.

31. Would you consider this a worthwhile investment?
(A) I did it for a while.
(B) The investigator is considerate.
(C) I'd have to study it first.

32. Do you know if this is aluminum or tin?
(A) I think it's a little bit of both.
(B) No, I haven't seen either of them.
(C) I'm sure it isn't ammonia.

33. Have the shipping clerks been notified?
(A) It will cost about five dollars.
(B) The harbor is very busy.
(C) I contacted them earlier today.

34. Can I invest in all three companies?
(A) I wouldn't, but you can.
(B) My vest is missing two buttons.
(C) I could sure use some company.

35. What did the accounting office say about the missing invoice?
(A) They weren't very pleased.
(B) She lost her voice.
(C) He'll recount it.

36. Is this the human resources division?
(A) This environment is not safe.
(B) Yes, are you applying for a job?
(C) No, human life is priceless.

37. Why should the furnace be left on?
(A) I left them at the station.
(B) If you put this on, it won't burn.
(C) It will dry the room out.

38. Can I have another look at those guidelines?
(A) I saw it again.
(B) Here, you can keep this copy.
(C) We're looking for good people.

39. When did your plane arrive?
(A) I prefer to drive.
(B) At the international airport.
(C) Minutes before the storm started.

40. Haven't you ordered dictionaries for the office?
(A) I was told we need atlases.
(B) I can't find my office copy.
(C) I'm looking for a glossary.

41. When may I drive you home?
(A) I always drive in the daytime.
(B) My home is on Fifth and Lane.
(C) After this speech, if you wouldn't mind.

42. What accounts for the drop in water pressure?
(A) Sales dropped rapidly after that.
(B) It was a very tough deadline.
(C) One of the main pipes burst.

43. You were supposed to meet Mrs. Baldwin at ten, weren't you?
(A) Oh no, I forgot all about it.
(B) She'll meet the plane at ten.
(C) They met at the station.

44. Does this plane fly direct to Botswana?
    (A) Let me check.
    (B) The plane leaves from Rome.
    (C) They're boarding now.

45. Are the elevators working again?
    (A) He's out of work again.
    (B) They fixed them last night.
    (C) She elevates her feet at work.

46. How will this car perform in very hot climates?
    (A) The theater has air-conditioning.
    (B) We were near the equator.
    (C) It's been designed just for that.

47. Do you think two hundred seats will be sufficient?
    (A) We sold enough tickets.
    (B) Well, we only invited a hundred and fifty people.
    (C) There was standing room only.

48. How do you suppose we'll get there?
    (A) We can dispose of them on the way.
    (B) I suppose they're good.
    (C) I was told a bus has been chartered.

49. Your cellular phone is working, isn't it?
    (A) He'll be at work this afternoon.
    (B) Let me test it.
    (C) She called from her cell.

50. Is the elevator out of order again?
    (A) It's gaining.
    (B) No, I ordered a new one.
    (C) Unfortunately it is.

PART III

51.
Woman   Did you hear about the new pipeline debate?
Man   Yes, something about an oil line going through the north side of town.
Woman   That's right, and commuter traffic will be re-routed for months.

52.
Woman A You know, I can't get this fax to go through.
Woman B Maybe there's one coming in.
Woman A Oh, I didn't realize it worked that way.

53.
Man   Have you noticed that off-the-street parking is getting more and more difficult?
Woman   I sure have, Steve. It's that new high rise about two blocks down the street.
Man   I think they miscalculated how large their parking lot needed to be.

54.
Woman A Did you hear? We're getting new uniforms.
Woman B Even the banquet staff?
Woman A Yes, from room service to the front desk.

55.
Man   Beth, do you know where the key to the supply room is?
Woman   It should be hanging on the wall right behind you.
Man   There are several color-coded keys here. Which one is it?

56.
Woman   It's boiling in here. We've got to get this air-conditioner working again.
Man   I can't stand this heat. I'm calling the repair man right now.
Woman   Good. Then we can turn these noisy fans off.

57.
Woman   How is the income from the computer sales?
Man   Well, we still haven't met this week's quota, but we sold more than last week.
Woman   Let's call in John and tell him we'll up his bonus if we meet the quota.

58.
Man   How was the test drive?
Woman   Very smooth and I liked the way it grips the road on the turns. It even has a CD player.
Man   Good. Did you notice how much room there is in the trunk?

59.
Man   Do you know what kind of an adapter I'll need for my computer when I go to Poland?
Woman   I'm not sure Paul, but I can call a friend of mine who travels a lot with his lap top.
Man   If he knows, could you also ask him where I can get one?

60.
Man   They're selling the old bakery, you know.
Woman   I wonder what it will be used for now?
Man   I've been told it was bought by a fast food chain.

61.
Woman   What triggers the signal to the police?
Man   Any movement in the building.
Woman   And do you use numbers or letters for the code?

62.
Man   Is the train station too far to walk to from here?
Woman   No, but in this heat you might want to take the subway. It takes you right into the station.
Man   That's a good idea, but I think I'll just take a taxi.

63.
Man   The city has really worked on its public transportation.
Woman   Yes, the train cars are much cleaner and the buses are running right on schedule.
Man   I'm even thinking of taking the bus to work and leaving my car at home.

64.

Man: Our electric bill is much higher than it ever has been.

Woman: Well, Tom, we may have underestimated how much energy these new computers need.

Man: Of course, it could also be the constant use of the central air-conditioning.

65.

Man: All four of these forms should be filled out in triplicate.

Woman: Who gets the copies?

Man: One goes to the treasurer's office, one to accounting, and we keep the original.

66.

Man: Twenty-five of us are going to the seminar.

Woman: How? Will we drive, take the train, or charter a bus?

Man: Didn't you hear? The company got a great deal with the airlines. We'll fly.

67.

Woman: Yes, the car runs now, but it won't pass the safety inspection because of the faulty turn signal.

Man: Can you fix that, too, Barbara?

Woman: I can, but I have to do a test drive first.

68.

Man: Susan, I'll need all the financial reports before I leave for Hong Kong on Monday.

Woman: That's fine. I'm just waiting on some tax data that should be coming in the mail today.

Man: Could you just leave them on my desk?

69.

Man: I can't read these little numbers. Can you set this for me?

Woman: For what time?

Man: To turn on at ten p.m. and to go off at four a.m.

70.

Man: I'd like to talk with Mr. Braun before we go in to the meeting.

Woman: He just left a message, Mr. Tam. He's stuck in traffic and will be a little late.

Man: Have him come to my office when he gets in. Then reschedule the meeting for after lunch.

71.

Man: I'm looking for the large-print edition of the New York Times.

Woman: It's to the left of the foreign periodicals.

Man: Do you also carry large print books? My sight is impaired.

72.

Woman: Did you know we lost that big desk order?

Man: No, I didn't. What happened?

Woman: The company ran out of funds and construction of the office building came to a standstill, so they don't require the desks now.

73.

Man: The president wants all management and finance personnel to participate in the conference call at five p.m.

Woman: But I'll still be uptown then, and besides the vice president will be with me.

Man: I'm sorry, but you really need to get back on time for the teleconference.

74.

Man: Could you tell me what price range you're interested in?

Woman: Around the $150,000 mark.

Man: Well, I can show you some spacious properties on the waterfront.

75.

Man: Isn't this the second cell phone you bought that doesn't recharge properly?

Woman: Yes, and I've missed several important business calls because of it.

Man: Check your warranty and go back to where you bought it.

76.

Man: But the sale is only this weekend, Maria.

Woman: I know, but Friday night we've been invited to dinner.

Man: OK, but Saturday and Sunday are still open.

77.

Man: We're spending all this money on computer equipment, but how do we know it won't be outdated next year?

Woman: We don't, Fred, but certain computers account for that and let you add on.

Man: I trust that's the kind we're buying.

78.

Woman: I'm going to computerize my address book.

Man: Who's going to enter all the data?

Woman: I'm going to hire a temp.

79.

Man: Why isn't Cathy going to the banquet?

Woman: Her father got sick. She's at the hospital with him.

Man: We should send him a get well card.

80.

Man: Margaret, did you know I'm going to Tokyo on business next week?

Woman: Could you pick me up a book on local customs?

Man: Sure. I also want to get a pictorial history of the city.

PART IV

Questions 81 through 83 refer to the following announcement.

Welcome to the New York Public Library. Anyone who resides, works, pays property taxes, or attends school in New York City, is eligible for a borrower's card. Most books can be borrowed for 28 days. These may be renewed once for 10 days if no one else is waiting. More popular books are due back in 14 days. Patrons must follow library instructions for the use of equipment. Many branches have coin-operated photocopying machines. Use of personal equipment, such as radios, portable cassette players, tape recorders, typewriters, cell phones and personal computers is not allowed.

Questions 84 through 86 refer to the following bulletin.

Controlling temperature is a must to keep food safe. Foods need to be kept cold (below 40 degrees) or hot (above 140 degrees). Lunch foods most likely to cause illness are those made with meat, poultry, fish, eggs and milk. Bread, fruits and vegetables do not pose a serious problem. Contrary to what you may think, adding commercial mayonnaise does not increase the risk of food poisoning. The negative associations with mayonnaise, stem from the fact that meat, fish, poultry and eggs, which are often mixed with mayonnaise, are usually chopped, sliced or diced, allowing greater exposure to bacteria.

Questions 87 and 88 refer to the following introduction.

The best way to learn how to run a bed and breakfast would be to talk with someone who has done it. Tonight you'll have that opportunity. Jeanne and Tom Taylor not only run a successful B&B, but now also offer advice for those considering a similar venture. Jeanne and Tom started out by renting out a room in their home. They now have a booming 24-room bed and breakfast in a little coastal town in Maine.

Questions 89 through 91 refer to the following notice.

Local anglers will be able to show off their fishing skills in several tournaments scheduled throughout the fall. The Mallory Beach Tournament and the Cape Troll Tournament are both sponsored by the New York Fishermen's Association. These tournaments are guaranteed to reel in the area's top fishermen, who will compete for cash and prizes. Pre-registration booklets are available at local tackle shops and at the Mallory Beach Chamber of Commerce. The 18th Annual Myrtle Beach Tournament will also dole out the prize money to local anglers. Special three-day beach vehicle tags will be available at the Myrtle Beach Town Hall.

Questions 92 through 94 refer to the following news story.

Six district elementary schools will receive a combined total of more than 50,000 francs worth of library books donated by Parisian Intercontinental Hotels. The number of books donated was based on the number of guests who stayed at the five Intercontinental Hotels in Paris. Hotel employees, students, parents and leaders of the Parisian Literacy Crusade will help unload and shelve the books this coming week.

Questions 95 through 97 refer to the following talk.

Before we end today's meeting, I'd like you to know I have read your suggestions. Your message is loud and clear. We all want air-conditioners for the offices. I am considering equipping all the branch offices with room air-conditioners and ours with central air. I have also noted the dining room is not well ventilated and tends to get quite warm from the kitchen. However, I am not fully convinced we need central air there. Please fill out the survey you have before you. If you are familiar with air-conditioner brands and sizes, please include that and any other technical information.

Questions 98 through 100 refer to the following advertisement.

In 1457, James II tried to outlaw golf because it distracted his subjects from practising their archery. Archery was the preferred aristocratic sport at the time. Despite this initial hostility, Scotland has been considered the home of golf for many years. Now everyone knows that St. Andrew's Old Course is the finest course in the country, if not the world. It isn't the only one in Scotland. There are dozens of courses to choose from. For a complete listing, call 1-800 PLA-GOLF, and we'll also send you a free Tours of Scotland golfing brochure.

Tapescript Practice Test Three

PART I

Sample question:

(A) They're looking out the window.
(B) They're having a meeting.
(C) They're eating in a restaurant.
(D) They're moving the furniture.

1. (A) They're at a reception.
   (B) She's soaking the coffee beans.
   (C) The customers are at the long table.
   (D) The woman is sitting at a round table.

2. (A) The monitors are connected to his heart.
   (B) The apparatus is off the ground.
   (C) The machine is being cleaned.
   (D) The man is buying a motor.

3. (A) The tags are being removed.
   (B) The bags are being delivered.
   (C) The luggage is being checked through.
   (D) The suits are being altered.

4. (A) They're moving the cement.
   (B) They're constructing a plan.
   (C) They're standing side by side.
   (D) They're building a relationship.

5. (A) It's a happy occasion.
   (B) The people are very solemn.
   (C) The group is cheering its team.
   (D) They're looking up to the sky.

6. (A) The tray is empty.
   (B) Food is on the table.
   (C) The roast is on a plate.
   (D) Four cups of tea are set.

7. (A) He's looking at the scene.
   (B) He's attending to the guests.
   (C) He's working at the desk.
   (D) He's arranging the flowers.

8. (A) He's handing over the accounts.
   (B) He's sneezing into the handkerchief.
   (C) He's welcoming the travelers.
   (D) He's blowing his clothes dry.

9. (A) They're dancing in the nightclub.
   (B) They're wearing feathers on their heads.
   (C) The costumes are plain.
   (D) The dancers are fully covered.

10. (A) The hotel receptionist welcomes the guest.
    (B) The flight attendant checks her seat.
    (C) The agent assists the traveler.
    (D) The parking officer issues a ticket.

11. (A) The group leader is hiking.
    (B) The instrument hangs from the ceiling.
    (C) His hand is wrapped around the food.
    (D) He's holding the mike.

12. (A) The hot water is for tea.
    (B) He's taking out the tables.
    (C) One man is behind the counter.
    (D) The men are going out.

13. (A) The mask covers the tubes.
    (B) His hand is on the knob.
    (C) The flask is full.
    (D) The bottles are in a row.

14. (A) All the fans have gone.
    (B) The flags cover the field.
    (C) The players are filing in.
    (D) The spectators are watching the action.

15. (A) The emergency workers enter the room.
    (B) The cleaning lady holds the mop.
    (C) The dentist examines the patient's mouth.
    (D) The hygienist sits next to the doctor.

16. (A) His collar is open.
    (B) His work is suspended.
    (C) He is making notes on the board.
    (D) He is gazing out the window.

17. (A) The men have their backs to the machines.
    (B) The devices are all the same.
    (C) The receiver is off the hook.
    (D) The machines dispense tickets.

18. (A) The assembly is meeting in the large room.
    (B) The ensemble is gathering at the back.
    (C) He is replacing the circuit board.
    (D) He is lifting the plate from the table.

19. (A) The plates are stacked neatly.
    (B) The coffee is poured.
    (C) The trays are in the kitchen.
    (D) The food is in the oven.

20. (A) The divers tighten the wire.
    (B) The fighters enter the ring.
    (C) The army enters the battle.
    (D) The firefighters are at the blaze.

PART II

Sample question:

Good morning, John. How are you?
(A) I am fine, thank you.
(B) I am in the living room.
(C) My name is John.

21. The music director approved it, didn't he?
     (A) They liked the music.
     (B) He did, but with a few changes.
     (C) He couldn't prove it.

22. How long will the taxi strike last?
     (A) It was about three feet.
     (B) They last longer in the plastic.
     (C) I think it'll be over next week.

23. Why are you changing professions?
     (A) I'm taking different lessons.
     (B) I have the same professor.
     (C) I'd like to try the medical field.

24. Who's going to do the driving?
     (A) Betty offered to.
     (B) She drove there.
     (C) I'm going to the drive-in.

25. Where's the doctor in charge of emergencies?
     (A) The emergence was sudden.
     (B) He wants to become a doctor.
     (C) She's in the emergency room.

26. Why should she turn the porch light on?
     (A) She lit the torch again.
     (B) They want to sit outside.
     (C) I would turn it over.

27. Would you help me start my car?
     (A) Yes, let me take a look at it.
     (B) No, the traffic isn't moving at all.
     (C) The new cars started selling fast.

28. Are you ready to take the typing exam?
     (A) Yes, I've been practising all week.
     (B) I took the exams to the printer.
     (C) I'll type it for you.

29. Do you have a truck driver's license?
     (A) No, but I can get one.
     (B) My driver is late.
     (C) I'll get a new license plate tomorrow.

30. What about changing the hiring requirements?
     (A) We hired all new staff.
     (B) The tires need to be changed.
     (C) I think they're fine as they are.

31. Where are the copier supplies stored?
     (A) I keep them in the cupboard.
     (B) The store was out of supplies.
     (C) We buy them every week.

32. Do you know of any problems on that route?
     (A) The roots are all entangled.
     (B) The traffic problem in cities is growing.
     (C) It was fine this morning.

33. Where should we go on vacation?
     (A) We pick up Egyptian stations.
     (B) I'd like to go to the shore.
     (C) She went to the Bahamas.

34. Would you like to sit here or there?
     (A) I'll be there later.
     (B) I bought them here.
     (C) I'd like to sit by the window.

35. Don't you have any credit cards?
     (A) I can't find my car.
     (B) I used to have excellent credit.
     (C) Several, but I try not to use them.

36. Would you rather inspect the electrical connections first?
     (A) I missed my connecting flight.
     (B) I'd rather go first class.
     (C) Yes, could you turn the power on?

37. Has he been forced to sell the family store?
     (A) His family owns the store.
     (B) That's what his brother told me.
     (C) He only sells brand names.

38. Is the loan officer I spoke with available?
     (A) He just stepped out for a minute.
     (B) My office will be available soon.
     (C) I didn't say anything about the loan.

39. Can I pick up the tickets at the box office?
     (A) The boxes are in the upstairs office.
     (B) Yes, or you can have them sent by mail.
     (C) No, you should take it to your office.

40. When did flight 779 depart?
     (A) Tomorrow.
     (B) At 2:15.
     (C) In five minutes.

41. Do you know how to type?
     (A) I don't have that type.
     (B) I can do sixty words a minute.
     (C) I can't read the type.

42. What will the advisory board recommend?
     (A) We'll know tomorrow.
     (B) I took the recommended dosage.
     (C) There's a winter advisory in effect.

43. You updated the officer's report, didn't you?
     (A) He wasn't sure of the date.
     (B) I did it first thing this morning.
     (C) She reported the incident.

44. Do these transmission parts fit your car?
     (A) Let me ask my mechanic.
     (B) My transmission is broken.
     (C) Car parts are expensive.

45. Would you like to see the test results?
    (A) If you have them.
    (B) I see what she means.
    (C) We're testing them now.

46. Do you think they'll offer me the secretarial job today?
    (A) You'll like the job.
    (B) I don't see why not.
    (C) My secretary was offered a better job.

47. You were shown the changes in the contract, weren't you?
    (A) She changed the contract.
    (B) I didn't know there were any.
    (C) No one showed up.

48. Could you send your new catalog to my office?
    (A) I have the log book.
    (B) What's the address?
    (C) We're sending you to a new office.

49. How can I fire him after all these years?
    (A) We put the fire out.
    (B) He's known him for many years.
    (C) Tell him we're downsizing.

50. You met the deadline, didn't you?
    (A) With minutes to spare.
    (B) We're not at a dead end.
    (C) I didn't know he was in town.

PART III

51.
Woman Mr. Barasso, your brakes need to be replaced. Can you leave your car here this afternoon?
Man   If they're that bad, I guess I'll have to.
Woman We could have it ready by five o'clock.

52.
Man   When will Ahmet land in Cairo?
Woman If he was able to catch that early flight, he'll be there by noon.
Man   I hope so. I'll be in Cairo for just the afternoon and I'd like to meet up with him.

53.
Man   Your ad is really attracting a lot of new customers.
Woman Thanks, but Marcy deserves half the credit.
Man   Well, the boss is sure to give you both a hefty bonus.

54.
Man   There's a meeting at five o'clock, but I don't think I can go.
Woman Do you have another appointment?
Man   Yes, I have to go to the doctor at four.

55.
Woman We're almost on empty. Shouldn't we find a gas station?
Man   Yes, but the tank is still good for another thirty miles.
Woman Fine, but the next town may be forty miles from here.

56.
Woman Do you think you could have these slides ready by this afternoon?
Man   Yes, but there will be a ten dollar charge for the express service.
Woman That's fine. I have to make an important presentation to the Board of Directors tomorrow evening.

57.
Man   Jeanie, could you call me a taxi? I have to go to the airport.
Woman Let me take you. It's on my way and besides, you have so much luggage.
Man   Gee, that's awfully nice. Would you be able to go now?

58.
Man   I'm sorry, Mrs. Blair, but your favorite hotel won't be taking any more reservations for the next few weeks. They've got no space.
Woman Oh, that's all right. There's probably a conference on and they're full up.
Man   Let me try the Crystal View. Remember how much you enjoyed your last stay there?

59.
Man   Is the theater on Second or Third Avenue?
Woman Neither, the newspaper said "First".
Man   Well, let's leave now. The movie starts at four and we may need a little time to find the place.

60.
Man   I'd like a monthly commuter pass for forty-five dollars.
Woman That price is only for senior citizens, sir.
Man   Oh, then what is the regular fare, please?

61.
Woman George, were there any messages for me?
Man   Yes, a Mr. Cowell called about the beachfront property he saw advertised.
Woman Would you please write down his name on my calendar?

62.
Man   This screw came out of the hinge on my glasses.
Woman That's not a problem. We can fix that in a few minutes.
Man   Really? Then maybe you could also adjust the nose piece?

63.

Man   We're going to the Seychelles this summer on business.

Woman   Why don't you combine it with your vacation?

Man   I would, but I can't afford it. We're putting an addition on the house this year.

64.

Man   On second thought, I think I'd rather have the 200 model printer.

Woman   That's fine, sir, but we'd have to order that.

Man   Maybe one of your branches has it in stock? Would you mind calling?

65.

Man   It's time for me to start my own business. I'm not going to hang around waiting to become vice president.

Woman   But you've only been in this position for one year.

Man   True, but I have lots of education and experience, and I'm going to come up with a good business plan.

66.

Man   You know, that restaurant investment went sour after all.

Woman   Yes, I heard it turned out to be a bad location – no foot traffic.

Man   The manager didn't help any either.

67.

Man   I like this model, the dials turn so smoothly.

Woman   Shall we crank up the bass?

Man   Why not? I bet the speakers are good.

68.

Man   I'd like to cash this check please.

Woman   We'll need two forms of ID if you don't have an account with us.

Man   Will my driver's license and a credit card do?

69.

Woman   Do you want to go to the open house that Worldwide Pharmaceutical is having?

Man   I do, but aren't they doing that for high school and college students?

Woman   Yes, but the sign does say that all are invited.

70.

Man   Sorry it's so late. The taxis were on strike so I decided to walk.

Woman   Why didn't you call? We could have picked you up.

Man   It felt good to walk after that long ride on the train. Actually, the walk took less time than that train trip.

71.

Man   The shipping department's softball team is challenging ours.

Woman   Count me out. I hate sports.

Man   Oh, come on. It's just for fun. Besides, we have a great coach.

72.

Woman   Are you looking for any book in particular?

Man   No. I'm actually trying to find a local map of this city.

Woman   Oh, maps are right behind you to the left of stationery.

73.

Woman   We'll need a special beaker to mix these acids.

Man   Will it be heated?

Woman   No, heat may cause the chemicals to react.

74.

Man   I like this style, but they're a little tight on my heel.

Woman   Let me get the next size up.

Man   Yes, that's fine. I'll take them and some polish if you have it.

75.

Man   I'll be right back, Mary. I'm just going to get a haircut.

Woman   The barber's closed on Monday, Jack.

Man   Oh, that's right. Well, it'll have to wait until Thursday. I have meetings all day Tuesday and Wednesday.

76.

Man   Joan, I'm not going to have time to get to the art store.

Woman   What do you need, Tom? I'm going to the dentist, which is just up the street from it.

Man   I need two large poster boards for those signs and a black marker.

77.

Man   I'm going to give my wife a special surprise for her birthday.

Woman   What do you have planned for her this year?

Man   I'm taking her to see the opera Madame Butterfly. She's always wanted to go.

78.

Man   That will be seventeen dollars and thirty-five cents, please.

Woman   But the sales sign said fourteen dollars.

Man   That's only if you have a coupon. And then there's seventy-five cents tax.

79.

Man   We have to get a new light switch. It's annoying how the light keeps flickering.

Woman   It could be the bulb, too. Fluorescent lights have a tendency to do that.

Man   Could you call the electrician and ask her to look at it?

80.

Man   I'm looking for 1801 Calvert Street. I see 1800 across the street.

Woman   Well, this is 1803. It should be right next door.

Man   That's odd. It goes right to 1799. I have the number. I'm going to call them.

PART IV

Questions 81 through 83 refer to the following announcement.

Our friends at Oklahoma City National Bank have informed us that a volunteer organization of local Woodside residents, the Neighborhood Corps, Incorporated will be hosting a fund-raiser to benefit home builders. This organization has been restoring and building attractive inner-city houses in the Bedford area for low-income families for almost ten years. The beautiful Fitzgerald house on Eighth Street is only one of many examples. The event will be held at the Macomb Club in Marlboro on Tuesday, September 2, from 6 p.m. to 8 p.m.

Questions 84 through 86 refer to the following report.

The world's worst nuclear accident happened years ago in Chernobyl, but the long term effects of the radiation fall-out are still unclear. Although humans and animals who were directly exposed did suffer genetic damage, it is still uncertain whether it will be passed on to their offspring. What has been discovered, though, is that birds near the accident have been found to have unusually high incidences of a condition that appears as splotches of white feathers. Swedish and French scientists also noted that birds with this condition are generally weaker and less likely to survive to breeding age.

Questions 87 and 88 refer to the following introduction.

Mr. Yan has come here today to answer your questions about the business customs of the Chinese people. This information should be of special interest to the many of you who will be attending this year's annual Trade and Commerce Convention in Hong Kong. Mr. Yan has been the Director of Public Affairs for the Bank of China for the last twenty-three years. He has given hundreds of seminars educating businessmen and women in the manners and business protocol of the Chinese. Please take advantage of his vast wisdom to address any questions or concerns you may have.

Questions 89 through 91 refer to the following notice.

If you have ever used a major credit card, you probably have a record at a consumer reporting agency, often called a *credit bureau*. This record allows creditors to check your payment history before they give you credit. If you have been denied credit because of information supplied by a *credit bureau*, the Fair Credit Reporting Act requires the creditor to give you the name and address of the bureau. If you contact that bureau within thirty days of receiving a denial notice, the agency must provide you with a copy of your full credit report, free of charge.

Questions 92 through 94 refer to the following news story.

Japan's Ebara Corporation is going to build water treatment facilities in Port Pacifica this year. Ebara, using its own breakthrough treatment technology, has joined with Vinacon, a Swedish construction firm. According to Ebara sources, the joint venture should bring the two countries over $40 million within five years. Together the firms also plan to enter the waste disposal business in Brazil. Analysts predict that the cooperation of the Japanese water disposal company and Swedish-owned construction firm will produce an efficient partnership.

Questions 95 through 97 refer to the following talk.

Good evening, ladies and gentlemen. Welcome to the Village Theater's production of Hamlet. Tonight, we celebrate our fourth year in entertaining our local community. In consideration of the cast members and the audience, we ask that you please turn off any cellular phones, beepers or electronic devices that could cause disruption. Also, if you have small children that require attention, we would appreciate your bringing them to the lobby. We hope you will join us downstairs at intermission for coffee and dessert. All sales will benefit the Village Theater. Thank you again and enjoy the show.

Questions 98 through 100 refer to the following announcement.

If you're just starting on your evening commute, we recommend loosening your tie and enjoying the music. With the holiday rush approaching, everyone is traveling tonight. I-5 is backed up from the Ship Canal Bridge all the way to Everett in both directions. If you're heading eastbound, it's a coin-toss between 520 and I-90. Westbound I-90 is moving at a turtle's pace, and 520 heading west has slow-downs from the Madison Exit to Roanoke. The S-curves are backed up on 405 both ways and it is stop and go approaching Pacific Highway at 180th. Stay tuned for another update. Here's the *Rolling Stones* with *Satisfaction*.

Tapescript Practice Test Four

PART I

Sample question:

(A) They're looking out the window.
(B) They're having a meeting.
(C) They're eating in a restaurant.
(D) They're moving the furniture.

1. (A) The receptionist is taking a message.
   (B) The executive is talking on the phone.
   (C) The manager is writing his material.
   (D) The entertainer is answering the reporters.

2. (A) The waiter is about to pour the beverage.
   (B) The waiter is being served a meal.
   (C) They're dining in front of mountains.
   (D) Their table has been cleared.

3. (A) He's bidding on the chair.
   (B) He's resetting the ignition.
   (C) He's handling the watch.
   (D) He's operating the machine.

4. (A) The service is not good.
   (B) Water is coming out of the hose.
   (C) He's filling the tank.
   (D) He's washing his car.

5. (A) The trainee is sitting at his station.
   (B) The train is at the station.
   (C) The passenger is waiting on the platform.
   (D) The plane is on the tarmac.

6. (A) She's choosing a jar.
   (B) She's looking at the selection.
   (C) She's resting her hand on the cabinet.
   (D) She's drinking the wine.

7. (A) He's using a knife and a spoon.
   (B) The bowls are full.
   (C) A bottle is by his hand.
   (D) He's clearing away the table.

8. (A) He is using a forklift to lift the barrel.
   (B) He's pouring oil from the container.
   (C) The blade is rotating.
   (D) The jet is landing.

9. (A) They're adjourning the meeting.
   (B) They're sitting at a small desk.
   (C) The displays are on easels.
   (D) The training is for accountants.

10. (A) The engine is being repaired.
    (B) One wheel is rotating.
    (C) The lumber supports the machines.
    (D) One of the belts is broken.

11. (A) He's at the departure gate.
    (B) His bags are on his back.
    (C) He's checking the list.
    (D) His plane is leaving now.

12. (A) His joints are improving.
    (B) The metal beams are connected.
    (C) The seams are ripped.
    (D) His foot is resting on the wall.

13. (A) They're heading towards the garage.
    (B) They're throwing out the trash.
    (C) The trash is piled up against the building.
    (D) The waste is thrown into the can.

14. (A) The lawyer is testing her case.
    (B) The sanitation worker is filling the dump.
    (C) The nurse is making her rounds.
    (D) The scientist is holding a bottle.

15. (A) It's a sunny day.
    (B) The newspaper is under his arm.
    (C) He's putting his umbrella away.
    (D) He's taking off his coat.

16. (A) Most of the tables are empty.
    (B) The people are running through the square.
    (C) The crowd is controlled by the police.
    (D) There are people sitting in the square.

17. (A) They're cutting down trees.
    (B) They're building a house.
    (C) They have nothing in their hands.
    (D) The hut has windows on every side.

18. (A) The cruise ship is leaving the harbor.
    (B) One boat is smaller than the other.
    (C) Sailors are running on board.
    (D) The shops are next to the dock.

19. (A) The gates are not open.
    (B) The doors are constructed of wood.
    (C) The entrance is guarded at night.
    (D) The passage is enclosed.

20. (A) Both women have shortish wavy hair.
    (B) Neither woman is wearing jewelry.
    (C) One of the women is standing on the stage.
    (D) Both of the women are unhappy.

PART II

Sample question:

Good morning, John. How are you?
(A) I am fine, thank you.
(B) I am in the living room.
(C) My name is John.

21. The charter bus leaves at 6 p.m., doesn't it?
(A) I left them on the bus.
(B) That's what the schedule says.
(C) He'll leave six of them for you.

22. My appointment wasn't at nine, was it?
(A) No, it has a dull point.
(B) I'm sure he meant it.
(C) Yes, but it's not a problem.

23. What do you find is the most popular item?
(A) The lamps sold out right away.
(B) She's more popular than I am.
(C) I find it everywhere.

24. How much gas does your tank hold?
(A) I can't hold it much longer.
(B) We need a new tank.
(C) I never really noticed.

25. Would you consider leasing a car?
(A) My lease is up next month.
(B) If the company were paying, yes.
(C) He's very considerate.

26. You helped them renovate the store, didn't you?
(A) They let me store it downstairs.
(B) The store was old anyway.
(C) I did the wallpapering.

27. Can't you test that loudspeaker outside?
(A) They're taking a test inside.
(B) I'll speak to her tonight.
(C) I would but it's raining.

28. How do you know which paper to buy?
(A) I went right by your office.
(B) It tells you on the order form.
(C) I like to read the paper over breakfast.

29. You were at the sales meeting, weren't you?
(A) I won't be able to make it.
(B) We're meeting them later.
(C) I was there for part of it.

30. Why would demand fall off so suddenly?
(A) His demands seem sudden.
(B) Sales always drop in the Autumn.
(C) She hadn't given me any notice.

31. Are you comfortable with this arrangement?
(A) These shoes don't fit.
(B) They're very relaxing.
(C) I would prefer a lower monthly payment.

32. Do you have any glue?
(A) I have too much to do.
(B) No, I have a red one.
(C) Over there in my drawer.

33. Have you offered Mrs. Dano the position?
(A) She's lying down.
(B) Yes, she wasn't interested.
(C) It's an offer I can't refuse.

34. Can't you show them something in a lower price range?
(A) I'm giving it to them at cost.
(B) The show was downtown.
(C) The lower range is broken.

35. She's the art director, isn't she?
(A) I like his art.
(B) He likes to direct musicals.
(C) Yes, she was just promoted.

36. Did you know she passed the bar?
(A) No, but I'm meeting her there tonight.
(B) Now she can start to practise.
(C) She didn't pass the ball.

37. Haven't you spoken with the hospital personnel?
(A) We're meeting with them tonight.
(B) I spoke with my friend in the hospital.
(C) The innkeeper was very hospitable.

38. Why should the media be invited?
(A) We need the exposure.
(B) All middle management was invited.
(C) Let's go together.

39. That's the Taj Mahal, isn't it?
(A) There's no one here.
(B) It's very comfortable.
(C) Yes, isn't it remarkable?

40. What did you think of the department's performance?
(A) I'm recommending bonuses for the entire team.
(B) The show had one intermission.
(C) I was thinking of them just yesterday.

41. Would you rather have someone else look at it?
(A) I can't see it.
(B) No, I trust your judgment.
(C) We're looking for someone.

42. What about ordering a six-month supply?
(A) It's a six-man team.
(B) I can supply a reference.
(C) I bet they would give us a discount.

43. You'll notify the marketing department, won't you?
(A) I just got off the phone with them.
(B) I went to the market yesterday.
(C) The police notified me.

44. Where can I find a translating service?
(A) You'll find they have an excellent service.
(B) I believe there's one on Hilton Street.
(C) I found something nice to wear.

45. Are you opening an office in Hong Kong?
(A) We've decided to keep it open.
(B) There will be officers at the port.
(C) It will be either Hong Kong or Japan.

46. How is this new engine more efficient?
(A) It uses much less fuel.
(B) They always arrive on time.
(C) The old engine blew up.

47. Can I apply for membership over the phone?
(A) The price is lower now.
(B) I remember which ship it was.
(C) If you have a major credit card, yes.

48. Who's making the return-trip reservations?
(A) That was an unnecessary trip.
(B) I think they've already been taken care of.
(C) You didn't have to return them.

49. How many reference books did you buy?
(A) More than I should have.
(B) I went by the library today.
(C) We spent the day at the bookstore.

50. Don't you recognize this writing style?
(A) I like to ride side-saddle.
(B) She knew immediately who I was.
(C) It's very familiar, but I can't place it.

PART III

51.
Woman   I had to take my car to the shop.
Man   What was wrong with it?
Woman   The mechanic told me he wasn't sure.

52.
Man   What kind of dog do you have?
Woman   She's a beagle.
Man   I'd like to get a dog myself, but my wife doesn't like them.

53.
Woman   The supermarket down the street closed yesterday, Mr. Wong.
Man   Where should I go to buy my groceries?
Woman   There's another store around the corner that has good prices.

54.
Man   When did you buy the furniture?
Woman   I only got a new couch. Everything else is old.
Man   That's funny. I don't remember that coffee table or the desk.

55.
Man   I just found out that John is leaving the company.
Woman   Does he have a new job yet?
Man   No, he wants to take some time off. He'll start looking soon.

56.
Woman   You look much thinner. Have you lost weight?
Man   Yes, I've been on a diet for several months.
Woman   That's great. You must be really proud of yourself. I must try and exercise more.

57.
Man   I'd like the steak with mashed potatoes on the side.
Woman   Are you sure you don't want the French fries?
Man   Yes. I had some for lunch.

58.
Man   I can't believe it, Betty. This pen leaked.
Woman   The cleaners can get it out.
Man   But I need this suit for an important meeting this weekend.

59.
Man   My pen just ran out. Do you have another?
Woman   Let me check in my purse. Oh, here's one you can borrow.
Man   Thanks. I'll give it back as soon as I'm done.

60.
Man   How long were you in Beijing for?
Woman   Six weeks. I was supposed to stay longer, a couple of months, but my husband got sick.
Man   That's too bad. Six weeks isn't very long.

61.
Man   It's for you, Susan. I think it's your aunt.
Woman   Can you tell her I'm in the shower?
Man   Sure. I'll tell her to call you back later.

62.
Man   I can't tell if this is the keyboard, printer or fax cable.
Woman   It can be confusing. I once had my phone and fax cables all mixed up.
Man   I just have to get this report to print out. I need it this afternoon.

63.
Man   Has Paul ever been to Boston?
Woman   I don't think so. Maybe we'll go this year.
Man   It's a beautiful city, especially in the Autumn. You should try to get there if you have the chance.

64.
Man   Do you know who got the job?
Woman   I think that they gave it to Mr. Dupont.
Man   That's too bad. I was hoping that Carol would get it.

65.
Man   This copy machine has a paper jam. Can you help me fix it?
Woman   I don't know anything about those things. You should ask Rebecca.
Man   She stepped out of the office. I don't know where she is.

66.
Man   He said he was going to check on the price of the wallpaper, but he hasn't come back yet.
Woman Well, let's go over and pick out some shelving while we're waiting.
Man   OK, but I also want to look at some kitchen and bathroom accessories in aisle ten.

67.
Man   How much does this sweater cost?
Woman It's fifty dollars. Don't you like the color?
Man   I do, and it fits well. But I think I'll pick out something else that's cheaper.

68.
Man   I played tennis for three hours yesterday.
Woman Did Michelle beat you, or did you win?
Man   It was a tie, so we're playing again tomorrow.

69.
Woman Your table will be ready in fifteen minutes.
Man   But our reservation was for eight o'clock.
Woman I'm sorry, would you mind waiting in the bar?

70.
Man   Now that I have my own business, I'm home almost all the time.
Woman You're lucky. It's a great house in a great neighborhood.
Man   Yes, but it's getting cramped. I may do an add-on above the garage.

71.
Man   Could you press five, please?
Woman Certainly. You must work in the law firm.
Man   Yes, I do. Oh, here's my floor.

72.
Woman I'm really tired. I think I'll go to bed early tonight.
Man   Aren't you upset you'll miss the show?
Woman Could you tape it for me?

73.
Man   No matter what I do, the kitchen doesn't stay clean.
Woman Would you like me to put away the dishes?
Man   That would be a big help.

74.
Woman My boss said I'm next in line for a promotion.
Man   Congratulations! Will you be getting a raise?
Woman I suppose I will, if it comes through.

75.
Man   I thought the test was impossible. How did you do?
Woman It's hard to tell. I know I didn't get everything correct.
Man   I just hope I passed, or I might fail the course.

76.
Woman Sales are seriously down, John.
Man   I know. I went over all the reports last night.
Woman We have to turn this around immediately or we'll find ourselves in bankruptcy court.

77.
Man   Can you leave it on this station? My favorite show's on next.
Woman But there's something else I want to listen to.
Man   That's not fair. You got to choose yesterday.

78.
Man   How many candles should I put on the cake?
Woman I don't know how old he is tomorrow.
Man   Then I'll just put one for good luck.

79.
Man   I don't like this song. This group is pretty bad.
Woman Didn't you used to like them?
Man   That was before their music got so terrible.

80.
Man   If you go to the store, can you pick up some things for me?
Woman Just tell me what you need.
Man   Orange juice, cereal, milk and some bread. That's all.

PART IV

Questions 81 through 83 refer to the following announcement.

Our offices are closing early for the long weekend. Those of you who are responsible for the monthly reports should complete them and leave a copy on the treasurer's desk before leaving. And please remember, when we come back, we may have to work some overtime. Our client is going to want all the TV ads ready by the end of the week, and all newspaper and magazine ads by mid week.

Questions 84 through 86 refer to the following report.

A widely used drug for high blood pressure and heart disease, the XR2 channel blocker, has been associated with an increased risk of breast cancer. A study suggests that women over 65 who take XR2 may be twice as likely to develop breast cancer. However, the results are far from conclusive. Women who are currently taking this medication are advised to continue taking the drug, as its potential merits may outweigh the risks. Of the four thousand women who were studied, those who took calcium channel blockers ran twice the risk of developing breast cancer as those who took no blood pressure drugs.

Questions 87 and 88 refer to the following introduction.

Mr. Gupta has been kind enough to speak to us tonight, even though his plane from New Delhi landed just hours ago. We understand there was quite a delay in the Paris airport. As you all know, the magnitude of the upcoming trade fairs in India is considerable. Mr. Gupta is here tonight to tell us exactly how these fairs will contribute to India's industrial prominence.

Questions 89 through 91 refer to the following notice.

The city of Houston is slowly but surely completing the Biltmore Turnpike repairs. The Mystic Waterfront Park Commission is laying the groundwork for the long-awaited Mystic Waterfront Park, which is adjacent to the turnpike. Former town councilwoman Shirley May is leading the all-volunteer commission. Among other things, they are currently working on funding for the park as well as for parking, and on the construction of the boathouse and other water amusement facilities.

Questions 92 through 94 refer to the following news story.

Comptor is the world's largest maker of computer chips. In March of last year, Comptor opened its first representative office in Spain in Madrid. It is now opening another office in Barcelona. Comserve and CPT are the only authorized distributors for marketing Comptor products in Spain. Together with Comptor, they will be sponsoring computer training and other educational programs in Spain. Milan, in Italy, is being considered as a future site for manufacturing with a distributorship in Rome. Milan officials are eager to see Comptor pursue manufacturing in Italy.

Questions 95 through 97 refer to the following talk.

I'd like to pass on some tips for finding an apartment that may be helpful when we relocate to Kansas City. First consider networking. Call friends or business associates to see if they know of any available apartments. Some of our staff who are already there, have compiled a list of possible connections. You can also look in the classified ads of the local newspaper where you might find other things you need like cars and appliances. Otherwise try the phone book under "Real Estate". Many real estate offices have an array of listings for available apartments.

Questions 98 through 100 refer to the following advertisement.

The Russian Sports Massage is a painless approach prescribed by Russian physicians in thousands of clinics worldwide. This method has been used for over fifty years with astonishing results. While the rest of the world was concentrating their efforts on pharmaceutical drugs, the USSR educated hundreds of physicians in the art of natural healing. Physical therapists are medical doctors with PhDs in physical therapy. Massage has become one of the major forms of treatment in traditional Russian medicine. The treatment is accompanied by lowered levels of stress hormones and reports of reduced anxiety and depression.

Answer Key

Answer Key

Practice Test One

In the following Answer Key, the first explanation provided for each question is the correct option.

PART I

1. (D) There are signs advertising *stores*, or shops, on the left and on the right, so they are on *both sides* of where the people are walking. (A) There are a lot of *shops*, but they are not full of *flowers*, the street is. (B) People are passing each other in the street. There are no *cars* in the picture. (C) There are *pedestrians*, people on foot, but there is no *fountain* in the picture.

2. (A) The *deck*, or the upper floor of the boat, is where you can see the people standing and sitting. (B) The picture shows people *sailing* the boat, not *docking* it. They are at sea not in a harbor. (C) The passengers are on the deck, not *disembarking*, or leaving it. (D) There are no sails in this picture. An engine provides the power for the boat.

3. (B) The man is *playing* a musical instrument, the *saxophone*. (A) He's *playing* the instrument, not putting it away. There is no *case* in the picture. (C) *Fax* sounds similar to *sax* and is therefore easily confused. (D) A saxophone is a type of *horn* instrument, but a motorist would *honk the horn* of a car. There is no car in this picture.

4. (D) The men are both wearing *eye glasses*. (A) One man is *handing* something to the other man, but it is not possible to hand over a *business* in this way. (B) One man may be tipping the other, but they're not both *giving tips* to *customers*. This option refers to a minimum of four people (*they* and *customers*). (C) The man on the left may be a *conductor* because of the uniform he is wearing. However, there is only one *passenger* in the picture and the conductor is not *calling* him.

5. (C) The picture shows some stalls at a *market*. We know it is *outside* because shadows from the sun are visible. (A) Fruits and vegetables are sold in a *grocery store*, but a grocery store would be *inside* and this is outside. (B) The picture shows *vegetables*, but they are fresh, not *frozen*. (D) There are fruits and vegetables in the *baskets*, but no *meat*.

6. (B) The ship is not moving, it is *at the dock*. (A) A passenger *rides* on a ship, but there are no visible passengers and the ship is not moving. (C) *Loading* is associated with docks and ships, but there are no cars being put *onto the ship*. (D) A *canoe* is a type of small boat. The ship in this picture is much bigger than a canoe.

7. (D) The people are standing in line to buy, or *purchase*, cappuccino, or another kind of coffee, *to drink*. (A) They *are* standing in line, but not to buy tickets for a *movie*. (B) Although the people are in a line to buy a *beverage*, there is no beverage pictured. (C) *Caps* sounds like an abbreviation for *cappuccino*, but it isn't, and the sign has the word *bar* on it. There are no *caps*, or *hats*, visible.

8. (A) The *dentist* has her instruments in the patient's mouth and is looking at, or *checking*, her teeth. (B) A dentist is a type of *doctor*, but *operating* involves cutting something open and there is no evidence of cutting in this picture. (C) The picture may show a *hygienist*, somebody who cleans people's teeth, but she is not *washing her hands*. (D) *Patients* make appointments with receptionists, but there is no *receptionist* in the picture.

9. (A) The flight attendant is *serving drinks* on a tray to passengers on the plane. (B) The passengers are all *awake*, not *asleep*. (C) Nobody is eating in the picture, and they're not in a *car*, they are in a *plane*. (D) She is *serving drinks*, not *selling goods*.

10. (B) The *nurse* is taking the lid off, or *uncovering*, the food, for the patient. (A) The patient is in hospital and is being served a meal by a *nurse*, not a *waiter* who serves in a restaurant. (C) The patient is sitting up in bed about to eat a meal, she is not *getting out* of bed. (D) *Technicians* can be found in hospitals, but the tray in this picture is not being *adjusted*, or moved.

11. (B) Two men are *looking over* the woman's *shoulders* at the computer screen. (A) There are two men in the picture, not one, and they are looking at something so they can *both* see. (C) The woman is *sitting* at the computer. (D) The three of them are a *group* and they may be *reading a report* on the screen, but they aren't *presenting* one to other people.

12. (C) The picture is of an exercise *bike* which is designed to stay in one place, or be *stationary*. (A) A *tricycle* has three wheels (*tri-* meaning three). The bike in the picture doesn't have *any* wheels, but is shaped like a triangle. (B) A *motorcycle* is a type of bike which has an engine. The bike in this picture is not a motorcycle. (D) The bicycle in the picture may have *gears*, which are used to alter the speed or power, but it is not possible to know how many.

13. (D) She is withdrawing, or *taking money out* of the machine. (A) She's at a *bank*, but she is not waiting in a line of people. (B) *Check* (a means of payment) and *deposit* (to put money into an account) are both words associated with money and banking, but there's no *check* visible in this picture. Also, she's at a *bank*, not a *store*. (C) You *fill out* forms etc. at a bank, but she's not *filling* her bag with *bills* (paper money).

14. (B) The machines are *tractors* and they are in a *warehouse*, a room used for storing things. (A) *Lawnmowers* are also machines, but they are much smaller than tractors. (C) A tractor is a piece of *farm equipment*, but there aren't any *trailers* carrying anything in the picture. (D) The engines are *in* the machines, not *above* them.

15. (A) The hard hat indicates that the man is a *construction worker* and he's looking at some drawings, or *plans*. (B) The man may be an *architect*, and he may be looking at some *measurements*, but he is not *taking* them. (C) The man in the picture may be a *foreman*, but there is nothing to indicate he is looking for *more space*. (D) *Designers* are associated with buildings, but the picture shows the *exterior* (outside), not *interior* (inside) of the building.

16. (C) The castle is on the other side, or *across*, the *river*. (A) *Fortress* is another word for *castle*, but there is no *ocean* in the picture. (B) A castle is a *building*, but a *desert* is a dry, sandy place without any water or trees, both of which are in this picture. (D) The building in this picture may be used as a *palace*, but there are not enough trees visible for this to be a *forest*.

17. (D) The *cook*, or the chef, is *stirring*, or mixing something in the pot. (A) There might be *stew* in the pot, but this food is still being made. It is not being *served* to someone. (B) The man could be a cook on a ship and therefore a *sailor*, but he is not *cleaning the pot*, he is cooking something in it. (C) The man in the picture is a *worker*, but this option confuses the sound of *soap*, something that is used for cleaning, with *soup*, which is something to eat.

18. (C) She's *typing* on a lap-top computer and using what she has written on her notepad, her *notes*. (A) She is sitting *at* the table, not *searching* for it. (B) *Taping* sounds like *typing* and is therefore easily confused. She is typing on the computer, but would need a microphone and tape recorder to do any *taping*. (D) There is a cup on her desk which may have coffee in it, but she is not *sipping*, or drinking, it.

19. (C) A *conference* is being held and lots of people are present, or are *attending* it. (A) The people who attend a conference could be called the *participants*, but they are not talking to each other. (B) The room is *full* of people, but there is no *orchestra*, or group of musicians, in the picture. (D) Somebody may be *presenting* something, but there are no *dancers* in the picture.

20. (A) The man is *holding* the phone *receiver* between his *shoulder* and head, so his hands are free for him to write. (B) The *wire* in the picture connects the receiver, the part of the phone that you speak into, to the rest of the phone. There are no computers visible. (C) The *phone* is not in his *hand*, it is on his *shoulder*. (D) This option confuses the sounds of *bone* and *phone*.

PART II

21. (B) The funds should be *set aside*, or kept, for an *emergency*. (A) This option confuses the sounds of *funds* and *fundamentals*. (C) This option confuses the sounds of *funds* and *fun*.

22. (C) *Several feet* answers *how much snow* is expected according to the forecast. (A) Snow is often associated with blocking routes, but this option does not answer the question. (B) This option simply repeats the information in the question rather than answering it.

23. (A) The respondent *would* prefer to travel first-class, but only on the *return trip*. (B) *Class* is used in the question and the reply, but with different meanings. The question does not refer to a lesson. (C) This option confuses the sounds of *prefer* and *refer*, and the fact that *travel* can be associated with *agency*.

24. (B) If the package *did* arrive, the person does not know it. (A) *Package* is repeated, and this option confuses the sounds of *arrive* and *drive*. (C) *Package* is associated with *luggage*, but in this case the two are not connected.

25. (B) The respondent decides to ask the waiter for a new napkin. (A) *Fresh* is used in both the question and the reply, and *waiter* can be associated with *coffee*. However, coffee is not what is required. (C) This option confuses the words *waiter* and *wait*.

26. (A) By calling the *1-800 number* (a free call number), you can get tickets. (B) This response does not answer the question. (C) This option confuses the sound of *tickets* with *bigots*.

27. (B) Not only did the respondent look at the blueprints, he thought they were *excellent*. (A) *No* is a logical response to a tag question, and *blue* is repeated. However, this option does not answer the question. (C) The words *blueprints* and *footprints* are confused because they have the same root.

28. (C) The *accident* is the cause of the delays. (A) This option confuses the sounds of *delays* and *long days*. Her tiredness could be the *cause* of something, but not the delays. (B) *Because* would be a logical answer to *why?* not *what?*

29. (C) Some business is conducted, but the respondent would like it to be more. (A) *Businessmen* is associated with *business*, and *overseas* can be associated with *Japan*. However, this option is incorrect. (B) *Overseas* can be associated with *Austria*, but the words *conduct* and *conductor* are confused because they have the same root.

30. (A) The *joint* seems to be the location of the leak. (B) *Line* is used in both the question and the option, but with different meanings. (C) *Gas* is repeated, and *leaking* may sound like *locked*. However, this option does not answer the question.

31. (A) The respondent *has* participated in the negotiations, as a *consultant*. (B) This option confuses the words *participate* and *part* because they have the same root, and also the sounds of *negotiations* and *negation*. (C) *Negotiations* and *classifications* may be confused because they have the same suffix, but they have different meanings.

32. (A) The respondent must *check with the architect* before changing the height. (B) *Height* is repeated, but in the option it refers to a person. (C) *Need* is repeated, but the sounds of *height* and *fight* are confused, making this option incorrect.

33. (C) She was *promised* a raise, so she should be *getting* it. (A) This option confuses the sounds of *raise* and *praised*, and if she is getting a raise, it would be logical for her work to be praised, but this option does not answer the question. (B) *She* and *raise* are both repeated, but the meanings of *raise* are different.

34. (B) The *efficient management* is the reason they decided on a merger. (A) *Decide* is repeated, but the option does not answer the question. (C) The sounds of *merge* and *surge* are confused, and *gas* is a form of *power*, but this is not an appropriate response to the question.

35. (C) The *rain* will not stop construction, but the *high winds* will. In this question, the speaker's assumption is only partly correct – that construction will be halted. The respondent clarifies the reason for the halt. (A) *Halted* relates to *stops*. However, the sounds of *rain* and *train* are confused. (B) *Constructed* is used in the answer, but the option confuses the sounds of *halted* and *vaults*.

36. (B) We know that Mr. Tan *will* be attending, because everybody in the department has to. (A) *Attending* could be associated with *punctual*, and *Mr. Tan* can be referred to by the pronoun *he*. However, his punctuality is not in question. (C) The words *attending* and *tend* may be confused because they have the same root.

37. (B) It looks like it *is* the approval code and after checking, they will know. (A) *Approve* is used in the option and *approval* in the question, but the contexts are different. (C) *Code* is repeated, but the *dress code* is not the topic.

38. (A) Losing his job was the explanation he gave. (B) The words *explanation* and *clarification* may be confused because they have the same suffix. (C) The words *explanation* and *explorations* may be confused because they have the same prefix and suffix.

39. (C) Neither faxing *nor* mailing will be necessary, because the respondent will *pick it up* today. (A) This option confuses the sounds of *fax* and *facts*, making this option incorrect. (B) *Mail* is used in both the question and the option, but the *mail box* is not the topic.

40. (B) An *improvement* will be seen in *several days*. (A) *Improvements* is repeated, but this option would answer *What improvements are being made?* (C) *Tonight* is an attractive answer to *when?* but the question is not asking about a person.

41. (A) Their home is *in the north* in Saudi Arabia. (B) This option would answer *What do they wear in Saudi Arabia?* (C) This option would answer *When did they live in Saudi Arabia?*

42. (C) The pen needs to be refilled after *a good month.* This means a whole month or even longer. (A) *Often* is repeated, but the question is not about a pencil. (B) This option confuses the sounds of *pen* and *pin*.

43. (A) The speaker would like to drink an *iced tea*. (B) *Anything* and *I* are both repeated, but the question remains unanswered. (C) *Drink* is repeated, but this answer would logically include the pronoun *I*, not *she*.

44. (C) *Jennifer* has been asked to prepare the final draft. (A) *No one* is a logical response to *who?* and *ready* might be associated with *preparing*. However, this option is incorrect. (B) *Final* is associated with *last*, but the option confuses the sounds of *raft* and *draft*.

45. (A) *Just over the border* answers *how far south* the warehouse is. (B) *South* may be associated with being *hot*, but the weather is not the topic. (C) This option may confuse *warehouse* and *house* which have the same root. The question is about *distance* not *size*.

46. (B) *Normally* promotional mail *is* sent out. (A) *Sent* is the past tense of *send,* and *mail* is associated with *letter*, but this option does not answer the question. (C) *Promotional* and *promoted* might be confused because they have the same root. However, the question is not concerned with somebody's promotion at work.

47. (B) The lease will be signed after a *deposit* has been paid. (A) *He* is used in both the question and the option. However, the sounds of *lease* (a rental agreement) and *leash* (a dog's lead) are confused. (C) *Signing* is used in the question and *sign* in the option, but the meanings are different.

48. (B) They earned more than *eighty-thousand dollars* last year. (A) This option confuses the sounds of *earn* and *learned*, making it incorrect. (C) *Years* is repeated, but this option answers *how long?* not *how much?*

49. (C) *At least a dozen times* is how many times the reporter has called. A *dozen* means *twelve*. (A) *Reports* and *reporter* may be confused, and *she* could be the reporter, but this option does not answer the question. (B) This option does not answer the question.

50. (A) The respondent was *thinking* about buying a new computer. (B) *Buying* is associated with *sales*, but this is not the topic. (C) *Computer* is associated with *technology*, but this is not the topic either.

PART III

51. (A) The flight departs at *8:30*. (B), (C) and (D) These options are all mentioned in the dialog. (B) *11:00* is the flight's *arrival* time. (C) The woman is trying to get to Manila *before noon*. (D) The meeting is at *12:30*.

52. (B) *Boarding time* and *runway* are indications of an *airport*. (A) *Files* are associated with an *office*, but the women are looking at them somewhere else. (C) *Waiting area* is associated with a *doctor's office*, but there is no other indication. (D) *Drinking coffee* is associated with a *restaurant*, but they intend to drink it in the *waiting area*.

53. (D) *Terminal* and *mouse pad* are *computer* words. (A) *Training* sounds like *train*, and *trains* are associated with *travel*, but this is not the correct option. (B) *Terminal* can be associated with a *bus station*, but not in this context. (C) *Mouse pad* could seem to relate to *rodents*, but the answer is incorrect.

54. (C) The woman wants the meeting to end on time so that she can get to the bowling championship. *Championship* means *match*. (A) The woman wonders when the meeting will be *over*, not when it *starts*. (B) The chairman is described as liking to talk, so he *will* be at the meeting. (D) *Championship* is associated with *contest*, but the game has not been played yet, so who won cannot be known.

55. (D) The company has its *own delivery service*. (A), (B) and (C) These options are all mentioned in the dialog. (A) The *mailman* delivered several boxes, but they did not contain the fax paper. (B) The *supply clerk* ordered the paper. (C) The man will check with the *receptionist*.

56. (D) The man is worried about *Dania's health* because she may have worked too hard during the heat wave. (A) The *heat wave* is over, and the man is not concerned about it now. (B) It is *Dania's* work that is referred to in the dialog. (C) *Several days* and *worked too hard … last week* could be associated with *work schedules*, but the man is not concerned about the work schedules.

57. (A) *Starch, lost suits,* and *trousers with double creases* are associated with the *dry cleaners*. (B) and (C) *Suits* and *trousers* could be associated with a *tailor* or a *clothing store*, but neither of these options is correct. (D) Losing something could be associated with *a courier*, but there is no other indication of this.

58. (C) The woman will be *taking them* to the airport and has a roof rack for *luggage*. These are indicators of a *taxi*. (A) *Empty* and *room* are both used in the dialog and the option, but since they want to go to the airport, it is clear they are getting into a vehicle. (B) The man apologizes for keeping her *waiting* and *room* is repeated, but this is not the correct option. (D) They are on their way to the *airport* to catch a *flight*, but they aren't *getting on* the aeroplane now.

59. (B) The ad will be placed in the classified section of the newspaper. (A) and (C) *TV* and *stereos (*which normally have *radios)* are mentioned in the dialog as products they sell, not as places for the ad. (D) *Personnel* and *human resources* have the same meaning, but *personnel* will be called to see how much ads usually cost.

60. (A) The man reminds the women that it's only *Wednesday*. (B), (C) and (D) These options are all mentioned in the dialog. (B) and (C) The woman is reminded she has *Thursday and Friday* to prepare. (D) The hockey game is this *weekend*, which would include *Saturday*.

61. (C) The supplier told them that six binders were *backordered*. Items are *backordered* when they are *out of stock*. (A) They *know* Mary ordered them. (B) The supplier did not have the binders in stock, but he did not *misroute* them. (D) They *know* Mary ordered enough.

62. (A) The company has included *dental care* in its health care package. (B*) Bridge* is repeated in both the dialog and the option, but the *bridge work* the woman refers to is a *tooth bridge*. (C) The man mentions *cleaning* in relation to his teeth. (D) *Free physicals* are not referred to in the dialog.

63. (B) The man says that the elevator *goes up fine*. (A) *Five* might be confused with *fifth* which is mentioned in the dialog. (C) It's the *elevator* that gets *stuck*, not the *door*. (D) The elevator gets stuck going down, but it does work when it's going up.

64. (C) The man needs a different model. He wants a printer that goes with the Computer 500 series. (A) Actually, the man *likes* the printer in this store, but it does not work with his computer. (B) The store does not carry the printer he wants, so it cannot be *out of stock*. (D) The printer in the store *works*, it just does not work with the Computer 500 series.

65. (C) The secretaries will be taking *computer classes*. (A) This option may confuse *jobs* with *jog*. (B) Going to the *west coast* could be associated with *vacation*, but the secretaries will be working there. (D) Sending the staff to the west coast could be associated with *transferring*, but they are only going for training.

66. (D) Marie thinks that they should pay their last *bill* before ordering chairs. (A) *Messenger* may be associated with *driver*, but nobody is *late*. (B) Marie is worried that they *owe* money, but since Jack offers to send a check right over, there is no indication that they can't get any. (C) There is no suggestion that the rental company *needs more notice*.

67. (B) The man says his wallet is *upstairs*, and they are *ordering wine*, so they must be in a *hotel restaurant*. (A) In the dialog, Joan gives the man the key to his room. They are not in a *key store*. (C) The man would not need his *wallet* if they were at a friend's house, and his room would not require a *key*. (D) *Wine* and *liquor* are associated, but the man would not have a room upstairs in a *liquor store*.

68. (D) When complaining about service, one usually talks to *a customer service representative*. (A) The new *building* is referred to in the dialog, but there is no indication that she is a *building manager*. (B) *Office* is repeated in both the dialog and the option, but the woman is not a *receptionist*. (C) The man *wants* an answering service provided for the day they rewire, he is not talking to an answering service now.

69. (C) *Press* and *iron* have the same meaning. (A) The woman needs a *dry cleaner* for her skirt, not a *house cleaner*. (B) The woman is talking about a *skirt*, not a *dress*. The sound of *dress* and express might be confused. (D) *Express* is repeated, but transport is not the topic.

70. (C) The woman remembers that the man liked the *front porch* a lot. (A) and (B) It was because of the *garage* and the *basement* that they decided *against* the brick house because they needed a lot of work. (D) The *location* was not good because the man was worried about commuting.

71. (B) The woman says that the manager will be back after *lunch*. (A) His *assistant* is available to be spoken to, so the manager cannot be with him/her. (C) There is no mention that the manager is with a *customer*. (D) The manager is only out for *lunch*, not the whole day, and there is no mention of his being *sick*.

72. (A) *Packing*, *unpacking* and *front desk* are associated with a *hotel*. (B) The man may *go* to a drugstore, he is not in one now. (C) The *front desk* could be associated with the *reception area*, but they are unpacking which suggests they are in their room. (D) *On the corner* could be associated with an *intersection*, but this is where the man may go to find the drugstore.

73. (D) *Cleaning* and *loose filling* are both associated with a *dentist*. (A) and (B) *Cleaning* is used in both the dialog and these options, but the dialog is about cleaning *teeth*. (C) *Filling* could be associated with cakes or buns, but there is no other indication of a *baker*.

74. (B) The *car* has a *dead battery*. (A) and (C) *Music store* and *battery* are associated with CDs and cassette players, but neither of these options is correct. (D) The *driveway* is where the car has broken down, but it is not the topic of discussion.

75. (B) The man asks about the building of the new *subway system*. (A) and (C) *Construction* is associated with *buildings* and *bridges*, but neither of these options is correct. (D) They have *already* had a bond program for a *mountain tunnel*.

76. (C) The man wants to *buy* an umbrella, so we can assume that he's in a *department store* talking to a *salesperson*. (A) *Full-size* or *compact* can be associated with cars and car rental agencies, the man also says he travels a lot. However, this option is not correct. (B) *Travel* is repeated, but the man is not talking to a *travel agent*. (D) A person who is going camping may want an umbrella, but there is no indication that the man is talking to a *camping gear sales rep*.

77. (A) Sonya is reading up on the *new spreadsheet software*. (B) *Read* is repeated, but she is not reading a report. (C) *Technical* is used in both the dialog and the option, but there is no mention of further study. (D) The man is hoping that Sonya will *explain* the software to him later, but this is not what she is doing now.

78. (A) The woman is asking John to do research on *alarm systems*. (B) A new office building is mentioned in the dialog, but there is no mention of finding *more space*. (C) John is asked to *do* research, not to interview the research department. (D) *Consumer reports* could be related to *customer services*, but John is not going to work there.

79. (B) There are *two* full-time positions vacant. (A) *One* is not mentioned. (C) and (D) There are *five* or *six* part-time positions.

80. (C) *Books* and a *borrower's card* are associated with *libraries*. (A) You do not have to return books to a *book store*. (B) The card mentioned in the dialog is the woman's *borrower's card*. (D) *Borrower* can be associated with *a bank*, but you wouldn't take books out of a bank.

PART IV

81. (D) The *Animal Rescue League* is holding the clinic and giving the announcement. (A) *Pet owners* are invited to come. (B) The clinic is *next to* the *Department of Health* building. (C) The *City Town Hall* is where you go for proof of residency.

82. (C) *Rabies vaccinations* are being provided. (A) *Clinic*, *good health* and *vaccinations* are all associated with *medical check-ups*, but this is not what is being provided. (B) The announcement states the animals which are being vaccinated must be *at least five months old*. (D) Vaccinations are part of the *proper care of house pets*, but a seminar on this subject is not being given.

83. (A) The participants are being told they will need to *fill out paperwork*. (B) They will be *part of* a five-minute screening themselves. They are not being asked to screen other participants. (C) The clinic is *next to* the *Department of Health*, but participants are not required to *register their pets* there. (D) Proof of *City residency* is required, not of *pet ownership*.

84. (B) An accident at a substation in Manila resulted in its power supply being halved. (A) *Accident* is used in the report, but there is no mention of a *traffic accident*. (C) *Electrical* problems are the subject, and *downtown* is repeated in the report and the option, but there is no mention of *costs*. (D) *Customers* are referred to in the report, but not in relation to a *rebate program*.

85. (C) The managers were asked to take *voluntary steps* to consume *less power*. (A) The accident *halved* the power supplied, but there is no mention of turning off any *office lights*. (B) They were asked to *shut down* elevators. There is no mention of *installing* them. (D) *Maintenance* could be associated with *cleaning up*, and *accident* is repeated, but this is not what the managers were asked to do.

86. (A) The power of *one* substation was cut in half. (B) *Halved* is associated with *two*, but this is not the correct option. (C) There are *three* transformers on Pacific Street, but the question is asking about the number of *substations* affected. (D) *Square (square blocks)* may be associated with *four*, but this is not the correct option.

87. (A) Mr. Wiley is introduced as Hamford's new *Director of Marketing*. (B) Mr. Wiley's *old job* was department head in Chicago. (C) Mr. Wiley was marketing assistant in Chicago, and he won the *Marlboro district's Salesman of the Year Award*, but he is not a *sales assistant* now. (D) *Federal Highway* is mentioned only as the location of their used car center.

88. (D) Mr. Wiley will be running a *monthly training seminar* for the workers in the used car center on Federal Highway. A *seminar* is a *session*. (A) *Hamford* is where Mr. Wiley's current position is, and *Marlboro* is used elsewhere in the introduction. However, he will not be liaising between the two places. (B) Mr. Wiley will not be expected to *inspect* the cars at the center. (C) Mr. Wiley has worked as a *marketing assistant*, and he is currently at *Hamford*, but there is no mention of him devising a new plan.

89. (A) This notice gives advice to people who are moving. (B) *Long distance calling plans* are referred to, but *long distance callers* are not being targeted by the notice. (C) *Moving companies* are associated with people who move house. However, the practical advice is directed at the people who are moving. (D) *Electricity and other utilities* are mentioned in the notice, but the advice given would not help personnel.

90. (C) This notice gives *information* about moving. (A) The notice contains the warning that you will be charged extra by the cable company to have your control box picked up after the service has been disconnected. However, the main purpose of the notice is to inform movers of a variety of moving-related issues. (B) There are a lot of changes to be made when moving, but this notice does not *announce* a change. (D) *A week before* could make you think of a *previous notice*, but there is no other indication.

91. (C) The notice reminds you to have the cable company *take the control box*. If they have to come back, they will charge extra. (A) When you call the cable company you are told to have them disconnect the service at your *old address*, but there is no mention of giving them your new one. (B) There may be an *extra charge* for picking up your control box, but it is not said that you should ask about extra charges in general. (D) *Deposits* is repeated in the announcement and the option, but it is not said that you should ask how much they are.

92. (B) This story describes a new CD manufacturing plant in Norway. (A) We don't know whether Oslo disks has any new CDs. (C) *Norway* is the location of the factory and the manufacturing system was purchased from *Japan*, but this story is not about *trade relations*. (D) The *Hillside District* is where the factory is, but there is no mention of *improvements*.

93. (A) The system was purchased from *Japan's Wadushi Corporation*. (B), (C) and (D) *Norway*, *Germany* and *Denmark* are all mentioned in the story, but these are not the countries that produced the technology.

94. (B) Oslo Disks has been negotiating with *Germany's World Records* for the right to distribute products. (A) *Oslo Disks* is trying to *gain* distribution rights, not *sell* them. (C) The *Wadushi Corporation* sold the manufacturing system. It is not interested in distribution rights. (D) *Euro Records* was part of the merger with Oslo Disks.

95. (A) A *manager* would most likely be discussing times an employee could come see him/her, and a manager would also have a secretary. (B) *Staff member* is mentioned in the talk, but a *fellow staff member* would not use this tone, would probably not be addressing a mass of employees, and would be unlikely to have office hours set for equal colleagues. (C) The speaker refers to everyone meeting their *new department heads*, so is probably not one himself. (D) The speaker refers to a *secretary*, a secretary is not talking.

96. (C) This talk is to let staff members know the speaker's available times to meet. (A) The employees *will* be meeting their new department heads, and this is a talk *before* that happens. (B) The speaker gives hours when he is available, but there is no mention of a *change in office hours*. (D) Alex, the secretary, is mentioned, but not in an introductory fashion.

97. (D) The speaker's office is on the *seventh floor,* in *suite 700.* (A) The *elevator* is referred to in the talk, but the speaker's office is not to the left of it. (B) The *water fountain* is mentioned in the talk, but *right after* means just, or immediately, after. It does not refer to direction. (C) The *seventh floor* is mentioned, but there is no indication that it is the *top floor*.

98. (C) The advertisement says that the AJGA is *dedicated to the overall growth and development of aspiring junior golfers.* (A) *Professional golfers* have *emerged* from the AJGA, and several are named, but *training* them is not the association's stated purpose. (B) *International* and *foreign* have similar meanings, but there is no mention of promoting and funding competitions. (D) This advertisement sounds like a public relations announcement, but PR is not the purpose of the AJGA.

99. (B) The AJGA provides *positive life experiences through competitive golf.* (A) The advertisement mentions its membership in *ten foreign countries*, but the opportunity to *play abroad* is not stated. (C) The AJGA may help members gain *college golf scholarships* through *exposure*, but this is different from getting accepted into college. (D) The AJGA has membership in all fifty of the United States, but getting the opportunity to *travel all over the U.S.* is not stated.

100. (A) These people are *alumni* of the AJGA. *Alumni* means *graduate*, or *former member*.
(B), (C) and (D) There is no mention that they were *founders*, *trainers*, or *Members of the Board of Directors.*

PART V

101. (C) *A standstill* indicates that the union and the management cannot come to an agreement. (A) The gerund form *stalling* does not follow the article *a*. (B)*Point* is illogical in this context. (D) A *draw* occurs when an event finishes with equal scores.

102. (B) The town *pays for* something. (A) *Pay out* is an informal way of saying *distribute*. (C) An individual *pays into* a fund. (D) You might have to *pay by* the end of the month.

103. (B) An *apprentice* is someone who is learning how to do a job. (A) An *appellant* is a person who is appealing something. (C) An *applicant* is someone who applies for a job. (D) *Appendant*, from the verb *append*, means *attached*.

104. (A) The past tense of the verb think, *thought*, is used. (B) *Pondered* means *to think about*. (C) *Liked* is illogical in this context. (D)*Wondered* is usually followed by *if*.

105. (A) *Pollutants* is a plural, count noun and therefore is modified by *fewer*. (B) *Less* is used for non-count nouns. (C)*Lower* indicates height or level. (D) *Than* indicates that a comparative form is needed.

106. (C) The representatives were invited by someone; hence the passive voice is used. (A) *Been* is the past participle and must follow another form of a verb. (B) *Representatives* is plural and must be followed by the plural form; *was* is the singular form. (D) *Had invited* indicates an active voice.

107. (B) *Nor* follows *neither*. (A) *Or* follows *either*. (C) and (D)The conjunctions *and* and *but* do not follow *neither*.

108. (D) The infinitive *to hire* follows the verb *force*. (A) *Hired* is the past participle. (B) *Hiring* is the gerund form. (C) *Hire* is the base form.

109. (C) *Relegated to* means *passed down to*. (A) *Formulated with* is illogical in this context. (B) *Finished at* is illogical. (D) In the context *moved over* would need to be followed by the preposition *to*.

110. (A) *Us* is the indirect object form of the pronoun *we*. (B) *Our* is the possessive form of the pronoun *we*. (C) *We* is the subject pronoun. (D) *Ourselves* is the reflexive form of the pronoun *we*.

111. (A) The *if*-clause in the past perfect is followed by *would* plus the perfect infinitive, *have seen*. (B) The progressive form is not used in this type of conditional sentence. (C) *Had seen* is the past perfect. (D)*Saw* is the past tense.

112. (C) *Partner* is the noun referring to a person. (A) *Partnering* is the gerund and does not refer to a person. (B) *Partnership* does not correspond with the subject pronoun *we*. (D) The article *a* indicates that the noun is singular.

113. (D) *That* is the relative pronoun that introduces the clause. (A) *It* is redundant as it refers to the train. (B) *Who* is used for people and not things. (C) *What* cannot be used as a relative pronoun in this sentence.

114. (B) *Discreet* in this context means *careful*. (A) and (D) *Discrepant* and *dissonant* mean that there was some disagreement. (C) *Dissolute* means *without restraint* and would not be logical in this context.

115. (B) A *sense* or *a feeling of duty* motivated him. (A) *Motion* means *movement* and is illogical in this sentence. (C) and (D) Neither *touch* nor *manner* is used with *duty*.

116. (D) *Soil* refers to *earth* in general. (A) *Soils* suggests that there are different varieties of soil. (B) *Soiling* refers to *dirt* and not *earth*. (C) *Soiled* is the past participle which does not fit in this context.

117. (D) She offered to get the hall ready or *prepare* the hall. (A) *Precede* means *to go before*. (B) *Presume* means *to take for granted*. (C) *Predate* means *to happen before a certain time*.

118. (B) A specific association is being referred to; therefore the article *the* must be used. (A) The article *a* does not refer to a specific association. (C) No capital letters would be used with the article *one*. (D) The two prepositions *of* and *for* cannot be used together.

119. (B) The verb *darken* means *to get darker in color*. (A) and (C) The noun forms, but not the verb forms, of *shade* and *shadow* refer to darkening. (D) The verb *heighten* means *to get taller*.

120. (C) Someone is *rewarded with* something. (A) *Granted* means *to give*, but cannot be followed by the preposition *with*. (B) The verb *offered* cannot be used with the preposition *with*. (D) *Awarded* means *to give*, but cannot be followed by the preposition *with*.

121. (A) The past tense is needed after the passive voice, past tense *were given*. (B) In this sentence *were* needs to accompany *enjoying* to form the past progressive tense. (C) *Having enjoyed* is the gerund followed by the past tense of the verb. (D) *Enjoyable* is the adjective form.

122. (A) *Than* indicates that a comparative form is needed. (B) *Very entertaining* is not a comparative form. (C) *Most entertaining* is the superlative form. (D) We can say *Professor Haage is the more entertaining speaker*, but not *Professor Haage is the more entertaining than ...* .

123. (A) The gerund *meeting* replaces the relative clause, *which meet*. (B) *Met* is the past tense form and cannot be used with the future *will*. (C) *Will meet* is the future tense. (D) *To meet* is the infinitive form.

124. (D) The passive voice is used, because the subject of the signing is not specified. (A) *Sign* is the simple present form. (B) *Signed* is the past participle form. (C) *Was signing* is the active voice, past continuous form.

125. (A) *Prohibited* means *against the law.*
(B) and (C) *Professed* and *proclaimed* mean *declared* and are illogical. (D) *Procured* means *obtained.*

126. (A) *Than* indicates that the comparative, *more easily,* should be used. (B) and (D) *Some* and *any* do not precede adverbs. (C) *Most* is the superlative form.

127. (C) *It* is used as a 'preparatory subject' referring to (the fact) *that someone had tampered with the speedometer.* (A) and (D) *They were* and *those were* would refer to *the pistons.* (B) *She* cannot combine with *to her.*

128. (B) The gerund *visiting* replaces the relative clause *who are visiting.* (A) *Visits* is the third person singular form of the verb. (C) *Visit* is the base form of the verb. (D) *Visited* is the past tense.

129. (B) *Sometime* is an adverb describing an unspecified time. (A) *Some* is an adjective and does not answer the question *when?* (C) *Something* refers to an object and not a time. (D) *Somewhat* refers to the degree or extent of something.

130. (A) *Need* is followed by the infinitive. (B) *Will maintain* is the future tense. (C) *Maintain* is the base form of the verb. (D) The base form of the verb, *be,* cannot follow *need* in this context.

131. (D) *Explicit instructions* are precise and clear.
(A) *Old instructions* is illogical. (B) *Insignificant* means *not important* and does not fit in this context. (C) *Delayed* means *late* and does not fit in this context.

132. (C) The preposition *in* is used with specific locations.
(A) *Between* is used with two objects. (B) *To* is used to indicate motion towards something. (D) *Aside* is an adverb.

133. (D) The modal *should* in this context is used instead of *if.* (A) The gerund *considering* cannot precede the pronoun *you* in this context. (B) *Must* is a modal, but cannot be used in this context. (C) If the first clause used *would,* then *were* could be used, but the infinitive *to decide* would need to follow *you.*

134. (C) *Timely* is an adjective meaning *on time.*
(A), (B) and (D) *Quickly, hastily* and *promptly* are adverbs and do not precede the noun.

135. (C) The past tense *lost* is needed. (A) The sentence is in the past tense, and *lose* is the base form. (B) *Was losing* is the past progressive. (D) The infinitive *to lose* cannot follow the pronoun *that.*

136. (A) *Together* combines with *with.* (B) The preposition *to* follows *according.* (C) The preposition *of* follows *instead.* (D) No preposition follows *besides.*

137. (A) *If* is used to form a conditional sentence. (B) *Which* is a relative pronoun. (C) *Under* is a preposition which is followed by an object. (D) *How* is used to ask questions.

138. (B) *After* indicates when the event occurred; *right after* means *immediately after.* (A) *Since* is used to explain why. (C) *At* should be followed by an object. (D) *Yet,* as a conjunction, means *nevertheless.*

139. (C) The conjunction *and* combines *taking* and *maintaining.* (A) *To* could be used with *from: from taking an inventory to maintaining inventory records.* (B) *Because* is a conjunction used to explain. (D) *With* something would explain how to take an inventory.

140. (A) *Dividing* means *to split in two.* (B) *Cutting* is not used in this context. (C) A lack of something would *limit* the party. (D) *Distributing* is illogical in this context.

PART VI

141. (C) The gerund *making* parallels *creating.* It does not need the *to* since it is not an infinitive. The *to* that precedes *creating* is part of the expression *everything from … to … .*
(A) *Covered* is the past tense. (B) *From* is the correct preposition. (D) *A database* is a compound noun.

142. (B) *They* refers to the subject *towns* and therefore is redundant. (A) *Towns* is the subject followed by the past tense form *affected.* (C) *Applied for* is the past tense verb plus preposition. (D) *Other emergency relief* is an object of the verb *applied for.*

143. (C) *Than* indicates the comparative form; therefore it should be *better suited.* (A) *Don't believe* is the negative present tense form. (B) The singular verb *is* refers to the singular pronoun *anyone.* (D) *Than Mrs. Marellis* indicates a comparison.

144. (B) *Difficulty* is the noun form, while the adjective form, *difficult,* is needed in this position. (A) *Proofreading* is the gerund used as the subject of the sentence.
(C) *Familiar* is an adjective. (D) The preposition *with* follows the adjective *familiar.*

145. (C) *Information* is a non-count noun and does not take the *-s* ending. (A) *Still* is used to indicate that an action continues. (B) *Avail themselves* is the present tense form of the verb plus the reflexive pronoun. (D) *Despite every effort* is a prepositional phrase.

146. (D) The verb refers to the singular noun *funding* and therefore should be *has been.* (A) The adverb *often* modifies the verb *find.* (B) *Too few* is the correct modifier for the count noun *members.* (C) *As* is used as a conjunction.

147. (A) This is a reduced relative clause, requiring the past participle *built,* meaning *which was built.* (B) *Who were living* describes the senators and congressmen. (C) *Is now open* refers to the Library of Congress. (D) *General public* is the object of the verb plus preposition, *open to.*

148. (D) The base form of the verb follows *will* : either *accompany* or *be accompanying.* (A) *Of* indicates which tour. (B) *Company's* is the possessive form of the singular noun. (C) *Administrative* is used to describe *assistant.*

149. (A) An adverb form is needed to precede the verb: *specifically trained*. (B) *Redesigned* is the past participle which with *have* forms the present perfect.
(C) *In accordance with* is a prepositional phrase. (D) *The client's* is the possessive form of the singular noun.

150. (C) The present progressive requires the present participle, *operating*, following the form of the verb *to be*. (A) *With* is the correct preposition. (B) *At their disposal* is a prepositional phrase. (D) *Undreamed of* is a reduced relative, meaning *which was undreamed of*.

151. (C) The gerund form, *hang gliding*, is required; this is a parallel structure with *mountain climbing*. (A) *As usual* is an adverbial phrase which modifies the verb. (B) *Will be encouraged* is the passive voice in the future tense. (D) The simple present is used after *when* to describe a future action.

152. (B) The passive voice is needed and is formed by adding the verb *to be*: *has been approved*. (A) The base form of the verb *tell* follows the modal *can*. (C) *As soon as* is used as a conjunction joining the two clauses.
(D) *Arrives* is the third person singular form of the verb.

153. (D) The article *the* must precede *world*. (A) *Being held* is the reduced relative clause: *which is being held*.
(B) *Will attract* is the future tense. (C) *Boating* describes the kind of *enthusiasts*.

154. (D) *Success* is the noun form, but the adjective form *successful* is needed to describe *export business*. (A) The gerund, *having*, plus passive, *been trained*, is used to introduce the adverbial clause. (B) The modal *can* is followed by the base form of the verb *attest* and then by a prepositional phrase. (C) The adjective, *crucial*, follows the form of the verb *to be*.

155. (B) When used as an adjective, *dozen* does not take the plural ending. (A) *Supervising* describes the type of *manager*. (C) *Main* describes which *table*. (D) *Mixed* describes *flowers*.

156. (A) The correct two-word verb is *look at*. (B) *Hundreds of documents* tells us that there were 200 or more documents. (C) *What* is used as a pronoun. (D) *Looking for* is a two-word verb meaning *searching for*.

157. (A) The gerund form *counting* is needed to begin the sentence. (B) *Continued* modifies *expansion*. (C) *Are issuing* is the present progressive form of the verb. (D) *No* quantifies the noun *inflation*.

158. (D) *Either* must be followed by *or*, so *both* is needed in this sentence. (A) *All* is a determiner, identifying which *harbors*. (B) and (C) *Have been ... closed* is the passive voice.

159. (B) The preposition *for* is correct; *issued to* would be followed by a person. (A) *Fishing* describes *permits*.
(C) *Season*, meaning *a certain period of the year*, is the object of the prepositional phrase. (D) *Limited* quantifies *number*.

160. (B) The sentence is in the past tense and therefore it should read *were purchased for*. (A) *Pressing* describes what kind of *supplies*. (C) *Mistakenly* is an adverb which modifies the verb form *left*. (D) *At the store* is a prepositional phrase.

PART VII

161. (B) The first sentence of the second paragraph refers to the *five categories of documents in the export industry*. (A) *The storage and retrieval of documents* is not mentioned. (C) The article is not about *how the export activity is documented*. (D) *The responsibility of the exporter to the importer* is not mentioned.

162. (D) The *dispatch document* covers the goods inside the originating country including the originating warehouse. (A) The *bank document* concerns payment.
(B) The *shipping document* is for transporting goods.
(C) The *customs document* is required by the importer.

163. (A) The writer of the memo wants to make sure that payment is made and collected. (B) *Credit requirements* may be changed, but that is not the main point of the memo. (C) Mr. Sidwell is asking staff to take some action, but he is not saying that they have not *followed policy*.
(D) There is no mention of the hotel *collapsing*.

164. (C) The letter refers to a program *where we can reduce our average collection period*. (A) *That no new hotels be financed* is not mentioned. (B) Collection time should be reduced, not *time spent on filing reports*.
(D) *Restaurant clients* are not mentioned.

165. (C) Icewine is made in smaller quantities in other places, but most abundantly produced in *Moldavia*.
(A), (B) and (D) It is made in smaller amounts in *Bavaria*, *New Hampshire* and *Oregon*.

166. (B) The last sentence indicates that the winters must be *harsh*, or *severely cold*. (A) The grapes are harvested just before *they become frozen solid*. (C) There are two growing seasons in Moldavia, but there is no mention that the vines must produce *two crops*. (D) There is no mention that *the vines are supported by nets*, rather that the nets are protective.

167. (A) It is *nearly impossible to produce* unless the winters are harsh, therefore *production is limited*. (B) The implication is that the *fragrance* of icewine helps to make it popular. (C) The article does not say whether *dessert wines are popular* or not. (D) There is no suggestion in the article that price prevents icewine from being more widely known.

168. (C) The hotel *proudly achieved recognition as the country's first officially accredited five star hotel*.
(A) and (B) The advertisement says that it used to *attract celebrities and dignitaries* and that *it used to be the center of attention*, but these are not given as the hotel's biggest accomplishments. (D) There are *multinational corporations* housed in the hotel complex.

169. (B) The building was *renovated* or *restored* to its original style and charm. (A) The advertisement does not mention when *colonial rule ended.* (C) The advertisement does not mention when the hotel *was accredited* with a five-star ranking. (D) The advertisement does not mention when the *embassies became part of the complex.*

170. (A) *The Bai Noi Trade Center* is adjacent to the hotel. (B) *The train station* is not mentioned. (C) *Ho Chi Minh City* is a 30 minute train ride. (D)The *Nha Trang industrial complex* is not mentioned.

171. (D) She writes that the *tax bill was $2,100 more than expected.* (A) She refers to the form *1040*, but there is no mention that it *arrived late.* (B) There is no mention that *her business had difficulties.* (C) She will pay *penalties and interest* in the next month.

172. (D) She is *writing to propose a payment schedule.* (A) She does *explain why the payment wasn't made,* but that is not the purpose of the letter. (B) She states, but does not *prove that an initial payment was made.* (C) She says that she will pay any *penalties*, but does not ask what they are.

173. (C) She states that *$2600* has already been paid. (A) *$350* is the proposed monthly payment starting in September. (B) *$2100* is the amount owed. (D) *$4700* is the total amount owed.

174. (C) *June* is the month following the date of the letter, *May.* (A) *January* is not mentioned. (B) In *February* she will finish making her payments. (D) She will begin the monthly installments in *September.*

175. (C) The second sentence says that Electrix is the leading manufacturer in *Spain.* (A) There are sales and distribution outlets in *Egypt.* (B) Most of the satellite communications equipment for Electrix is produced in *Venezuela.* (D) There is no mention that *Morocco* is the main producer of electronics.

176. (D) The first sentence indicates that this is an internal report to *members of the Electrix team.* (A) *Competing European electronics manufacturers* would not be addressed as *members of the Electrix team.* (B) Although *software engineers* might be employed by Electrix, the report has a wider audience. (C) *Business school students* are not mentioned.

177. (A) *The most recent company to join ... is the Softcomp Corporation.* (B) and (C) There is no mention of when *Electrix in South America* or *Telecor* joined. (D) *SpanElectrix* was the first manufacturing plant.

178. (C) No companies are mentioned in *Asia.* (A) Electrix is in *Venezuela, South America.* (B) Telecor, an Electrix company is in *Morocco, North Africa* and there are outlets in Egypt. (D) The first Electrix company was in *Spain, Europe.*

179. (B) Office equipment is manufactured in *Caracas.* (A) The report does not say what specifically is manufactured in *Madrid.* (C) Software is made in *New York City.* (D) Capacitors, semiconductors and transistors are manufactured in *Rabat.*

180. (D) The announcement gives a range of information about a *loan.* (A) and (C) A hotel is being built, but there is no mention of the *growth of tourism* nor of *hotel services.* (B) *Debt* is not mentioned.

181. (B) The *Madrid Credit Corporation* is providing $35 million. (A) The *ILC* is providing $9.5 million. (C) There is no mention of whether the *Gartala Hotel* will provide part of the loan. (D)*Saudi Finances* is providing $2.5 million.

182. (D) The hotel is being built by the Gartala Hotel, Dimond and Blue Orient Hotels. (A) The *ILC* is providing the financing. (B) The *Madrid Credit Corporation* is providing money, but not doing the building. (C) *The Dhiba Dimond Hotel* is the name of the new hotel.

183. (D) The first sentence is *Attention all passengers!* (A), (B) and (C) *Security personnel, customs officials* and *porters* are not mentioned.

184. (D) The notice does not mention *ticket class* as one of the factors. (A) The notice says that *if room allows* more carry-on luggage may be allowed. (B) and (C) The second sentence mentions *weight* and *dimensions* or *size.*

185. (A) Passengers should identify baggage both inside and out, or *put name tags on them.* (B) You do not *check in* carry-on bags. (C) Passengers may or may not be asked to *identify them for security personnel.* (D) *Valuables* should be in carry-on luggage.

186. (A) *Out-of-date luggage tags* or *old identifying labels* should be removed. (B) *Combination locks* should not be removed, they *are advisable.* (C) *Personal effects (cash, jewelry … important documents) should be carried in your hand luggage.* (D) *Combustible items* are not mentioned.

187. (B) The last sentence states that *This order is non-transferable,* which means that *only the recipient can place an order on it.* (A) The order is subject to *credit approval.* (C) *The payment terms* are on another page. (D) The products can be returned and the customer owes nothing.

188. (C) The products can be returned *within 30 days* and the customer owes nothing. (A) *Apply for credit according to the payment terms* is not mentioned. (B) The customer keeps the *free gift.* (D) *Requesting a refund* is not mentioned.

189. (D) The order form asks for the *page number.* (A) There is no request for *billing address.* (B) The order is subject to *credit approval;* however the number is not requested. (C) The customer is ordering products, not *returning* them.

190. (B) Pensions paid in Year 2 were *$24.8 million.* (A) *$5.5 million* is the amount of employee contributions. (C) *$62 million* is the amount of company contributions. (D) *$191.4 million* is the total amount owed to pensioners.

191. (C) Participants not yet retired are *future retirees* and *$748.9 million* was set aside. (A) *$20.7 million* is the employee contribution in Year 1. (B) *$174.6 million* is how much is owed to pensioners. (D) *$923.5 million* is the total liabilities and reserves.

192. (A) Employee contributions were *$5.5 million.* (B) *$19.4 million* were other assets. (C) *$24.8 million* is the amount of pensions paid. (D) *$191.4 million* is the total amount owed to pensioners.

193. (D) The subject line informs the reader that the purpose is *to explain sales figures* for month ending February 2000. (A) He does not *criticize the sales force.* (B) Not all of the areas have experienced *a drop in sales.* (C) *Marlboro* is only one area that he discusses.

194. (C) *West Grammit* went from $26,057 to $26,387. (A), (B) and (D) *Carrington* fell in sales as did *Marlboro and Abidole.*

195. (B) He mentions that *there is a new sales supervisor.* (A) The *competition* is not mentioned. (C) Half of the salesforce is inexperienced, but they do not only *have half of the salesforce.* (D) The memo does not indicate whether or not *the staff has been given enough help.*

196. (D) Jerry Baldwin is a *troubleshooter* which means he will *find the reason for the drop in sales.* (A) *Training* is not mentioned. (B) Joseph Bradigan says that he will *assist the sales supervisor.* (C) Jerry Baldwin is not involved with *the shipment from Mali.*

197. (C) The last sentence indicates that *the EDF is providing real assistance to southeast Los Angeles.* (A) *Gas-powered vehicles* are mentioned, but are not the main point. (B) and (D) *Improved air quality* and *reduced traffic congestion* are mentioned among a list of several benefits.

198. (D) The shuttle service takes workers to the nearest *train station.* (A) *Testing the efficiency of the gas-powered engines* is not mentioned. (B) The goal was not to *promote commuting by train,* although that is one of the outcomes. (C) The goal was to allow low-income workers to have more access to jobs, but there is no mention of *second jobs.*

199. (B) He is an *economic analyst.* (A) The *Director of Train 'n Wheels* is not mentioned. (C) *A systems analyst* works with computers. (D) *An employment specialist* is not mentioned.

200. (A) The Southeast Community Development Corporation is *the primary sponsor* or *the main source of money.* (B) No *partners of the Environmental Defense Fund* are mentioned. (C) The EDF may *study the effects of pollution on Los Angeles,* but there is no suggestion that the SCDC do this. (D) *An employment resource center* is not mentioned.

Answer Key

Practice Test Two

In the following Answer Key, the first explanation provided for each question is the correct option.

PART I

1. (D) She's taking the lid off her drink. (A) The woman in the picture may be *resting*, but she's not on a *stool*. A *stool* is a type of seat, without a back or arms, for one person. (B) *Trench* sounds like *bench*. A *bench* is a long seat for several people whereas a *trench* is a long hole in the ground which soldiers might dig. (C) The beverage she is drinking may be coffee and *cream* is associated with coffee, but it is not a pot of cream from which the lid can be removed.

2. (B) The two screens are next to each other, or *side by side*, on the desk. (A) The manual control is on his *right*, not his *left*. (C) The desk is not *straight*, it is at an angle. (D) There is a *loudspeaker* above the monitor which sound comes out of, not a *fan*, which is used to cool people down.

3. (C) The men are standing on the street *corner*, waiting for something. (A) *Goods* are things that are sold. Some of the men are *carrying* goods which can be bought at a *market*, but they are not *selling* them. (B) The men may be *waiting* for a bus, but they are not *hurrying to catch* the bus. (D) The men are *waiting*, not *pushing through* a lot of people.

4. (B) His hand is resting on the *notebook,* or ring binder. (A) One man is *wearing* a watch and it may be touching the *table*, but this option implies it is not being worn. (C) The man is *wearing* a suit and may keep it in a *closet* at home, but there is no closet in this picture. (D) His shirt is *striped,* but there are no *shorts* visible in the picture.

5. (C) The five *laborers*, or workmen, are *working together* on the same job. (A) One man may be using a machine to drill, but we have no way of knowing if he is *drilling for oil*. (B) This option confuses the sound of *tires* with *wires*. We can see *wires* in the picture. (D) One man may be the *boss*, but there is no way of knowing if it is the man who is holding the wire.

6. (C) The man is a *doctor* because he has a stethoscope round his neck. He is reaching into a cabinet full of small boxes which could be medicine. (A) This man could be a *naval officer* because of his uniform, but he is not outside, on the *deck* of a ship. (B) The man could be a *pilot*, but he is not *flying a plane* in the picture. (D) The man may be a *pharmacist*, but he is not putting anything into, or *filling*, the boxes.

7. (C) There is a pair of *glasses* on the counter. She is *not wearing* any. (A) She *is* sitting at the desk. (B) *Riding* sounds like *writing* (which she is doing). She is not on a *horse*. (D) She may be *studying*, but she is not in a *library*. There are no books on the shelves behind her. She may be in a store.

8. (C) Tickets can be bought at a *train station*, either from a clerk or a machine, as in the picture. Also the screen shows information about departures and arrivals. (A) The men may be passengers waiting for their transport, but a *passenger lounge* would have chairs in it and there are no chairs in this picture. (B) *Admissions* is used for entrance to a school or a stay in hospital, not for a *form of transport*. (D) The machines in the picture have *self-service* written on them, but it is obviously not a restaurant.

9. (B) The woman in the picture may be a *chemist* because of her protective coat and surroundings. She is *examining*, or looking at, the glass *flask*. (A) *Experiences* sounds similar to *experiments* (tests carried out by scientists). This woman is *examining*, not *explaining*, something. (C) She's holding a glass container, but not *weighing* it on a scale. (D) She may be *measuring* something in the container, but it does not look like *food* and she is not in a kitchen. She is a scientist, not a *cook*.

10. (A) The man is vacuuming, or cleaning, so the floor must be *dirty*. (B) There is a *carpet* in the picture but it is laid out on the floor, not *rolled up*. (C) There are *chairs* around the tables, they are not *stacked* on top of each other. (D) The *floor*, not the *door*, is being cleaned.

11. (C) There is a *candle* on the table, but it is not *lit*. There is no flame visible. (A) These people are eating, possibly in a *restaurant*, but we can only see one table so we do not know if the place is *full*. (B) There is a *candle* on the table, not a *handle*. (D) The glass of wine *is* in the woman's hand.

12. (A) The man appears to be checking in at the reception desk, and the women are *assisting*, or helping him. (B) The women work at the *Executive Club*, which is written on the screen behind them, they are not *executives*. (C) The man is *checking in*, not *checking through his baggage*. There is no *baggage* in this picture. (D) This option confuses the sound of *pub* with *club*, which is written on the wall behind the women.

13. (D) The artist has included *trees* in his *work* (his picture). (A) The artist and his painting are *in front of* the building, not *behind* it, or *at the rear*. (B) Although *drawing* is associated with painting, here it means to choose something at random, as in a raffle draw. *Winner* is easily confused with *winter* which is the season in the picture. (C) Artists use a *brush* to apply paint to something. This man has a brush in his *hand*, not in a *pot of paint*.

14. (B) The *boats*, or yachts, are racing each other. You can see they are moving at speed. (A) They are *sailing* the boats, not *selling* them. (C) There are *sails* on the boats, but they are up, not *coming down*. (D) A *kayak* is a type of boat designed for one or two people. The boats in the picture are much bigger than a *kayak*.

15. (C) The man is doing something to the *motor*, so we can assume he's *working on* it. (A) There are two *belts* on the motor, but not the same kind of belt that is worn with pants. We do not know if the man is or is not wearing a belt. (B) The motor is *made of* metal, but it is not in sheet form now. (D) He's working on an *engine*, but it is not under the *hood* of a car.

16. (A) The tables are ready for customers and each place at the table is *set* with glasses, silverware, plates, etc. (B) There are no *customers* sitting at any of the tables in the picture. The waiter is standing *near* the first table. (C) There are *wine glasses* on the tables, but they are *empty*, not *full*. (D) The curtains are *open*, not *drawn* (*closed*).

17. (C) The man is on a stretcher, with straps around his body so that he cannot move. (A) The men may be firemen, but they are not *fighting a fire*, they are helping the injured person. (B) The injured man is wearing a shirt, but it is not *striped*, it is *plain*. *Stripe* sounds similar to *strap* so this could be confusing. (D) The man may be on his way to a hospital for an operation, but they are not in a hospital now, and there are no doctors visible.

18. (B) The *receivers* (the part you speak into) of the phones which are not being used, are hanging on their hooks. (A) Faxes and phones are both machines which you dial numbers into, but there is no *fax machine* in this picture. (C) The woman is *talking on the phone*, but not at *home*. She is on a public pay phone. (D) The *phones* are next to each other, but this option refers to two or more *people* (*they*) and there is only *one person* in the picture.

19. (C) The crowd, or the *fans*, are waving and *moving their hands*. (A) The people in the crowd are happy, they are not *fighting*. (B) The people may be *supporters*, but they are waving their *hands*, not *flags*. (D) The *crowd* may be cheering the *entertainers*, but not vice versa.

20. (B) The signs say *passengers only*, which indicates that beyond the doors is a *restricted area*. Only certain people are allowed to enter. (A) This option is incorrect because passengers *can* enter the room. (C) *Passport* is written on the sign, but there is no passport visible in the picture with a stamp on it. (D) Arrows on the doors indicate *movement to the left* and also *to the right*.

PART II

21. (C) The speaker both answers the question (*yes, he is the captain*) and adds new information (*I talked with him earlier*). (A) *He* and *ship* are repeated, but the question is not asking about location. (B) *He* is repeated, and *seat* sounds like *sea*, which is associated with ship captains, but this option does not answer the question.

22. (B) The company will have *seventy-five employees* by the end of the year. (A) This option answers *who* they employ, not *how many*. (C) *Employ*er relates to *employees*, but this option does not answer the question.

23. (A) The speaker has *already* taken the action that is suggested – adding an extra car. (B) *Because* is a common way to start answering *why not?* but this option confuses the sounds of *rush* and *rash*. (C) *Rush* is repeated, but this option does not answer the question.

24. (A) The speaker implies that in the upcoming demonstration, the *new features* will be shown. (B) *Talked* is repeated in the option, but it does not answer the question. (C) *Features* is repeated in both the question and the option, but with different meanings.

25. (C) The speaker predicts that electrical services will not be back until morning. (A) *Service* is repeated in the question and the option, and *prompt* is a likely answer to *when?* However, this option does not answer the question. (B) *Restored* and *store*, and *electric* and *electricity*, have the same root. However, this option does not answer the question.

26. (B) The speaker *may* be interested in studying financial planning. They want to know more about it before making a decision. (A) *Yes* is a likely response to a *yes/no* question, and *financial plan* is repeated. However, the question remains unanswered. (C) *Financial* is repeated in both the question and the option, but in different contexts.

27. (C) The department has already *set aside*, or reserved, funds for *this purchase*. (A) *Purchase* and *buy* are related. However, the pronoun *she* does not relate to the department, and the question refers to *one* purchase and the option to *two*. (B) *Purchase* and *sale* are related, but this option confuses the sound of *apartment* with *department*.

28. (C) The option answers the question by giving additional information – the respondent does data entry in his job. In the TOEIC, answers which *imply* a response are common. For example, in this situation, the speaker is answering *Yes, I do have experience*, by explaining *where* the experience comes from. (A) *Entry* is repeated in both the question and the option, and *no* could be a response to the question. However, this option does not answer the question. (B) *Data* is repeated in both the question and the option. *I'm* is a likely response to a question about *you*, but the question is not answered correctly.

29. (B) The speaker does not think that the new contract is too *lengthy*, but that it is too *complex*. (A) The speaker may like the *title* of the new contract, but this question refers to the *length* of the contract. (C) Contracts are usually typed documents, and they may require *re-typing*, but the question does not ask for this information.

30. (A) The respondent does not want to hire temporary staff for the event. Rather than saying so directly, the answer gives the reason – paying the existing staff *overtime*. (B) This response indicates *when* an event will end, but that is not the question. (C) This option confuses the words *hire* and *fire* which have similar sounds but opposite meanings.

31. (C) The speaker does not know if the investment is worthwhile, without studying it first. (A) This option is attractive, because without the pronoun *it*, it would be a reasonable answer to the question. However, the *it* makes it a meaningless response to the question. (B) *Considerate* has the same root as *consider*, and *investigator* sounds similar to *investment*, but somebody's personality is not the question.

32. (A) The speaker thinks that the item contains both aluminum *and* tin. (B) *No* is an appropriate answer, and *either of them* could refer to the two metals, but the option does not answer the question. (C) This option may confuse the sounds of *aluminum* and *ammonia*.

33. (C) The speaker implies that the clerks have been notified by saying that they were contacted earlier today. (A) This response does not answer the question. (B) *Harbor* and *shipping* are associated, but this option does not answer the question.

34. (A) The respondent advises *against* investing in all three companies, but realizes it's not his decision. (B) This option confuses the sounds of *invest* and *vest*. (C) *Company* is repeated in the question and the option, but with different meanings.

35. (A) The accounting office was not pleased about the missing invoice. The question what did someone *say* about something, does not always literally mean what exactly was said. It often means how did someone *feel* or *react*. (B) *Missing* and *lost* can be synonyms, and *voice* sounds similar to *invoice*, but this option does not refer to accountancy matters. (C) *Accounting* and *recount* have the same root, but if something is *missing* it cannot be *recounted*.

36. (B) This option answers the original question and then asks a further question. (A) The response does not relate to the question. (C) *Human* is repeated in both the question and the response, but *human life* is not the topic.

37. (C) The furnace is left on to *dry the room out*. (A) Although *left* is repeated, this option does not relate to the question. (B) *On* is repeated in the question and option, and *furnace* can be associated with *burn*. However, the option does not answer the question.

38. (B) The speaker gives a copy of the guidelines to the person to keep. This indicates that they can be looked at again. (A) *Look* and *saw* have similar meanings, but the question is not answered correctly. (C) *Look* is repeated in both the question and the option, but *looking for good people* is not the topic.

39. (C) The plane arrived just before the storm started. (A) *Plane* and *drive* are both associated with transportation, but the question is not about preference. (B) This response answers *where* the plane arrived, not *when* it arrived.

40. (A) The reason why *dictionaries* were not ordered is because the speaker was told *atlases* were required. (B) *Dictionaries* and *office copy* may be related, but the question remains unanswered. (C) A *dictionary* has a *glossary*, but this option does not answer the question.

41. (C) The speaker would like a ride after the speech. (A) *Drive* is repeated in the question and the option, but the question is not about the driver's habits. (B) *Home* is repeated in the question and the option, but in this option the speaker says *where* her home is, not when she wants to *go home*.

42. (C) The *burst pipeline* explains the *drop in water pressure*. (A) *Drop* is repeated in both the question and the option, but *sales* is not the topic. (B) *Pressure* (having a lot to do in a short time) and *deadline* can be associated, but the question refers to *water pressure*.

43. (A) The speaker forgot about the meeting with Mrs. Baldwin. *Oh no* is an expression of surprise and disappointment. It does not actually mean *no*. (B) *Meet* and *ten* are repeated in the option, but the option refers to a time in the *future* whereas the question refers to the *past*. (C) *Met* is repeated, but the question remains unanswered.

44. (A) The speaker will find out whether the plane flies direct to Botswana. (B) *Plane* is repeated, but the question is asking about the plane's *destination* not from where it is traveling. (C) *Plane* and *boarding* are associated, but the question is not about the boarding time.

45. (B) The speaker implies that all of the elevators are working again, because they were fixed last night. (A) *Work* is repeated in the question and the option, but in different contexts, and this option refers to a person whereas the question is about an object. (C) *Work* is repeated in the question and the option. *Elevator* and *elevate* have the same root, but the meanings are different and the question is not asking about somebody's feet.

46. (C) The speaker implies that the car will do well because it was specifically designed to perform in a very hot climate. (A) *Hot* and *air-conditioning* are associated, but the question is not about a theater. (B) *Hot climates* and *equator* are associated, but the option does not answer the question.

47. (B) The speaker implies that 200 seats will be sufficient because only 150 people were invited. (A) *Sufficient* and *enough* are synonyms, but the option does not answer the question. (C) Insufficient seats could lead to *standing-room only*, but the question is about what is *going to* happen, so an answer in the past is unlikely.

48. (C) The speaker thinks a bus has been hired, or *chartered*, to get them there. (A) *Get there* and *on the way* may be associated, but this option confuses the sounds of *suppose* and *dispose* and does not answer the question. (B) *Suppose* is repeated, but the response does not answer the question.

49. (B) The speaker needs to *test* the cellular phone to check it's working. (A) *Work* is repeated in the question and the option, but the question does not refer to a man's job. (C) *Call* is associated with *cellular phones*, and *cell* is repeated, but in a different context.

50. (C) Unfortunately the elevator *is* out of order again. (A) The pronoun *it* is a likely way to start a response to this question, but the option confuses the sounds of *again* and *gaining*. (B) *No* might seem like the most appropriate response, but this option does not answer the question.

PART III

51. (A) The debate is about the *new pipeline*. (B) *Traffic disruption* is mentioned in the dialog, but as a result of possible building work, it is not the subject of the debate. (C) This option repeats the *location* of the pipeline, but this is not the topic of the debate. (D) An *oil line* is mentioned in the dialog, but there is no reference to an *oil spill*.

52. (C) The woman is having a problem sending her fax. (A) Making a call is not the topic, although she is trying to communicate with somebody. (B) Although *facts* may sound like *fax*, they have different meanings. (D) *Coming in* and *entering* are synonymous, but nobody is going into a house in the dialog.

53. (B) They're discussing the new parking problems; parking is becoming more difficult. (A) Discussion of the location of the new high rise may be confused with giving directions. (C) *Street* and *road* can be synonymous, but there is no mention of the condition of the road. (D) The new high rise may be an *apartment building*, but it is not the topic of their discussion.

54. (C) A hotel has both *room service* and *front desk* workers, so we know that a hotel is being referred to. (A) A *restaurant* may have *banquet staff* and a *front desk*, but not *room service*. (B) There is nothing to associate a *furniture manufacturer* with this conversation. (D) *Room service* could be confused with a *cleaning company*, but a cleaning company would not have *banquet staff*.

55. (C) The man asks Beth how to find the key. (A) *Color* is repeated in both the dialog and the option, but there is no mention of *paint*. (B) *Hang* is repeated in both the dialog and the option, but the man is not trying to *hang a picture*. (D) In the dialog, it is the *supply room* which is mentioned. There are no references to *buying supplies*.

56. (B) The speakers are discussing the *air-conditioner*, which needs fixing. (A) *Boiling* and *boiler* might be confused. (C) The fans are operating and do not need fixing. (D) *Heat* is mentioned in the dialog, but a *heater* is not what is required.

57. (C) The speakers plan to ask John to sell more computers in order to *meet the quota*. (A) *Computer* is repeated, and *buy* is associated with *sell*, but this is not what John will be asked to do. (B) *Sales* is repeated in both the dialog and the option, but there is no mention of a seminar. (D) *Sales* is repeated, but there is no mention of *setting a new record*.

58. (C) *Drive, road, turns,* and *trunk* are all associated with a *car*. (A) A *CD player* is mentioned, but the woman is not *testing* one. (B) A *computer* may *have a* CD player, but this is not what is being tested. (D) A *truck* would not have a *trunk*, so this option is not possible.

59. (C) The woman offers to ask a friend what kind of adapter Paul will need. (A) *Computer* is repeated, but Paul does not need to borrow one. (B) *Adapter* is repeated and Paul is going to *buy* one, but she does not offer to *sell* him anything. (D) Paul needs to get an adapter, and finally he'll have to go to a *store*, but sending him to one is not what the woman offers to do.

60. (B) The speakers are discussing the sale of a *building*. (A) The building mentioned in the dialog is a bakery, but *baked goods* is not the topic of their conversation. (C) The *old bakery* may become a *restaurant* because it has been bought by a fast food chain, but this is not discussed. (D) *Food* is repeated, but the *price of food* is not the topic.

61. (A) *Triggers a signal to the police*, and *code*, are associated with *alarm systems*. (B), (C) and (D) These options may all have *numbers* and *letters*, but none would *trigger a signal to the police*.

62. (A) The man wants to go to the *train station*, and he is trying to figure out the best way to get there. (B) *Heat* is repeated in both the dialog and the option, but *getting out of the heat* is not his goal. (C) We do not know if the man wants to *leave town* or not. He could be leaving from the train station, but he may also be meeting someone there. (D) *Train, subway,* and *taxi* are all forms of *transportation*, but the man is not doing a comparison.

63. (D) The man says that the city has *worked on*, or improved, *public transport*, and the woman agrees that the trains are *cleaner* and the buses are *running on schedule* now. (A) *Train* is repeated in both the dialog and the option. However, the dialog talks about the trains being *cleaner*, it does not mention *safety*. (B) *House* and *home* can be synonymous, but *cleanliness* refers to the trains in the dialog. (C) *Running* is repeated in the dialog and the option, but in different contexts. The man's *car* is mentioned, but not its *state*.

64. (C) The man thinks that the constant use of the *air conditioning* could explain the high electric bill. (A) *Bill* is repeated, but the man does not mention thinking that the bill is incorrect. (B) *Computers* are mentioned in the dialog, but not in terms of *needing repair*. (D) *Electric* is used in the dialog and *electrical* in the option, but there is no mention of *faulty wiring*.

65. (C) *Triplicate* means *three*. In this dialog, it is worth guessing at the word triplicate, even if you are not sure. Notice the prefix, *tri-*. (A) *One* copy goes to the treasurer's office, *one* to accounting and *one* is kept, so there are three copies in total. (B) *Two* is not mentioned in the dialog, but may attract you if you do not know the meaning of the word *triplicate*. (D) There are *four* forms, but *three* copies are needed of each, so this option is incorrect.

66. (C) The man says that the group will *fly* because they got a good deal with the airlines. (A), (B) and (D) These options are mentioned in the dialog as possibilities, but in the end, the group will go *by plane*.

67. (A) Barbara is a *mechanic* because she's planning to fix the *turn signal* and do a *test drive*. (B) *Inspection* is used in the dialog, but Barbara is helping the car to *pass* an inspection, she is not an inspector herself. (C) and (D) A *chauffeur* and a *bus driver* are both associated with *driving*, but there is no reason to think that one of these is Barbara's job.

68. (C) Susan is waiting for tax data in order to finish the reports and give them to the man. (A) The man may be the *boss*, but he does not have the reports. Susan will leave them *on his desk* when they are complete. (B) *Hong Kong* is where the man is going. The reports are not there. (D) Susan is waiting for the *data* to arrive in the mail, not the *reports*.

69. (D) The man wants to set a light to *turn on* at one time and *go off* later. This could be to deter burglars. (A) People do not set *train schedules* individually. (B) A *watch* cannot be set to go on and then off, so this option is not possible. (C) *Work schedules* may be *set*, but they are not turned on and off.

70. (A) Mr. Tam wants to talk with Mr. Braun. *Talk with* is similar to *see* in an office environment. (B) *Traffic* is mentioned in the dialog as something Mr. Braun is *stuck in*, not as something Mr. Tam wishes to avoid himself. (C) Mr. Tam's *office* is mentioned in the dialog, but there is no mention of *changing offices*. (D) *Lunch* is only referred to in terms of when the meeting will be rescheduled.

71. (A) The man requests *large-print* literature and describes his vision as *impaired*. (B) The *New York Times* is a *newspaper*, but there's no mention that it has *sold out*. (C) *New York* is repeated. *Foreign* is similar in meaning to *overseas*. However, flights is not the topic. (D) *Magazines* are the same as *periodicals*, but there is no mention of *English language magazines*.

72. (A) Because they lost an order for *desks*, we can conclude that they have a *furniture company*. (B) Construction of a building is mentioned in the dialog, but the people talking are not responsible for it. (C) *Funds* and *finance* have similar meanings, but they do not have a finance company. (D) Constructing a building requires *real estate*, but a *real estate company* is not likely to sell desks.

73. (D) *Teleconference* and *phone conference* mean the same. (A) *Management* are required to take part in the call, but *management* is not the topic of discussion. (B) *Finance personnel* are mentioned, but *finances* is not the subject under discussion. (C) The *vice president* is mentioned in the dialog, but he or she is not being discussed.

74. (B) Because the man has *spacious properties on the waterfront* to show, we can conclude that they are for sale and he is a *real estate agent*. (A) There is no mention of his being a *broker*. (C) *Waterfront* and *boat* may seem associated, but the man does not sell boats. (D) The dollar figure may make you think of a *banker*, but bankers do not usually take people to see properties for sale.

75. (B) The man implies that the woman should return her phone by telling her to go back to the store. (A) *Charge* is repeated in both the dialog and the option, and charging the battery may be a good idea, but it is not the man's suggestion. (C) The man suggests checking the *warranty,* not the *phone*. (D) Calling the *Better Business Bureau* may be a good idea, but it is not the man's suggestion.

76. (B) The sale is only for the *weekend*. (A) Only the *weekend* is mentioned in the dialog, not the *week*. (C) *Friday* is the night of the dinner, not the only day of the sale. (D) *Monday through Friday* would not include the *weekend*, which is when the sale is.

77. (D) They are talking about computer costs, which are a *business expenditure*. (A) The *accounting department* is connected with spending money, but *accounting procedures* are not being discussed. (B) *Money* is repeated in both the dialog and the option, but *money market funds* is not the topic. (C) *Computers* may be associated with *offices*, but there is no mention of a *new office design*.

78. (D) The person wants to *computerize her address book*, which means she wants to put her addresses onto the computer. (A) She wants to *hire* a temp, not get a job as one. (B) *Computer* is repeated in both the dialog and the option, but she does not mention buying a new one. (C) *Data* is repeated in both the dialog and the option, but she wants to *enter* it, not *verify* it.

79. (B) Cathy is at the *hospital* with her father. (A) There is going to be a *banquet*, but that is not where Cathy is now. (C) The speakers want to *give* Cathy's father a card, nobody is in a *store*. (D) The sounds of *bank* and *banquet* may be confused.

80. (A) The man is going to Tokyo *on business* which means he is going to *work*. (B) The man may *go into* a shop in Tokyo to buy some books, but he is not going to *open* one. (C) *Local* is repeated in both the dialog and the option, but with reference to different things. (D) *Pictorial* and *photograph* have similar meanings, but there is no mention of taking any photos.

PART IV

81. (A) Anyone who *attends school in New York City* is among those *eligible* for a borrower's card. *Eligible* means *qualified*. (B) The announcement only mentions those who pay *property taxes*. (C) and (D) It would be nice to think that people who study in the library and / or need its services were eligible, but this is not the case.

82. (D) Most books may be checked out for *twenty-eight days* with a possible *ten-day* extension, totaling *thirty-eight days*. (A) *Ten days* is the length of the *extension*. (B) *Fourteen days* is the check-out period for *more popular books*. (C) *Twenty-eight days* is not the longest time.

83. (B) There are *coin-operated photocopying machines* available in many library branches. (A), (C) and (D) These pieces of equipment are named in the announcement, but none of them is allowed in the library.

84. (C) The bulletin emphasizes the need to *maintain* appropriate temperature. (A) *Mayonnaise* is repeated in both the bulletin and the option, and many people think that mayonnaise causes food poisoning, but the bulletin says that it is *not* a key factor. (B) *Meat* and *poultry* are mentioned as being likely causes of illness, especially if they are chopped up, but serving them whole is not mentioned. (D) While *washing hands* is considered by most people as a good idea, this is not mentioned as the key to keeping food safe.

85. (B) *Poultry* includes *chicken* and is named as one of the foods most likely to cause illness. (A) *Mayonnaise* is mentioned in the bulletin as *not* directly increasing risk. (C) *Vegetables* are mentioned in the bulletin. However, they are specifically identified as *not* posing a serious threat. (D) *Hot* relates to *temperature*, which is mentioned in the bulletin, but *hot foods* are not identified as more likely to cause illness.

86. (C) The bulletin says that *chopping, slicing* or *dicing* meats allows *greater exposure to bacteria*. (A) *Mayonnaise* is mentioned in the bulletin as *not* directly increasing risk. (B) *Vegetables* are mentioned in the bulletin, but not *vegetable dips*. (D) *Fruits* are mentioned in the bulletin, but not *fruit fillings*.

87. (B) *Entrepreneurs* would be most interested in learning how to run a bed and breakfast. (A) *Vacationers* may stay at a bed and breakfast, but they would be unlikely to want to learn how to run one. (C) Students learn, but this talk is not aimed at *college students*. (D) A bed and breakfast may *hire* a chef, but the talk is about *running* a bed and breakfast. Chefs do not normally run such places.

88. (B) The speakers, two *successful* bed and breakfast operators, will talk about *how to run* a bed and breakfast. (A) *Renting a room* is mentioned in the introduction, but this is not the topic. (C) The B&B is *in* Maine, but traveling there is not the topic. (D) *Adventure* sounds similar to *venture*, but its meaning is different.

89. (A) The notice is for *fishermen* who may want to compete in a tournament. (B) Some fishing tournaments are *fund-raisers*, but not the ones mentioned in this notice. (C) *Beach* is repeated in the notice and the option, and we might expect *beach officials* at the tournament, but this notice is not for them. (D) *Vacationers* often enjoy fishing, and some may attend these events, but the notice is not for them.

90. (D) *Registration materials* are available at *local tackle shops*. (A), (B) and (C) These locations are mentioned in the notice, but you cannot register at any of them.

91. (C) The event is sponsored by the *New York Fishermen's Association*. (A) and (B) These are both mentioned in the notice, but are not the sponsors. (D) *Cape Troll* is the name of one of the tournaments, but its residents are not the sponsers.

92. (C) The news story is about books being *donated* to six schools. (A) *Parisian Intercontinental Hotels* is donating the books, but their growth is not the topic. (B) Elementary schools are receiving the books. *Books* and *curriculum* are associated. However, this is not what the story is about. (D) *50,000 francs* relates to *finances*, and *books* relate to *libraries*, but this is not the correct option.

93. (D) The story says that the number of books donated was based on the number of guests who stayed in the hotels. (A) In the story, *hotel employees* are only referred to as people who will help with unloading. (B) The six elementary schools will *receive* the books. (C) The *leaders* of the *Parisian Literacy Crusade* are referred to as people who will help with unloading.

94. (B) *Leaders* of the *Parisian Literacy Crusade* have agreed to *unload and shelve* the books. (A) It is *Parisian Intercontinental Hotels* who are doing the donating. (C) There is no mention of *promoting* the *Intercontinental Hotels*. (D) *Donated* is associated with *free*, and *elementary schools* is repeated, but *free tutoring* is not mentioned in the story.

95. (A) The topic is the *purchase of air conditioners*. (B) *Central air* is mentioned in the talk, but the difference between it and *single units* is not mentioned. (C) Air-conditioners may *cause* noise, but this is not mentioned in the talk. (D) People present at the meeting are asked for *technical information*, but this is not the focus.

96. (D) By proposing air conditioners for the *branch offices*, the speaker is addressing suggestions made by many of the *office workers*. (A) The *kitchen* is only mentioned as a source of heat. (B) Ultimately, *building engineers* may need to be consulted, but they are not mentioned in this talk. (C) The *dining room* is only mentioned as a place which is not well-ventilated.

97. (C) The speaker asks for *technical information* about air conditioners including *brands and sizes*. This information is likely to help *educate decision-makers*. (A) *Opinions* has a similar meaning to *suggestions*. The *kitchen* and *dining room* are mentioned, but what people think about the *menu*, is not asked for. (B) While the speaker is obviously wondering how many units to buy, this information is not being requested. (D) While the systems will need to be financed, this information is not being requested.

98. (A) The advertisement is for *golf courses in Scotland*. *(B) Archery* is mentioned in historical terms. There is no reference to *training*. (C) *Scottish* is the adjectival form of *Scotland*, but *antiques* are not the topic. (D) *Scotland* is the country which is being advertised, but *tours* are not mentioned.

99. (B) The verb *outlaw* means *forbid* and *1457* was the year James II tried to outlaw golf. *(A) Archery* is repeated in both the advertisement and the option, but we do not know if this was the year of its peak. (C) *Aristocrats* is repeated, but there is no mention of rules being developed.
(D) *James II* tried to *outlaw* the sport. He did not become an *outlaw* himself. An *outlaw* is somebody who is running from the law.

100. (B) It is described as the *finest course in the country*.
(A) *Many years* could refer to *hundreds of years*, but the age of the course is not stated. (C) *Preferred* may relate to *aristocratic* and *finest*, but this is not the correct option.
(D) The *Tours of Scotland golfing brochure* is mentioned, but there is no reference to any tours of *St Andrew's*.

PART V

101. (A) You *take action against* something or someone. (B), (C) and (D) The verbs *do, give* and *make* are not used with the noun *action.*

102. (B) The article *the* indicates that the superlative *hardest* should be used. (A) *Hardly* is an adverb. (C) *Harder* is the comparative form. (D) *Hard* is the adjective form.

103. (A) A *prospectus* is a formal description of a proposed business venture. (B) *Prosecution* implies legal action. (C) A *prosthesis* is an artificial device to replace a body part. (D) *Prosperity* means *wealth* or *success.*

104. (B) The adverb *probably* modifies the verb *need.* (A) The verb *may* could replace *will*; however *maybe* cannot follow the verb *will.* (C) *Possible* is an adjective, and the adverb form is needed. (D) If *eventually* is used, then a specific time frame, *by week's end*, cannot be used.

105. (C) The adjective *admissible* follows the verb *to be* and describes what can be allowed in a court of law. (A) and (D) *Admission* and *admittance* are noun forms. (B) *Admit* is the verb form.

106. (D) The present perfect tense follows a clause beginning with *ever since.* (A) *Didn't go* is the negative form of the past tense. (B) *Weren't going* is the past progressive tense. (C) A negative form needs to be used with *anywhere,* and *went* is the simple past tense.

107. (A) The past perfect is used in the *if*-clause, when the result clause uses *would* plus perfect infinitive. (B) *Have not changed* is the present perfect. (C) and (D) A progressive tense is not used to describe a single action in the past.

108. (B) The verb *passing* is an abbreviation of the relative clause *who were passing.* (A) *Passed* is the past participle and cannot be used in this context. (C) *Passes* is the third person singular form of the verb. (D) *Pass* is the base form of the verb.

109. (D) The verb *were* refers to the plural noun *discoveries.* (A) *Was* is the singular form of the verb. (B) *It was* repeats the subject unnecessarily and uses the singular form. (C) *Had* would need to be followed by *been given* in order to be correct.

110. (D) *So* is a conjunction introducing an explanatory phrase. (A) The wiring is not put behind the walls *because* it is not visible, rather *because* it is visible. (B) *So that* is a possible combination, but not *for that.* (C) *To* is a preposition and cannot be used in this sentence.

111. (D) *Are considered* forms the passive voice. (A) The base form of the verb *consider* does not follow the form of *to be.* (B) *Are considering* would be the present progressive, but in this context, the passive voice is needed. (C) *Considerable* is the adjective.

112. (A) *Little* can be used with non-count nouns. (B) *Few* is used with plural nouns. (C) *Small amount* is possible, but not *small money.* (D) *Less money* indicates a comparison with another amount.

113. (B) The verb *be able to* is followed by the base form *run.* (A) *Running* is the participle and cannot follow the verb *be able to.* (C) The base form only follows another base form in the case of modals. (D) The simple form *run* does not follow *are able.*

114. (A) *Which* is used as a pronoun to indicate a limited choice. (B) *That* is used to refer to a specific object. (C) *Some* is a plural pronoun; therefore the verb *is* cannot follow it. (D) *What* is used to indicate an unlimited choice.

115. (D) You *print out* a document from the computer. (A) You *print with* a printer. (B) You *print on* paper. (C) *Print forth* is not possible.

116. (C) *Didn't* indicates the past tense negative, and is followed by the base form of the verb. (A) *Didn't* indicates the past tense, so the following verb is not in the past. (B) *Be closed* would follow a modal. (D) The infinitive *to close* does not follow the past tense form of the auxiliary.

117. (C) *Invaluable* means *extremely valuable* (literally, *of a value too high to be measured*). (A) *Industrious* and not *industrial* is used to refer to a person. (B) *Indigenous* means *native* or *belonging naturally to a place.* (D) *Inclement* means bad and is usually used to describe the weather.

118. (D) *Have to* means *must* and is followed by the base form *approve.* (A) The base form cannot follow *have* directly. (B) The passive voice cannot be used, as the agent (*Customer Service*) is the subject of the sentence. (C) The gerund *approving* does not follow the base form.

119. (A) *Postpone* means *to delay.* (B) You might *move the time* of the conference call. (C) *Hinder* means *to obstruct or to make more difficult.* (D) *Detain* is most commonly used with people.

120. (A) The third conditional uses the past perfect in the *if*-clause. (B) If *were* is used in the conditional, the result clause would use *would* plus the base form of the verb. (C) If *are* is used in the conditional, the result clause would use the future tense. (D) The past participle *been* cannot be used without an auxiliary.

121. (A) *Empty* means there was no more gas in the pumps. (B) *Used* could be replaced by *in use* or *being used* (consequently we could not get gas). (C) *Out of order* would be the correct phrase here. (D) *Being repaired* or *under repair* would be the correct phrases.

122. (C) *Than* indicates that the comparative *more* should be used. (A) and (B) *Most* and *best* are the superlative forms. (D) *Very* is not a comparative form.

123. (B) *In good repair* means *in good condition.* (C) *Good quality* cannot be used with *in.* (A) In order to use *state,* the article *a* must be used: *a good state.* (D) *Manner* is not used to describe the condition of physical objects.

124. (B) *Wander around* means *to walk around*. (A) She could *wander among* people. (C) The article *the* is not used with the proper noun *Lisbon*. (D) *Wander out* needs to be followed by another preposition, *into*.

125. (D) Only the past tense form of the verb, *spoke*, is needed. (A) If *who spoke* is used, the sentence would be incomplete. (B) *Was spoken* is the passive voice and this sentence is active: Mrs. Stein speaks. (C) *That she spoke* repeats the subject.

126. (B) The subject of the sentence is the plural noun *opinions* and is followed by the plural verb *are*. (A) *Is* is the third person, singular form of the verb. (C) *They* is redundant as the subject, *opinion*, begins the sentence. (D) *Have* is an incorrect verb.

127. (D) *Herself* is the reflexive pronoun for *she*. (A) *Himself* refers to a masculine subject. (B) *Itself* refers to an impersonal subject. (C) *Themselves* refers to a plural subject.

128. (D) *Populous* is an adjective and describes *areas*. (A) *Population* is the noun form. (B) *Populations* is the plural noun form. (C) *Populate* is the verb.

129. (A) *Tolerated* is the past participle used in the passive voice. (B) *Tolerate* is the base form of the verb. (C) *Tolerant* is the adjective form. (D) *Tolerance* is a noun.

130. (B) *Nor* follows *neither*. (A) *Or* follows *either*. (C) The conjunction *but* is illogical. (D) *Also* means *in addition to*.

131. (B) The reflexive pronoun *themselves* is used to refer back to the subject, *lawmakers*. (A) *Himself* is the reflexive pronoun for *he*. (C) *Herself* is the reflexive pronoun for *she*. (D) *Yourselves* is the plural reflexive pronoun for *you*.

132. (D) The adverb *not* is used to negate the verb. (A) *Though* is illogical. (B) *How* is an adverb that means *in what manner*. (C) *Yet* could be used following *not*.

133. (B) The phrase is *in light of*, meaning *considering*. (A) *To light* is the infinitive form and does not follow the preposition *in*. (C) and (D) *Lights on* and *lighted* do not make sense in this context.

134. (C) *Always* is an adverb meaning *all the time*. (A) *Almost* might be possible if *don't* were not in the sentence. (B) *Already* is used to indicate that something has happened. (D) *Also* is illogical.

135. (B) *Undervalued* means that the price of the shares was lower than it should have been. (A) *Undernourished* is used to talk about nutrition or diet. (C) *Undercharged* means that someone did not pay enough. (D) *Underdeveloped* means that something is lacking development.

136. (A) The preposition *to* indicates that the policies were designed for a particular purpose. (B) *So as to* would fit, but not *so*. (C) *That* could be used as a relative pronoun after the noun, but not following a verb. (D) The pronoun *what* does not fit in this context.

137. (C) *Since* is used to introduce a clause that happened first, followed by a clause describing the subsequent action. (A) *Before* would indicate that absenteeism declined first and then the managers started a new program. (B) *When* is used to indicate that two actions happen at the same time. (D) *During* is always followed by an expression indicating the time period.

138. (A) The gerund *being* is followed by the adjective *friendly*. (B), (C) and (D) *Politely*, *courteously* and *respectfully* are adverbs.

139. (B) *Which* refers to an object. (A) and (B) When used as pronouns, *that* and *this* do not follow the preposition *for*. (C) *Whom* is used to refer to people.

140. (B) *Highly recommended* means *spoken of very favorably*. (A) *Inferred* means *to conclude*. (C) *Conferred* means *to discuss with*. (D) *Referred* means *to direct someone to something or someone else*.

PART VI

141. (B) The adverb *less* should be used, not the adjective *lesser*. (A) *In larger cities* is a prepositional phrase. (C) *Has been given* is the passive voice in the present perfect. (D) *Over* is the correct preposition, following the noun *priority*, to compare *education* and *punishment*.

142. (B) The subject of the sentence is *merger*, therefore the verb should be *is*. (A) *Merger* is the singular subject. (C) *In the business community* is a prepositional phrase used to describe where. (D) *Media* is a plural noun.

143. (D) The adjective form required is *conservative*. (A) *These days* indicates the time frame. (B) *To deal with* is the infinitive plus a preposition. (C) *Revolving around real estate* is a reduced clause identifying which tax issues.

144. (C) The noun form *logistics* is needed. (A) *Would feel* indicates that this is a conditional sentence. (B) The subject plus the past tense of the verb is used in this *if*-clause. (D) *Before we left* is a prepositional phrase.

145. (B) The phrase *one of* is followed by a comparative, *more*, or a superlative, *most*. (A) *One of* is used to quantify *assets*. (C) *Assets* is a plural noun meaning *skills or good qualities*. (D) *His ability to say 'no'* is the object, i.e. the *valuable asset*.

146. (A) The noun form *diversity* must be used. (B) *Throughout* is used as a preposition. (C) *Many* modifies *Indonesian islands*. (D) *Their color* refers to the islands.

147. (B) The noun *agriculture* is needed. (A) *Is growing* is the present progressive. (C) *Its* is the correct use of the possessive pronoun, referring to Vietnam. (D) The adjective *economic* describes *mainstay*, which means *main part or component*.

148. (C) *Time* in this context is a non-count noun. (A) The first clause of the sentence uses *I* as the subject and *asked* as the past tense verb form. (B) The modal *could* is followed by the base form of the verb, *have*. (D) *For the meeting* is a prepositional phrase.

149. (D) The progressive form of the verb, *applying*, is needed. (A) *This year alone* means *only in the present year*. (B) *Over three thousand* quantifies the number of inventors. (C) *All over* describes what part of the country.

150. (A) *Any* should be used instead of *some*, to mean that no increase is acceptable. (B) *Will be met* is the future tense in the passive voice. (C) *Stiff* is an adjective describing *resistance*. (D) *From all sides* is a prepositional phrase.

151. (D) Either *a* or *per* should precede *dozen*. (A) The infinitive expressing purpose is used as a subject in this sentence. (B) *Is selling* is the present progressive tense. (C) *At* is a preposition, in this case meaning the same as *for*.

152. (C) When used as an adjective, the singular, *month*, is required. (A) The verb *was able to* is followed by the base form of the verb, *buy*. (B) *On* is a preposition. (D) *No* means the same as *zero*.

153. (D) The participle form *recalculated* is used following the verb *be* to form the passive voice. (A) *Due to* is a synonym for *because of*. (B) There is an increase *in* something. (C) *Pay* tells us what kind of *scales*.

154. (D) The article *the* is not used with *many*; *few* would be possible. (A) *Is being* is the present progressive tense in the passive voice. (B) A person is *briefed on* or *given advance information about*. (C) *Scheduled for* is a reduced clause: *which are scheduled for*.

155. (D) The conjunction used to tell us two pieces of information is *and*. (A) *One* is used to refer to the third person singular. (B) *It* refers to the information about the ice cream sales. (C) The verb *are* refers to the plural noun *sales*.

156. (B) *Data* is a non-count noun and should be followed by the singular pronoun *it*. (A) The modal *should* is followed by the base form of the verb *be* and the past participle *transferred*, indicating the passive voice. (C) Data is *stored* or *kept safe*. (D) *We* is the subject of the clause, followed by the present tense *need* and the pronoun *it*, referring to the *data*.

157. (D) The base form of the verb *forget* follows the modal *may* to refer to future time. (A) *It* is used as a preparatory subject to refer forward to *writing down appointments*. (B) The correct two-word verb is *write down*. (C) The phrase *as they come up*, meaning *as they occur*, gives us a time reference to *appointments*.

158. (C) *Every* is followed by a singular noun; *nearly all* is required in this context. (A) *It came as no surprise* means that they were expecting it. (B) *Discovered* is the past tense form of the verb. (D) The correct preposition is *prior to*, meaning *before*.

159. (C) In order to use the plural *thousands*, it must be followed with the preposition *of*. (A) *Hiring* is a gerund, used as the subject of the sentence. (B) The phrase *no different from* is synonymous with *the same as*. (D) *Public relations* is used as a compound adjective to describe the *campaign*.

160. (B) *News* is a singular noun, so it takes the singular verb form, *is*. (A) The prepositional phrase *by the time* indicates when. (C) The adverb *already* is correctly positioned between the auxilary and main verb. (D) The prepositional phrase *in the world* indicates where.

PART VII

161. (A) *"Free Dinner for Two"* means that they are offering *two complimentary meals*. (B) The offer is for people who may be flying to *Kuala Lumpur*. (C) The ticket agency has a *list of preferred dining locations*. (D) *Discounts at popular hotels* is not mentioned.

162. (D) The campaign is open to everyone flying *round trip* and is offered by *Singapore Airlines*. (A) One can get a list of restaurants by *visiting a travel agency*. (B) *Hotels* are not mentioned. (C) Any round trip ticket, economy or first class is eligible.

163. (D) The second sentence refers to *the reported blockage*. (A) There is no mention that the *cutting room workers are complaining*. (B) The *pallets* were found outside the cutting room. (C) *Technical difficulties* are not mentioned.

164. (B) He suggests allocating space in storage; in other words, *the wood could be moved*. (A) There is no indication that the *inspections* are not *taken seriously*. (C) Hans may believe that *nothing should be left outside the cutting room*; however, it is not his suggestion. (D) There is no mention that *John Stevens should meet with Jeremy*.

165. (D) The text states that it is a *power-cable plant*. (A), (B) and (C) *Heavy machinery, water filtration devices* and *electrical power* are not mentioned.

166. (B) *PB Cable and Chorny Electrical* own 48%. (A) *Buyuk Power and Water Machine Company* owns 47%. (C) *PB Group* owns 5%. (D) *PB Cable and Machinery, Ltd.* is a subsidiary of PB Group.

167. (C) The first sentence indicates the main purpose of the news item: *to announce a new factory*. (A) There is no indication that the new plant is controversial or that anyone is *protesting*. (B) The responsibilities of the investors are not mentioned. (D) *Business relations between Turkey and Russia* are not mentioned.

168. (A) The last three sentences *highlight the benefits of using Worldwide Watchers*. (B) Publications, which could include *newsletters*, are mentioned, but not for the purpose of selling them. (C) *Overseas investments* are mentioned, but not explained. (D) *Software systems* are mentioned, but *investing in software companies* is not.

169. (C) The ad talks about what a person has to do to be able to make money; therefore, it is aimed at *investors.* (A) Software systems are mentioned, but the ad is not aimed at *computer programmers.* (B) and (D) *Financial analysts* and *research analysts* would work for a company like Worldwide Watchers.

170. (D) *Currency fluctuations* means the same as *shifting exchange rates.* (A) *High costs* are not mentioned. (B) Investing is *unpredictable,* but there is no mention of *tides* (*rocky waters* is used figuratively). (C) *Changing investment patterns* is not mentioned.

171. (B) The last paragraph mentions his suggestion of a monthly installment plan. (A) Dr. Garcia is a doctor, not an insurance provider. (C) He does *report on his post-surgery progress,* but that is not the main purpose. (D) He does not dispute the bill.

172. (C) Juan thought that the surgery would be covered 100%, but his insurers will only pay 70% of the cost. (A) There is no mention that the *follow-up care was unexpectedly expensive.* (B) Juan thought he would be responsible for 0% of the cost. (D) The *type of surgery* was covered, just not the amount that he expected.

173. (D) *Increased range of motion* is the same as *more flexibility in his arm.* (A) The results of the surgery were *positive.* (B) Juan is still not working. (C) He has very little money after the *holidays.*

174. (B) The letter is dated *January* 13, and he says that he will pay $50 this month. (A) and (D) *December* and *March* are not mentioned. (C) He will start the monthly installment plan in *February.*

175. (A) The first sentence mentions *statistics that may heighten your interest* and the last refers to *something few businesses can ignore,* suggesting it would be for *companies wanting to expand their market reach.* (B) Languages are mentioned, but not *translators.* (C) The *natural rubber manufacturers* are already in the region. (D) *The Department of Labor* is not mentioned.

176. (C) 95% of the world's *silk* is found in the Pacific Basin. (A) 22% of the world's *oil* is found in the Pacific Basin. (B) 88% of the world's *rubber* is found in the Pacific Basin. (D) 64% of the world's *cotton* is found in the Pacific Basin.

177. (B) *Their market for advanced technology will expand,* or *grow.* (A) The report talks about *expanding economies,* which contradicts the idea of *little buying power.* (C) and (D) The report encourages the reader to see the Pacific Basin as a growing market, not as a *competitor* or *opponent.*

178. (A) The telecommunications industry, which would include *mobile phone manufacturers, ... will soon take off,* i.e. it will soon *excel.* (B) and (C) There is no mention of whether the *rubber tire and oil refinery* businesses are growing. (D) The silk industry is mentioned, but not *clothing manufacturers.*

179. (B) The last sentence mentions the area's unique advantage, which indicates that *it is well poised for great economic expansion.* (A) *The cost of labor* is not mentioned. (C) The region has an *educated labor force,* but there is no mention of whether the region has *superior educational standards.* (D) *Trade restrictions* are not mentioned.

180. (B) The first sentence of the second paragraph indicates that the purpose is *to inform the staff of heightened security measures.* (A) How *new IDs can be obtained* is not mentioned. (C) *The stolen goods* are described; however, it is not the purpose of the announcement. (D) The announcement does not place any *blame.*

181. (D) Things were stolen during normal working hours, i.e. *9 to 5.* (A) *9 to 11* are the visiting hours in the morning. (B) *11 to 2* is not mentioned. (C) *2 to 5* are the visiting hours in the afternoon.

182. (C) Visitors will have name tags *indicating which department they will be visiting.* (A) *Video phones* are to assist the staff. (B) The staff will *wear a photo ID at all times.* (D) *Submitting a visitor's form to their department* is not mentioned.

183. (D) People who are going to see films, or *show goers* would be most interested. (A) The Film Festival is in the *Victory Building,* but the workers would not necessarily be interested. (B) *Actors and actresses* probably would not need this information. (C) *Job applicants* are not mentioned.

184. (A) *365-8000* is the number for a *pre-recorded program* or a *listing of shows.* (B) *221-8937* is the number for phone orders. (C) *365-7786* is the number for reviews. (D) *800-EFF-SHOWS* is not mentioned.

185. (C) Members can reserve tickets five days in advance. (A) The notice says that *there is a limit of two member-price tickets ...* which means discounts not free tickets. (B) The notice mentions *screenings,* but that concerns when the box office is open. (D) *Parking is free* for everyone.

186. (B) The notice is about a film festival, or a *movie festival.* (A), (C) and (D) *A play,* a *boxing match* and a *car race* are not mentioned.

187. (C) The form is used to send a *registered* package. The postal department would insure the shipment and notify you when it was delivered. (A), (B) and (D) are not mentioned in the form.

188. (A) The customer must *declare full value of all shipped goods to receive insurance on items valued over $20.000.* (B), (C) and (D) are not mentioned as options.

189. (A) The form must be completed *legibly,* or *clearly.* (B) There is no mention of whether the form should be typed or handwritten *with a pen.* (C) There is no mention that there should be two copies of the form. (D) *Illegibly* is the opposite of *legibly.*

190. (B) Lydia Thornton has *run Mr. Sheldon's building*; therefore she is *a building manager.* (A) *A neighbor* complained, but it was not Lydia Thornton. (C) Mr. Sheldon is the *landlord.* (D) *A past tenant* was evicted.

191. (C) *Initially, the downstairs neighbors complained.* (A) *She found cigarette butts and ashes below the balcony* after the neighbors complained. (B) The fact that *other neighbors smoked* is not related to the first clue. (D) Lydia *has smelled smoke* since the neighbors complained.

192. (D) The tenants were given *thirty days' notice*, which means that *they were evicted.* (A) The tenants *lived in apartment 404B.* (B) The tenants did not *heed the warning*, they ignored it. (C) Lydia *takes the situation seriously.*

193. (B) Richard wants views on whether or not the booklet should be *reprinted.* (A) He is asking for improvements, but he is not *proposing* them. (C) He is asking for advice, not for *permission.* (D) *A meeting of managers* is not mentioned.

194. (D) The first sentence says that the booklet was issued for the *twentieth anniversary.* (A) *Offering opportunities to employees* is not mentioned. (B) The booklet has been requested by *high school students*, but this was not the original aim. (C) *College students* have requested the booklet, but this was not the original aim.

195. (B) Item 3 says that copies were distributed to *educational leaders.* (A), (C) and (D) There have been requests for the booklet from *private industries, private individuals* and *high school students.*

196. (C) The FYI (for your information) says that the request is being sent to *middle managers.* (A) and (D) *The company shareholders* and *employees* received the booklet. (B) *Community leaders* is not mentioned.

197. (A) The article lists examples of new power projects. (B) There is no mention that Argentina and Brazil are *sharing resources.* (C) *Germany is working with Brazil*, but that is not the main point. (D) The article does not state what percentage of power companies in Brazil are foreign-owned.

198. (D) *$300 million* of working capital is *already on hand*, or *available.* (A) *$60 million* is the amount the EVS paid. (B) and (C) *$130 to $140 million* is the expected cost for the Iguape Project.

199. (A) *20%* is the amount being possibly offered. (B) Nova Lima will sell EVS a *40% share.* (C) *60%* of costs for the Iguape project will be paid for by the World Bank. (D) *80%* is not mentioned.

200. (B) *The line will transmit ... from the Iguape Hydroelectric Power Plant.* (A) The power line will go to *Sao Paulo.* (C) *Electricity of Brazil* is not mentioned. (D) *Nova Lima Lignite* is a different project.

Answer Key

Practice Test Three

In the following Answer Key, the first explanation provided for each question is the correct option.

PART I

1. (D) The woman is sitting at a round table. (A) A *reception* is a formal gathering of people and is therefore associated with food and drink, but the picture shows a *restaurant*, not a *reception*. (B) There is a beverage, possibly *coffee*, on the table, but no *coffee beans* are visible. *Soaking* sounds like *smoking* and could be easily confused. (C) The customers are sitting at several *round* tables, not at one *long* table.

2. (B) The *apparatus*, or machine, is resting on a table, or bench, and is therefore *off the ground*. (A) There are monitoring machines in the foreground, but they are connected to the *machine*, not to the man's *heart*. (C) It is not clear exactly what the man is doing to the machine, but there is nothing to indicate he is *cleaning* it. (D) The machine may be a type of *motor*, but the man is not in a shop *buying* anything.

3. (B) The porter is taking the bags somewhere, possibly to the rooms of the guests who own them. (A) *Tags* sounds like *bags* and therefore could be confused. The *bags* may be being removed from the trolley, but not the *tags*. (C) The picture shows *luggage*, or bags, but it is not being *checked*, or looked, *through*. (D) *Suits* may be confused with *suitcases*, but there are neither in the picture.

4. (C) The two construction workers are standing *side by side*, or next to each other. (A) The men are *moving* something, but it is not *cement*. (B) The men are *construction workers* and are therefore building something from a *plan*, but they are not creating the plan itself. (D) They may be *building* something, but we do not know if they are *building a relationship* (making their friendship stronger).

5. (B) The people look very *solemn*, or serious. They are wearing dark, formal clothing and their expressions are not cheerful. (A) The people are not smiling and do not look *happy*. (C) *Team* and *cheering* imply a happy, sporting event. The *group* of people are too formally dressed to be watching a sports competition and they are not cheering. (D) Most of the people are looking *down*, not *up*.

6. (B) There is food (cereal, toast, and tea) on the table. (A) The woman is holding a tray, but there is something on it, so it is not *empty*. (C) *Roast* sounds similar to *toast*. There is *toast* on a plate, but no *roast* meat. (D) There is only *one* cup in the picture, not *four*.

7. (C) The man is sitting at the *desk* and is *working* on a computer. (A) This option confuses the sounds of *screen* and *scene*. The man is looking at the computer *screen*. (B) He may be working in a hotel, but there are no *guests* in the picture so it's not possible to know if he is *attending* to them. (D) There is a vase of flowers in the picture, but he is not *arranging* them.

8. (B) The man is holding the handkerchief to his nose to cover a *sneeze*. (A) *Handing over* means *giving someone something*, but the man is by himself. (C) He's walking through the station where there are other *travelers*, but he is not *welcoming* them. (D) This option confuses the sound of *clothes* with *nose*. *Blow* has different meanings; the wind blows and dries *clothes*, but you can also blow your *nose*.

9. (B) The performers *are wearing feathers on their heads* as part of their costume. (A) The people seem to be *dancing*, but outside, not in a *nightclub*. (C) The *costumes* are decorative and highly detailed, not *plain*. (D) The dancers are *not* fully covered. Their costumes reveal parts of their bodies.

10. (C) The *agent* is helping a customer, or *traveler,* at the counter. (A) The picture is of an airline office or counter, not a *hotel*. (B) A *flight attendant* works on an airplane so would not be checking what seats have been allocated. This option may also be confusing because a passenger would *check in* their luggage at the check-in desk, but the picture does not show this. (D) *Tickets* are associated with *airlines*, however, a *parking officer* gives *tickets* to car drivers, etc. which result in a fine or penalty.

11. (D) The tour guide is *holding* and talking into a microphone, or *mike*. (A) *Hike* is easily confused with *mike* because of the sound. The man speaking could be a *group leader*, but he is not *hiking*, or walking. (B) He's holding an *instrument*, a microphone, but it does not *hang from the ceiling*. There is a TV screen attached to the roof of the bus, but it is not an instrument. (C) His hand is wrapped around the *mike*, not *food*.

12. (C) There is one man behind the counter. (A) The water on display is cold, not *hot*, and there is no reference to *tea* in the picture. (B) *Take out* and *tables* are written on the sign, but nobody in the picture is *taking* out *the tables* . (D) *Go out* sounds like *take out*, but their meanings are different, and although there are two men in the picture, they are not *going* anywhere.

13. (B) The scientist's right hand is *on the knob* of the machine. (A) There are *tubes* coming out of the machine, and there is a *flask* on the left, but there is no *mask* anywhere. (C) The flask in the picture is *empty*, not *full*. (D) There is only *one* bottle or flask, and this option refers to more than one.

14. (D) The *action* is not shown, but the picture shows that the *spectators*, or fans, are looking intently at something. (A) The stadium is full of fans watching something, they have not *gone* anywhere. (B) Some of the people are waving flags in the seating area, but the *field* is not visible. (C) *Players* are associated with stadiums and fans, but the picture does not show any players.

15. (C) The dentist is looking into and *examining* the patient's mouth. (A) The patient may be having *emergency* treatment, but the people are *already* in the room, they are not in the process of *entering* it. (B) The woman may be *cleaning* the patient's teeth, but she is not a *cleaning lady* and she is not holding a *mop*. (D) The woman may be a *hygienist*, but she is *standing*, not *sitting*, next to the *dentist*, not *doctor*.

16. (A) The collar on the man's shirt is *open*. (B) The man is wearing *suspenders,* or braces, to keep his pants up, but they are not related to his *work*. (C) He is *making notes* in a notebook, not on a *board*. There is no board in the picture. (D) The man is looking at the notebook, not *gazing out the window*.

17. (D) There is a slot to insert money and buttons to select the ticket on each machine. The machine then *dispenses* the ticket. (A) The men have their backs to the *photographer*, not the *machines*. (B) *Three* of the devices, or machines, are *the same*. The fourth is *different*, it's a phone. (C) The phone receiver is *on* the hook.

18. (C) The man is *replacing,* or putting back, the circuit board into the machine. (A) Machines are *assembled*, or put together, but an *assembly* is a group of people. This picture does not show people *meeting*. (B) *Ensemble* sounds like *assemble*, but an *ensemble* is a group of musicians and there are none in the picture. (D) The man is lifting part of the machine, not a *plate*.

19. (A) The plates on the table are *stacked neatly* in two piles. (B) The coffee has *not* been poured yet, the cups are still on the tray waiting to be used. (C) The trays of food are on a table, not *in the kitchen*. (D) The food is *on the table*, not *in the oven*.

20. (D) There are four *firefighters* holding hoses, aimed at a *blaze*, or fire. (A) The tanks on the men's backs look like diving tanks, but they are *firefighters*, not *divers*. *Wire* could be confused with *fire*. (B) *Fighters entering the ring* would be *boxers*, but these men are *firefighters*.
(C) The firefighters are battling, or fighting, the fire, however, they are not in the *army*.

PART II

21. (B) The respondent affirms that the music director *approved it*, but adds the additional information *with a few changes*. (A) *Music* is repeated, but this option refers to *they*, not *he*. (C) This option confuses the words *approved* and *prove* which have the same root.

22. (C) The strike should be *over*, or finished, *next week*. (A) *Three feet* is a logical answer to *how long?* but the question is about *time*, not *length*. (B) *Long* and *last* are used in both the question and the answer, but the contexts are different, making this option incorrect.

23. (C) The reason for *changing professions* is that the respondent would like to try the *medical field*. (A) *Changing* is associated with *different*, but this option confuses the sound of *lessons* with *professions*. (B) This option confuses the words *professions* and *professor* which have the same stem, and contrasts *change* with *same*.

24. (A) *Betty* offered to do the driving. (B) *Drove* is the past tense of *drive*, and *she* is a logical answer to *who is?* However, this option does not answer the question. (C) *Going* is repeated, but this option confuses the sound of *drive-in* with *driving*.

25. (C) The doctor who is in charge of emergencies is in the emergency room. (A) This option confuses *emergence* with *emergency*. (B) *Doctor* is used in both the question and the option, but the question requires information about location.

26. (B) The porch light was turned on so that they could *sit outside*. (A) *Torch* rhymes with *porch*, and *light* is associated with *lit*, but this is not the correct option. (C) *Turn* is used in both the question and the option, but in different contexts.

27. (A) The respondent agrees to help start the car by taking a looking at it. (B) *No* is a logical response to *would you?* and *car* is associated with *traffic*. However, this option does not answer the question. (C) *Cars* is repeated and *start* is used in both the question and the option, but with different meanings.

28. (A) The respondent answers in the affirmative and adds the additional information that she has been *practising all week* in order to prepare. (B) *Exam* is used in the question and the option, and *took* is the past tense of *take*, but the question is about somebody *sitting* an exam, not the location of the exam *papers*. (C) The respondent is going to *take* a typing exam, not do some typing *now*.

29. (A) The respondent does not *have* a truck driver's license, but can get one. (B) *Driver* is repeated, but the topic is a *license*, not a person. (C) *License* is repeated, but a *new license plate* is not the topic.

30. (C) The respondent thinks the *current* hiring requirements are fine. (A) *Hired* is repeated, and *changing* is associated with *new*. However, this option refers to a specific event whereas the question asks about general requirements. (B) *Changed* is repeated, and this option may confuse the sound of *tires* with *hiring*, but the question is not about cars.

31. (A) The copier supplies are kept in the cupboard. (B) *Supplies* is repeated, but *store* is used with a different meaning, so this option is incorrect. (C) This option would answer *when* the copier supplies are bought.

32. (C) The route did not have problems this morning. It was *fine*. (A) This option confuses the sound of *root* with *route*, and *problems* is associated with *entangled*. (B) *Traffic* is associated with a *route*, and *problem* is used in both the question and the option, but this is a generalised comment and does not answer the specific question.

33. (B) The *shore* is where the respondent would like to go on vacation. (A) *Egypt* is a logical answer to *where?* but this option confuses the sounds of *vacation* and *station* and does not answer the question. (C) *The Bahamas* are associated with *vacations*, and *the Bahamas* is a logical answer to *where?* However, this option refers to the past and the question asks for suggestions for the future.

34. (C) The respondent would like to sit by the window. (A) and (B) *Here* and *there* are repeated, but neither answer is correct.

35. (C) The respondent has several credit cards, but tries not to use them. (A) This option confuses the sound of *car* with *card* and has no connection with the question. (B) *Credit cards* are associated with *excellent credit*, but the question is not answered correctly.

36. (C) The respondent *would* prefer to inspect the electrical connections first, and asks for the power to be turned on. (A) *Connecting* and *connections* have the same root, but the topic is not *flights*. (B) *First* and *rather* are used in both the question and the option, but the topic is not travel.

37. (B) His brother said that the person in question *had* been forced to sell the store. (A) *Family* and *store* are both repeated, but the question is not about ownership. (C) *Sell* is used in both the question and the option, but what he sells is not the topic of the question.

38. (A) The loan officer is not available right now because he has just *stepped out*, or left the building. (B) *Office* might be confused with *officer* and *available* is repeated, but this option is incorrect (C) *Loan* is repeated, but this is not the topic of the question, the loan *officer* is.

39. (B) The respondent confirms that you can pick up the tickets at the box office, then adds that you can also have them *sent by mail*. (A) *Box* is repeated in the question and the option, but the question is about *theater tickets*, not *boxes*. (C) *No* is a logical response to *can I?* and *office* is repeated. However, this option does not answer the question.

40. (B) The flight left at 2:15. (A) and (C) Both *tomorrow* and *in five minutes* are logical answers to *when?* but they refer to the future and the flight has already departed.

41. (B) The respondent knows how to type *sixty words a minute*. (A) and (C) The word *type* is repeated in both these answers, but neither option is correct.

42. (A) The advisory board's recommendation will come *tomorrow*. (B) *Recommended* is repeated, but the question is not about medicine. (C) *Advisory* is used in both the question and the option, but this option does not answer the question.

43. (B) The report *was* updated, *first thing this morning*. (A) This option may confuse the words *updated* and *date* which have the same root. (C) *Reported* is repeated, but the option refers to *she* whereas *I* would be a natural response to the *you* in the question.

44. (A) The respondent wants to ask the *mechanic* if the parts fit the car. (B) *Transmission* is repeated, but the *state* of the transmission is not the topic. (C) *Parts* and *car* are used in both the question and the option, but cost is not the topic.

45. (A) If the results are available, the respondent would like to see them. (B) *See* is used in the question and the option, but the context is different. (C) The test results are *already* available, they cannot be testing them *now*.

46. (B) The respondent sees no reason why they will not offer the speaker the job. (A) *Job* is repeated, but the option does not answer the question. (C) *Secretary* and *job* are both repeated, but the speaker's job is the subject, not the *respondent's secretary's* job.

47. (B) Not only was the respondent *not* shown the changes, but the respondent did not know there *were* any changes. (A) *Change* and *contract* are repeated, but the question is not about *who* made the changes. (C) *Shown* is used in the question and *showed* in the option, but the meanings are different.

48. (B) The respondent requests an address in order to be able to send the new catalog. (A) This option confuses *catalog* and *log*. (C) *Sending*, *new* and *office* are all repeated. However, the subject of the question is a new *catalog*, not a *new office*.

49. (C) In order to fire him, the respondent suggests saying they are *downsizing*. (A) *Fire* is used in both the question and the option, but in completely different contexts. The question deals with sacking somebody, not something that is burning. (B) *All these years* is associated with *many years*, and *him* is used in both the question and the option. However, this option does not answer the question.

50. (A) The deadline was only just met with *minutes to spare*. (B) This option may confuse the meanings of *dead end* with *deadline* and is incorrect. (C) *I didn't* is a logical answer to *didn't you?* but knowing somebody's location is not the subject of the question.

PART III

51. (C) The brakes need to be *replaced*, which implies that they are not working. They need to be *fixed*. (A) *Bad* might be associated with health and therefore with a *doctor*, but there is nothing to indicate that Mr Barasso is ill. (B) *Leave* his car and *get out of* the car could have similar meanings, but not in this case. (D) *Five o'clock* is repeated in the option, but in the dialog his car will be *ready* at that time. We are not told he is going to pick anybody up.

52. (C) If Ahmet takes an *early flight* to Cairo, the man will be able to meet up with him. (A) *Twelve o'clock* and *noon* have the same meaning, but that is when Ahmet would need to arrive, not leave. (B) *Early* is repeated in both the dialog and the option, but the meeting will take place *in* Cairo. If Ahmet leaves early it will not happen. (D) *Twelve o'clock* and *noon* have the same meaning, but again the meeting will take place *in* Cairo. If Ahmet leaves at noon it will not happen.

53. (D) They have created an ad which has *attracted* a lot of customers. (A) The women have written *one* ad, not a *series* of ads. (B) *Credit* is repeated in the dialog and in the option, but with different meanings, so this option is incorrect. (C) In the dialog, the woman *thanks* the man for the compliment, and the boss may *thank* the women with a bonus. However, there is no mention of the *women* thanking their *boss*.

54. (C) The meeting is at *five o'clock*. (A) There is no mention of *three o'clock*. (B) The man is due to go to the doctor at *four*. (D) There is no mention of *six o'clock*.

55. (A) We know that they are driving in a *car*, because they are worried they could run out of gas. (B) *Trains* do not fill up at gas stations. (C) They need to *go* to a gas station, it is not where they are now. (D) *Empty* is repeated in both the dialog and the option, but in the dialog it refers to the *tank* of the car, not their location.

56. (A) The woman wants the slides to be ready by *this afternoon*, so it must be *morning* when she brings them in. (B) and (C) *Afternoon* is repeated in both these options, but that is when she wants them to be ready. (D) *Evening* is when she is making the presentation.

57. (D) Jeanie offers to drive the man to the airport. (A) This is what the man *first* asks her to do. (B) *Airport* can be associated with *reservation*, but presumably the man already has one. (C) *Luggage* is repeated in both the dialog and the option, but Jeanie does not offer to carry it.

58. (B) The hotel will not be taking any reservations for the next few weeks, because they have got *no space*. (A) *Conference* is repeated in both the dialog and the option, but rooms being available or unavailable there is not mentioned. (C) *Reservations* and *Mrs. Blair* are repeated in both the dialog and the option, but not having remembered to *make* a reservation is not the problem. (D) The secretary knows the hotel has no space, so he must have remembered the name to be able to call them.

59. (A) The newspaper said that the theater was on *First Avenue*. (B) and (C) The man wonders if the theater is on *Second or Third* Avenue. (D) The movie starts at *four*, so this might be confused with *fourth*.

60. (C) The man is buying a *monthly commuter pass*. A *commuter* is a person who takes *public transportation to work*. (A) *Senior citizen* means *over 65*, but the man is clearly not because he cannot buy a pass at the cheaper rate. (B) This option confuses *fare* with *fair*. (D) The commuter pass may be *monthly*, but there is no mention of a *journal*.

61. (A) George takes phone messages and will write this one in his boss's calendar. These are *secretarial* duties. (B) A *telephone operator* may take messages, as George has done, but George has additional duties so he is not *only* a telephone operator. (C) *Beachfront property* and *real estate* are associated, but George is not an agent, although he may work for an agent. (D) *Beachfront property* could be part of an estate, but George is not a manager, although he may work for an Estate manager.

62. (C) A *hinge* and a *nose piece* are associated with *eye glasses*. (A) A door has *hinges*, but not *nose pieces*, so this is not what is being discussed. (B) *Glasses* are mentioned in the dialog, but not *glassware*. (D) It is common to *fix* and *adjust* machines, but a *machine* is not under discussion.

63. (C) The man cannot *afford* it because he has other financial commitments. He is putting an addition on his house. (A) *Business* is associated with *work*, but having to work is not mentioned as a reason why he cannot go on holiday. (B) *Vacation* is mentioned, and he discusses putting an addition on the *house*, but he does not say he wants to stay at home. (D) The man would combine his business trip with his vacation if he had the money, so he must have the time left.

64. (A) He decides he would rather have a different model; *the 200 model printer*. (B) The woman says they will have to *order* the model he wants, but *several orders* will not be necessary. (C) The man asks the *woman* to try another branch to find the printer, but he will not call them himself. (D) *Stock* is repeated, but a customer is unlikely to buy stock.

65. (C) *Start my own business* and *come up with a good business plan*, are indicators that the man intends to *open a company*. (A) *Vice president* is repeated, but there is no mention of the man talking to him or her. (B) *Position* is repeated in both the dialog and the option. He plans to leave, but not for a new position. (D) *Education* is repeated in both the dialog and the option, but the man does not talk about continuing his own.

66. (C) The speakers imply that the *bad location* left the restaurant with too few customers. (A) *Sour* is often associated with *bad food*, but not in this case. (B) *The manager* is mentioned, but not how often he was *absent*. (D) *Help* is mentioned in the dialog, but not in the context of getting enough.

67. (D) *Dials*, *bass* and *speakers* are all signs of a *stereo*. (A) *Computers* may have *dials* and sometimes *speakers*, and their *model* is often referred to. However, a computer is not being sold. (B) *Cars* are described as *models*, they often have *speakers* and *turn so smoothly* could describe the way a car runs. However, this option is incorrect. (C) *Dials* are associated with *telephones*, but not *bass* and *speakers*, so this option is also incorrect.

68. (A) This man is *cashing a check*, so we can conclude that he is in a *bank*. (B) A *driver's license* is mentioned in the dialog and this may be associated with *auto*, but a checkpoint would not require two forms of ID. (C) *Driver's license* may be associated with a *motor vehicle office*, but there is nothing to indicate this is where the conversation is taking place. (D) *Police* often check for *ID*, but people do not have *accounts* with the police.

69. (A) *Worldwide Pharmaceutical* is hosting the open house. *Pharmaceuticals* are *drugs*. (B) and (C) The open house is *aimed* at college and high school students, the students are not having an open day themselves. (D) This option may confuse *nautical* and *pharmaceutical* which have the same suffix, but different meanings.

70. (A) The man describes the train trip as a *long ride*. (B) The walk took *less time* than the train ride. (C) He did not take a taxi because they were on strike. (D) The woman mentions *picking him up*, but he didn't go in a car.

71. (C) Nathan wants the woman to join in the game against the shipping department's softball team. (A) The *shipping department* is mentioned only as the opposing team. (B) This dialog sounds as though it is taking place in a work environment, but it is not about the woman doing better work. (D) *Coach* and *team* are repeated in both the dialog and the option, but Nathan's team already has a coach.

72. (B) The man is looking for a local map of the city. (A) *Stationery* is mentioned in the dialog only in terms of where the man can find maps. (C) The woman asks him if he is looking for a *particular book*, but this is not what he wants to buy. (D) A *local map* is associated with *directions*, but he is already in the city, he is not trying to find it.

73. (C) *Beaker*, *acids* and *heat causing chemicals to react*, are all signs of a *scientist* at work. (A) This option may confuse the sound of *actress* with *acid*, but there is nothing in the dialog to indicate she is an actress. (B) *Beaker* might sound like *baker*, and *heat* is also associated with baking. However, this option is not correct. (D) This option could be attractive because *beaker* might be confused with *speaker*, and sound technicians *mix* music. However, this is not her profession.

74. (D) Shoes can be *tight*, they come in different *styles* and *sizes*, they have *heels* and they require *polish*. (A) One might *polish* cufflinks, but they do not come in different sizes. (B) Some silverware *requires* polish, but it cannot be described as *feeling tight*. (C) *Hats* come in different styles and sizes, and a *leather hat* could require *polish*. However, being tight on the *heel* would not be correct.

75. (A) Mary reminds Jack that he cannot go get a haircut right now because the barber is closed on *Monday*. (B) and (C) The man refers to the meetings he has on *Tuesday* and *Wednesday*, but they are not today. (D) *Friday* is not mentioned.

76. (C) Joan offers to go to the *art store* to pick up Tom's things. (A) *Art store*, *poster boards* and *black marker* are all associated with *art work*, but Joan is not going to make any. (B) Joan has a dental appointment herself, she does not offer to schedule one for Tom. (D) *Tom* is going to do the signs when he has the relevant material, not Joan.

77. (A) The man is going to surprise his wife for her *birthday*. (B) *This year* and *wife* could be associated with an *anniversary*. However, this is not the subject. (C) There is no mention of a *promotion* in this dialog. (D) *Birthday* is mentioned, but it is not his own, it is his wife's.

78. (D) The customer is charged *$17.35*. (A) The woman *thought* it would be fourteen dollars, but that is the total with a coupon and the woman does not have one. (B) If she had had a coupon, the woman could have paid *fourteen dollars* plus *seventy-five cents tax*. (C) *Seventeen dollars* is mentioned in the dialog, but it is not the total amount.

79. (B) The man complains about the *flickering light*. *Flicker* means continually going *on and off*. (A) *Switch* is repeated in both the dialog and the option, but with different meanings. The man is not expected to change the hours he works. (C) *Fluorescent lights* is repeated in both the dialog and the option, but we do not know whether he likes them or not. (D) The *electrician* would not have shown up yet because she has not been called out.

80. (D) The man cannot find building number 1801. (A) The man has found *Calvert Street*, but he cannot find a particular house there. (B) He has the *telephone number* and plans to call, but has not done so yet. (C) *Across the street* is repeated, but there is no mention of an *event* being moved.

PART IV

81. (D) The *Neighborhood Corps* is hosting a *fund-raiser*. Fund-raisers raise money. (A) The fund-raiser is intended to *benefit* home builders. (B) *Oklahoma City National Bank* may be *involved* in this restoration project, but it is not named as the fund-raiser. (C) The *Macomb Club* is the location of the fund-raiser.

82. (B) The organization restores and builds homes in the *Bedford area*. (A), (C) and (D) are all mentioned in the announcement, but none of them is the correct option.

83. (B) The Neighborhood Corps is made up of *local Woodside residents* who are *volunteers*. (A) *Restoring* and *building* could be associated with *construction*, but it is not *construction workers* who make up the Corps. (C) *Low-income families* benefit from the work to their homes, but they do not make up the group. (D) *Architects* are associated with *building*, but this is not the correct answer.

84. (D) Researchers are looking for the *long-term effects* of the radiation. (A) There is no mention of *reports* from radiation victims, although such reports could help the researchers. (B) The *cause* of the accident is not mentioned, although it may interest some researchers. (C) *Fall-out* is repeated in both the report and the option, but the *exact amount* is not mentioned.

85. (C) The report says that humans did suffer *genetic damage*. (A) *Passed on* and *offspring* are repeated in the report and the option. Also, *defects* are associated with *genetic damage*. However, it is not known if this will occur. (B) We do not know if the number of human offspring *has declined*. (D) Areas of white feathers have appeared on *birds*.

86. (A) Birds near the accident had high incidences of a condition, which appears as *splotches of white feathers*. *Splotches* means *areas*. (B) In the report it is stated that birds with this condition are *generally weaker*. It does not mention that this is the case for those near the accident. (C) This option confuses the sound of *blotches* with *splotches*. (D) In the report it is stated that, in general, fewer birds with this condition are likely to reach *breeding age*. It does not specifically mention the age of those *near the accident*.

87. (C) The talk is for *business people* who are going to China. (A) *Chinese* is repeated, but the introduction is not for students of the language. (B) *Public* is repeated in both the introduction and the option. However, while *public relations personnel* may benefit from the talk, they are not specified as the audience. (D) *The Bank of China* is mentioned in the introduction, but not *bankers* in general.

88. (B) Mr. Yan gives *seminars* and *answers questions* about *manners and business protocol*. (A) *Customs agents* may be associated with *trade*, but we are not told that Mr. Yan has ever been one. (C) Mr. Yan is answering questions from people who are *going* to the convention. He is not *managing* the convention. (D) Mr. Yan is connected with the *Bank of China*, but the *seminars* he gives are not about banking.

89. (D) The notice explains how to get a free credit history report. (A), (B) and (C) This notice is not about *applying for credit*, *keeping good credit*, or *correcting bad credit*.

90. (D) The *Fair Credit Reporting Act* requires creditors to give *information* to consumers who have been *denied credit*. (A) Keeping the bureaus *in business* is not how the act serves consumers. (B) Ensuring that all credit checks are reported is not the Act's concern. (C) *Credit* and *debt* may be associated, but this help is not given.

91. (C) The credit bureau may be asked to provide a copy of the credit report. (A) *Refund* may be associated with *free*, and *agency* is repeated in both the notice and the option. However, this option is not correct. (B) We are not told the creditor may be asked to review any data. (D) *Thirty days* is repeated in both the notice and the option, but this is the length of time someone has to *request* a full credit report.

92. (C) Water treatment facilities are going to be built this year in *Port Pacifica*. (A), (B) and (D) These options are all mentioned in the story, but none of them is correct. (A) *Japan* is the location of the *Ebara Corporation*. (B) *Sweden* is where *Vinacon*, a construction firm, is based. (D) *Brazil* is a site for future work.

93. (C) Ebara, the *Japanese* company, is using its *own breakthrough treatment technology*. (A) *Brazil* is a site for future work, it is not where the method was developed. (B) *Vietnam* sounds similar to *Vinacon* and could be confused. (D) *Vinacon* is a *Swedish* firm, but Sweden is not where the method of treatment was developed.

94. (C) *Vinacon* is a *construction firm*. (A) *Waste disposal* is mentioned in the story as a business the firms intend to enter. (B) It is intended that *water treatment facilities* be built, but this is not the kind of company *Vinacon* is. (D) While this project will surely require a huge *investment*, this topic is not mentioned in the story.

95. (C) The speaker is addressing the *ladies and gentlemen* of a theater *audience*. (A) *Ladies and gentlemen* would be a reasonable way to address *dignitaries*, however, this is not the correct option. (B) *Theaters* and *actors* are associated, but it is not actors who need to be given this type of information. (D) *Electronic devices* are named as being disruptive, but the listeners are not *manufacturers*.

96. (D) The speaker asks the audience to turn off devices and attend to children who could *cause disruption*. (A) *Cast members* is repeated in the talk and the option, but there is no mention of them being *professionals*. (B) Theaters often need *donations*. However, this request is not made. (C) The theater is relatively *new* being in its *fourth year*, but this is not the point of the talk.

97. (B) *Sweets* means *desserts*, and *beverages* refers to *coffee*. (A) *Tickets* and *T-shirts* are likely sale-items at a play, but these are not mentioned. (C) *Pagers* and *beepers* are mentioned as causes of *disruption*. They are not for sale. (D) *Proceeds* and *benefits* are often associated with theaters, but they are not something you can buy.

98. (D) The announcement is aimed at commuters in their cars, so we can guess that it is on the *radio*. (A) TV sometimes broadcasts traffic updates, but this announcement directly addresses the commuters themselves – the people in their cars. (B) *Sports events* are full of fast-paced announcements like this one, but in this case, there is no reference to sport. (C) Apart from the mention of music, there is no reason to think this announcement might take place in a *theater*.

99. (A) The broadcast is for *drivers* in their cars. (B) *Rush, a turtle's pace*, *slow-downs*, and *stop and go* may be associated with sports and athletes, however, this option is not correct. (C) The *Rolling Stones'* song, *Satisfaction*, might attract *music-lovers*, but they are not the target of the broadcast. (D) *Police officers* may be concerned with traffic conditions, but the broadcast is not aimed at them.

100. (B) The traffic is so bad that one could only feel *frustrated*. (A) Because lots of places are mentioned, you might think *worldly* is a good option. However, *wordly* means *experienced*, or having knowledge of the world. Therefore it is not an appropriate answer. (C) *Loosening your tie* and *enjoying the music* may sound *encouraging*, but the news which follows is not encouraging at all. (D) *Manipulated* is not a reasonable option.

PART V

101. (B) The gerund *marketing* is used as a noun. (A) *Marketing* does not take the plural ending *-s*. (C) *Markets* is a noun, but is not used to refer to the job title. (D) *Marketed* is the past participle.

102. (D) The verb *invited* is followed by the infinitive *to include*. (A) *Include* is the base form of the verb. (B) The prepositional phrase *for inclusion* is followed by another preposition, *in*. (C) *Including* is the gerund form.

103. (A) The *if*-clause is followed by *would* plus the base form. (B) *Will* indicates the future tense and is not used in this type of conditional sentence. (C) and (D) *Was collapse* and *were collapse* are incorrect forms.

104. (A) The expression is *to base an opinion on something*. (B) *Think our opinions* is repetitive. (C) and (D) You *have an opinion* or *give an opinion* on a particular subject.

105. (A) The base form of *make* follows the modal, *can*. (B) *Cause* could be used if followed by the infinitive *to seem*. (C) *Put* is not logical. (D) *Appear* is a synonym of *seem* and would therefore be redundant.

106. (D) *Analyze* means *to examine and study*. (A) *Empathize* means *to understand or identify with another person*. (B) *Catalyze* means *to cause a reaction*. (C) *Symbolize* means *to represent*.

107. (B) The zero conditional, describing a general truth, uses the simple present tense, *erodes*. (A) *Would erode* would be used if the verb in the *if*-clause were in the past tense. (C) The simple past is not used in the result clause of conditional sentences. (D) With a general truth, the future progressive, *will be eroding,* cannot be used.

108. (B) The simple present verb form, *persists* is needed. (A) *Persistence* is the noun form. (C) *Persisting* is the gerund form. (D) *Persistently* is the adverb form.

109. (D) The plural noun *decisions* is needed. (A) *Decisive* is an adjective. (B) *Deciding* is a gerund. (C) *Decides* is the third person singular form of the verb.

110. (A) *In* is the correct preposition to describe where. (B), (C) and (D) *For, at* and *over* are not the correct prepositions to use in this context.

111. (C) *Restored* means *to bring something back to its original form*. (A) *Reconstituted* means *to reorganize or restore to its original state*. (B) *Restructured* means *to change the organization of something*. (D) *Redone* is a past participle, not a simple past form.

112. (D) The simple past *explained* is needed. (A) *Explaining* is the progressive form. (B) *Are being explained* is the passive voice in the present progressive tense. (C) *Had been explained* is the passive voice in the past perfect tense.

113. (B) An *installment loan* is one in which the borrower repays the loan in regular amounts. (A) *Increment* means *a slight increase*. (C) *Internment* means *being confined*. (D) *Involvement* means *participation*.

114. (B) *As* is a synonym of *because* and explains the *two-week delay*. (A) *Ever since* is used to explain a cause. (C) The verb *was exhausted* would follow the conjunction *whenever*. (D) *Until* makes the sentence illogical.

115. (C) *Cable* is used as an adjective to describe what type of companies. (A) The noun is plural; however, the adjective used to describe the noun does not take a plural ending. (B) *Cabling* is a gerund. (D) *Cabled* could be used as an adjective; however it would mean that the companies were cabled, not that the company made cables.

116. (C) Employees *work under* certain conditions. (A) *Beneath* is not used in combination with *work* in this context. (B) *Besides* means *in addition to; beside* means *next to*. (D) *Over* is not used with *work* in this context.

117. (A) A comparison uses the conjunction, *than*. (B) and (D) *Until* and *from* are not used to make a comparison. (C) *Beside* is sometimes used to compare objects, but not *besides*.

118. (D) *No* is used as a determiner to describe *amount*. (A) *None* is a noun. (B) *Not* is an adverb. (C) *Such* is illogical in this sentence.

119. (D) *Quite* is an adverb meaning *fairly* or *to some extent*. (A) *Greatly* and *keenly* are adverbs; however, they are not used in this context. (C) *Moreover* is illogical.

120. (A) The future tense indicator *will* is followed by the base form of the verb, *lessen*. (B) *To lessen* is the infinitive. (C) *Will be lessened* is the passive voice. (D) *Lessening* is the progressive form.

121. (A) *Because* introduces a clause that explains why. (B) *So* introduces a clause that states why something else was done. (C) *Neither* is used with *nor* and refers to two or more objects. (D) *Or* indicates that there are two options, which is not the case in this sentence.

122. (D) *Eating away at* means *reducing little by little*. (A) and (B) *Eating down* and *eating on* are not used. (C) *Eating through* is possible; however, it is not followed by *at*.

123. (B) The third person singular verb in the present tense, *is*, is correct. (A) *It is* repeats the subject. (C) If *unless* is used, a second clause is needed. (D) The conjunction *and* cannot be used in this context.

124. (A) *Every* modifies a singular noun. (B) and (D) *All* and *other* modify plural nouns. (C) When *individual* is used to modify a noun, it is preceded by an article.

125. (B) *Look forward to* means *to anticipate*. (A) *Look up to* means *to respect someone*. (C) *Look over to* indicates the direction in which to look. (D) *Look above to* is not a correct combination.

126. (A) *Whereas* is a conjunction introducing a contrast or contradiction. (B) *Because* is used to explain why something happened. (C) *In case* means *in the event of*. (D) *Should* in this context means the same as *if*.

127. (A) Buying and selling describes an activity; therefore *something* is used. (B) *Somewhere* refers to a place. (C) *Somehow* indicates in some manner or way. (D) *Somewhat* means *to some extent* or *a little*.

128. (B) *Corruption* means *dishonesty*. (A) *Interruption* and *disruption* refer to breaking the continuity of, or upsetting, something. (C) An *eruption* is when something explodes.

129. (D) The preposition *of* is used to show possession. (A) and (B) *With* and *to* do not indicate possession. (C) The ballroom is *in* the hotel, not *on* the hotel.

130. (D) *Guarantee* is the verb form; the base form follows *can*. (A) *Guarantor* is the person. (B) *Guaranty* is a noun. (C) *Guaranteed* is the past participle.

131. (B) The article *the* refers to a specific object. (A) The article *a* does not specify which software, and the indefinite article cannot be used with an uncountable noun. (C) and (D) *These* and *those* are used for plural nouns.

132. (B) Prices go up or *increase*. (A) *Enlargement* means to make bigger, but is not used in reference to prices. (C) and (D) *Progress* and *growth* are synonyms, but are not used in this context.

133. (D) *As a result of* introduces a clause to explain the cause of an effect. (A) and (B) *With respect to* and *in regard to* refer to the subject that is being discussed. (C) *In light of* is similar in meaning to *as a result* ; however, it is not used in this context.

134. (B) *Draw up* means *to write out*. (A) *Draw out* means *to make something longer*. (C) *Draw in* means *to get shorter* (as in *the days are drawing in*). (D) You can *draw on* a piece of paper.

135. (B) *Renovation* means *rebuilding* or *restoring*. (A) *Fabrication* means *building* and would not form a logical combination with the word *original*. (C) *Manifestation* is something that is obvious or clear. (D) *Calculation* refers to numbers and is illogical.

136.(C) The verb *put* completes the set expression, *put it in writing*, meaning *to write something down*. (A) *Put off* means *to postpone*. (B) *Put away* means *to put something in a place of keeping*. (D) *Put up with* means *to tolerate*.

137. (D) *Will have been turned on* is the passive voice, in the future, as indicated by the expression *by that time*. (A) and (B) *Will* and *should* would be followed by the base form of the verb. (C) *By that time* indicates the future, whereas *is being* is the present progressive.

138. (A) *Would* is followed by the perfect infinitive, *have* plus the past participle, in this type of conditional sentence. (B) and (C) The past participles *had* and *done* are not used after *would*. (D) The past tense *did* does not follow *would*.

139. (C) *They* is the subject of the verb phrase *could not work*. The pronoun refers back to *employees*. (A) *Them* is not a subject pronoun. (B) The pronoun *he* refers to a singular, masculine noun. (D) *Those* is used to identify a specific group.

140. (D) The understood subject in the sentence is *you* and therefore the object pronoun, *me*, is used. (A) The pronoun *she* refers to *my wife*, so it is illogical. (B) *Us* refers to the husband and the wife, so it would be repetition. (C) *I* is the subject pronoun.

PART VI

141. (B) The infinitive form *to greet* is required, to express purpose. (A) The adjective *several* describes how many *delegates*. (C) *Ambassador* is a noun and identifies who will be greeted. (D) *Before the concert* is a prepositional phrase referring to the time period.

142. (B) When preceding a noun, *tax* is used as an adjective and does not carry the plural ending. (A) *Erroneously* is an adverb, meaning *mistakenly*. (C) *Wrong* modifies *agency*. (D) *Over* is a preposition describing the time span.

143. (D) The preposition *for* cannot end the sentence; *typed up* could be used. (A) *Simply* is an adverb, modifying the verb form *requested*. (B) *That the results* answers 'requested what?' (C) The subjunctive form *be* follows *requested that ...* .

144. (C) *It* repeats the subject *country*. (A) The prepositional phrase *by the time* indicates when. (B) *Is paid off* is the passive voice. (D) *In interest* is a prepositional phrase followed by the adverb *alone*, meaning that the two million dollars will just be interest.

145. (C) The superlative form *least* is needed, as the price of all pencils is being compared. (A) *Thousands* tells us how many *pencils*. (B) The conjunction *so* is used to explain why something was done. (D) *Ones* is a pronoun referring to the plural noun, *pencils*.

146. (D) The noun *economy* should be used. (A) *Work* is used as an adjective to describe which *force*. (B) *Integral* is an adjective, meaning that it is necessary for completeness. (C) *Of* is a preposition.

147. (A) The active voice *have regained* is needed. (B) *They* refers to *retailers* and *lost* is the past tense. (C) *Last year's* identifies which *slump*. (D)*Economic* describes *slump*.

148. (D) *Accompaniment* is a noun; the adjective *accompanying* should be used. (A) The past tense verb *worked* is followed by the preposition *through*. (B) *In an effort* is a prepositional phrase. (C) *Nationwide*, meaning *across the country*, is an adjective describing *strike*.

149. (D) *Recover* means *to get back* and therefore *back* is redundant. (A) The adverb *carefully* modifies the participle *devised*, which in this sentence is used to modify the *marketing plan*. (B) *That Tara put together* is a relative clause giving more information about the plan. (C) *Were able to* is the past tense form.

150. (B) The passive uses the past participle *developed*; *development* is the noun form. (A) *Solar*, meaning *of the sun*, is an adjective describing *technology*. (C) *To keep pace* is a two-word verb in the infinitive. (D) *Developing* describes *countries*.

151. (D) To refer to *last summer*, *past* (not *passing*) is used. (A) *Half the cost* is 50%. (B) *Memorable* is an adjective describing *trip*. (C) *On* is the preposition used for boats.

152. (B) *These* is used when there is a specific group present; *those* is needed in this context. (A) *Usually* is an adverb modifying *issued*. (C) The preposition *of* is followed by the gerund *paying*. (D) The prepositional phrase *on time* indicates how.

153. (A) The past tense form *worked out* is needed. (B) The phrase *that would take* introduces the relative clause. (C) *Into* is a preposition indicating where. (D) *Heart of China* tells us where in China.

154. (B) The present perfect tense, *has doubled*, is required in a sentence referring to ongoing time. (A) *Activity* is the subject of the sentence. (C) *Due to* is a synonym for *because of*. (D) *Its* is a pronoun referring back to *market*.

155. (A) The singular form *is* is used for the non-specified object. (B) *How much* refers to the amount of tax. (C) *Pays* is the third person singular form of the verb, which agrees with the impersonal subject, *one*. (D) The preposition *by* follows the verb *determined*.

156. (B) *Etiquette* is a non-count noun and therefore the singular form of the verb, *is*, should follow. (A) *According to* is a preposition. (C) *From country to country* describes the scope of an activity. (D) *Even* is used to add emphasis.

157. (D) If *entire* is used with a plural noun, *floors*, then the article *the* is not used. (A) The conjunction *because* introduces a clause explaining why. (B) *Had warped* is the past perfect tense. (C) The verb *begin* is followed by the infinitive in this case.

158. (C) *Refunded* and *paid back* are synonyms and therefore one is redundant. (A) *At all*, meaning *in any way*, quantifies the amount of *dissatisfaction*. (B) *With the product* is a prepositional phrase. (D) *Upon request* indicates how the money will be refunded.

159. (A) The gerund form *fearing* is needed. (B) *Not as willing* indicates that investors were more willing before. (C) *That have characterized* introduces the relative clause. (D) *The last six months* describes a time period.

160. (C) *Not only* is followed by the conjunction *but*. (A) *Not only* introduces the first clause. (B) *Did* indicates the past tense and therefore *call in* is in the base form. (D) *Was due her* is another way of saying *she was owed*.

PART VII

161. (C) The article describes *agricultural pollution* and how the ESB plans to deal with it. (A) *The need to protect waterways* is understood, but is not the main topic. (B) The article is about ways to *prevent run-off*, not problems in preventing it. (D) *The effectiveness of water filters* is not mentioned.

162. (A) Farmers will receive *an annual payment* or *financial compensation*. (B), (C) and (D) *More land to use*, *guaranteed renters* and *new crops* are not mentioned.

163. (A) The writer wants to do *better than $18,500 a year*. (B) The memo states that *the last inspection* was done by Briggs. (C) *The need for safety* is understood but this is not the purpose of the memo. (D) *Insurance agent* is mentioned in the text, but the writer is not looking for one.

164. (D) Briggs *submitted a cost estimate* of $200–300 for installation of each smoke detector. (A) Briggs did an inspection of the warehouse; there is no mention that he *issued a warning*. (B) Briggs inspected the building for the purpose of insuring the building. He is not responsible for the level of *coverage*. (C) Briggs quoted figures on *smoke detectors* but we do not know if he *inspected smoke detectors*.

165. (B) The money was paid to have exclusive status which means that there is no *competition*. (A) Lawson hopes *to buy a major league team* in the future. (C) The text says: *if a stadium is built*. (D) Lawson still has to pay to *lease the stadium for another year*.

166. (C) The *investor group* is funding the activity. (A) Lawson is an executive of a *computer company*. (B) *The state* is not mentioned. (D) *The New York Baseball Club* is the name of the future team.

167. (A) The stadium is *to be built by the state*. (B) *The New York Baseball Club* is an investor group. (C) *The stadium authority* has made an agreement with the New York Baseball Club. (D) Lawson is trying to buy *a major league team*.

168. (C) There is a manufacturing plant in *Seoul*. (A), (B) and (D) There are offices in *Pusan*, *Atlanta* and *Bonn*.

169. (D) The advertisement says that IRC *is a leader in the field of laptop computers.* (A) There is no mention of the *customer service* being the best. (B) IRC will expand over the next *three years.* (C) The central office is in Brisbane, Australia, not *Malaysia.*

170. (C) There are *2000 software* employees. (A) There are *4,500 sales and marketing* employees. (B) There is no mention of the number of *manufacturing* employees. (D) There are *2,500 clerical and financial,* or administrative, employees.

171. (A) The first sentence of the last paragraph indicates the purpose: *to request a refund.* (B) Ingrid knows that the *$400* was an overcharge. (C) The gate has already been *installed.* (D) The wall has been *complimented* on by neighbors, but it is not the purpose of the letter.

172. (B) The first sentence indicates that she first tried to reach him *by phone.* (A) She says that if she does not hear from him, she will contact *her lawyer.* (C) *E-mail* is not mentioned. (D) She is sending this letter by *registered mail.*

173. (C) She paid $5,500 plus a $400 overcharge. (A)*$4,000* is not mentioned. (B) *$5,500* was the agreed-upon price. (D) *$6,000* would be the agreed-upon price of $5,500 plus the repair of $500.

174. (A) The third paragraph says that *old fittings ... [must] ... be rearranged.* (B) There is no mention of *buying a new gate.* (C) The repairs will cost *$500 more.* (D) The wall must be opened, not *taken down.*

175. (C) The first sentence states that the report is *concerned primarily with construction of homes.* (A) There is no mention of *the rate of success of previous construction efforts.* (B) Some of the older housing needs repair, but the report does not *criticize the housing conditions in Haiphong.* (D) *Industrial activity* is mentioned, but is not the main topic.

176. (A) *The availability of public transportation* is not mentioned. (B), (C) and (D) The second sentence mentions economic activity, or *industrial activity, population growth,* and *current housing facilities.*

177. (A) The population of corporate Haiphong was *724,000.* (B) Metropolitan Haiphong's population was *922,000.* (C) *1,646,000* was the combined populations. (D) *198,000* is not mentioned.

178. (D) *25%* of the housing is *dilapidated* or in need of *repair.* (A) *10%* is the possible home construction increase. (B) *11%* was the increase over the Vietnam census figure. (C) The city's living area increased by *13%.*

179. (C) The Hunddei plant will *further develop the economy.* (A) There is no mention of *a rise in the price of homes in the area.* (B) Home construction should *go up 5–10%.* (D) There is no mention that *the company will help subsidize the repair of dilapidated homes.*

180. (A) Bulk trash will be picked up only *from residences that are serviced by the city for regular pick-ups.* (B) There is no *written application* mentioned. (C) *Items such as doors, broken chairs or pieces of machinery are* (also) *permissible.* (D) Not *anyone with non-combustible bulk trash* may have trash picked-up.

181. (A) *Turpentine* is a solvent. (B), (C) and (D) *Metal fence poles, transmission parts* and *doors* are acceptable items for bulk trash pick-up.

182. (C) Trash should be placed outside *after 6 p.m.* on the previous day. (A) *4 p.m.* is the closing time of the Environmental Safety Section. (B) *Do not place items outside for pick-up before 6 p.m.* (D) The Environmental Safety Section opens at *8 a.m.*

183. (B) The first sentence tells readers to be advised of the *changes in international travel.* (A) There is no mention of *construction work at Dorval airport.* (C) There are different airports, but not *additional services.* (D) There is no change *in the bus schedules.*

184. (D) The second sentence tells readers to *check* or *review their tickets carefully.* (A) The changes take effect *on September 20.* (B) *Charter flights* will leave from Dorval. (C) *Parking near the airport* is not mentioned.

185. (B) The code 'VRV' indicates Mirabel and 'TMT' indicates Dorval. (A) The purpose of the notice is to warn travelers that arrivals may be at a different airport from departures. (C) All *charter flights leave from Dorval*; it does not say where they land. (D) You could ask *an airport ticket agent,* but they will not provide reports.

186. (B) *A convenient shuttle bus connects Dorval and Mirabel and the city center.* (A) *Arriving passengers* may not land at the *airport of departure.* (C) You should not *leave your car at the airport you depart from* because you may land in another airport. (D)*Parking only in designated areas* is not mentioned.

187.(C) The first line states that the service *protects one's credit cards.* (A) The form is to sign up for the service, not to *extend the length of the card's validity.* (B) *The Watchguard* is a service, but you *subscribe* to a magazine. (D) There is no mention of the ability to *apply for additional debit cards.*

188. (D) Three years, at *$41.00,* is the longest time mentioned. (A) The form says *send no money,* which means you will be billed at a later date. (B) *$13.00* is the saving over three years. (C) *$18.00* is the price for one year.

189. (C) The last sentence says *in the membership kit I will be sent.* (A) The credit card account number is mentioned but not a *membership number.* (B) The customer's card will be charged; he will not receive a *bill.* (D)There is no mention of a *duplicate credit card.*

190. (B) The two tables indicate *the cost difference:* $15,000 vs. $1,250 (A) Only the first table *illustrates how much is being spent on wages.* (C) The second table does not show *how many days are spent.* (D) There is no *additional step shown if a printer is used.*

191. (D) The second chart shows *25 changes a month.* (A) *$.10* is the cost per change and the cost per mailing. (B) *$15 per day* is the wage for the worker. (C) *20* is the number of years.

192. (A) *$.10* is the cost per mailing. (B) *12* is the number of months. (C) *$15 per day* is the wage for the worker. (D) *25* is the number of changes per month.

193. (C) The subject line says: *Adherence to company policy*, which means that there is *an established procedure.* (A) *Membership of professional organizations* is encouraged; however, it is not the purpose of the memo. (B) *The use of uniforms* is not mentioned. (D) The subject line indicates that this is not a *new policy.*

194. (D) The company pays half the membership fees which means it *subsidizes membership.* (A) There is no indication that the *reimbursement process is being streamlined.* (B) *Employee benefits* remain the same. (C) The reimbursement voucher is taken to *the cashier's office.*

195. (A) The employee completes the voucher using *Form 33R5*; department heads will *sign* this voucher. (B) The department heads make sure that membership in an organization benefits the company, but the *fees* are not mentioned. (C) The employee *processes the paperwork.* (D) The department head does not interact with these organizations.

196. (A) Form 33R5 is used for *a reimbursement voucher* or to be *recompensed.* (B) A *specific membership form* is not mentioned. (C) *Department approval* is given before Form 33R5 is filled out. (D) There is no mention of *certain fees being waived.*

197. (C) The article is about the new countries admitted to ASEAN, so the main point is that *the membership is growing.* (A) The new member countries have *experienced civil unrest*; however that is not the main point. (B) There is no mention *that SLORC's position is weakened.* (D) There is no mention that *ASEAN tariffs have changed.*

198. (D) Cambodia will have low tariffs on exports, thereby *opening doors to economic cooperation.* (A) There is no mention of *enhanced trade with the European Union.* (B) *Opponents of the SLORC party* are mentioned, but not in relation to Cambodia. (C) Membership will lower not *raise tariffs.*

199. (C) The new countries have *10 years in which to lower their tariffs.* (A) Tariffs should be lowered, not *relinquished.* (B) *Proposing any needed changes to CEPT* is not mentioned. (D)The benefits of AFTA come into effect in *1998.*

200. (A) The first sentence in the last paragraph says that the goal has been *to have all nations of Southeast Asia as a part of its organization.* (B) There will be a ceremony in *Kuala Lumpur.* (C) There are now *ten member countries.* (D) The *European Union* did not want the new members admitted.

Answer Key

Practice Test Four

In the following Answer Key, the first explanation provided for each question is the correct option.

PART I

1. (B) The *executive* is at his desk, talking on the phone. (A) *Receptionists* are associated with telephones and this man is on the telephone. However, he is reading his notes, not *taking a message* because he is not holding a pen. (C) The man in the picture may be a *manager*, but he is not *writing* anything. (D) The man on the phone is not an *entertainer*, he is a businessman. He may be reading a report, but there are no *reporters*, or journalists, in the picture.

2. (A) The *waiter* has a bottle in his hand and is going to *pour the beverage*. (B) The waiter is *serving* a drink, not *being served* a meal. (C) They're dining outside, but not *in front of mountains*. (D) The tables still have glasses, plates, condiments, etc. so it has not *been cleared*.

3. (D) The man is *operating*, or performing some function on, the machine. (A) The man is *sitting* on the chair, not *bidding*. The two words sound similar and could be confused. (B) *Resetting* sounds similar to *sitting*, and *ignition* is associated with engines and machinery. However, we cannot know for certain that this is what the man is doing in the picture. (C) His *watch* is on his wrist, he is not *handling*, or holding, it.

4. (C) The man is using a hose to fill the *tank* of the car with gasoline from the pump. (A) The man is at a *service station*, but there is no indication of whether or not the service is *good*. (B) There is no *water* coming out of the hose. (D) The man is filling his car with gas, he is not *washing* it.

5. (B) The *train* has either just arrived at, or is about to depart from, the *station*. (A) There is a *station* in the picture, but this option confuses the sounds of *trainee* and *train*. Nobody is visible in the picture at all. (C) This option is incorrect because there are no *passengers* on the platform of the station. (D) This option confuses the sounds of *plane* and *train*.

6. (B) The woman is looking at the selection of alcoholic beverages. (A) She is choosing a *bottle* of something, not a *jar*. (C) Her hand is resting on a *shelf*, not on *a cabinet*. There is no cabinet visible. (D) *Wine* is a type of alcohol, which is displayed on the shelves in the picture, but she is *looking* at it not *drinking* it.

7. (C) There is a bottle on the table by the man's right hand. (A) The man is using a *knife* and a *fork* to eat the meat, not a *spoon*. (B) There are *plates* on the table, which are *full*, but no *bowls*. (D) The table is *set* and there is a lot of food on the plates. Nobody is *clearing it away*.

8. (A) One man is operating the forklift to raise, or *lift*, the barrels, while the other man is helping to either get it in, or out, of the helicopter. (B) *Oil* is often stored in barrels, but nothing is being poured out of, or removed from, the one in the picture. (C) The *blade* on top of the helicopter is not *rotating*, or moving. (D) The aircraft in the picture is a *helicopter*, not a *jet*. The helicopter has already landed.

9. (C) The display material on the left is resting *on easels*, or wooden frames. (A) They're *having* a meeting, and they'll *adjourn*, or finish it later. (B) The people are sitting around a *large* desk, not a *small* one. (D) From the photographs and the diagrams on the board, the *training* appears to be for *engineers*, not *accountants*.

10. (C) The machines are supported by pieces of wood, or *lumber*. (A) The machines may have *engines*, but there is nobody in the picture *repairing* them. (B) No *wheel* in the picture is moving, or *rotating*, they are all held still by the wood. (D) *Belts* are associated with engines and machines, but there are no *broken belts* visible in the picture.

11. (C) The man is reading, or *checking*, the list of departures on the screen. (A) The man is reading the *departure information*, he's not about to get on a plane at the *departure gate*. (B) His bags are on a *trolley* in front of him, not on his *back*. (D) The screen he is looking at gives *information* about when planes leave, or depart, but we do not know anything specific about *his* plane.

12. (B) The *metal beams* are joined together, or *connected*. (A) *His joints* refers to the joints he has in his body (in the ankle, wrist, finger, etc.) rather than *joints* in a building (structural points that connect). The picture cannot give any information about his own joints. (C) *Seams* sounds like *beams*, but means something different, and there is nothing in the picture that could be *ripped*. (D) His foot is resting on a part of the *beam*, not on a *wall*. There is no wall visible.

13. (C) Trash bags are *piled up* against the buildings, on the sidewalk. (A) It is not possible to see what the women are *heading towards*, but *garage* sounds like *garbage* (trash), and therefore could be confused. (B) The trash has *already* been thrown out, it is in the bags waiting to be picked up. (D) *Waste* is a synonym for *garbage*, which is pictured, but the bags are on the street, not in a *trash can*.

14. (D) The woman is holding a *bottle* in her right hand and a *syringe* in her left hand. We assume she is a *scientist* because of the equipment and her clothing. (A) *Testing* is associated with experiments and scientists, but the woman is not a *lawyer*. (B) The woman may be a *sanitation worker* judging by her clothing, but she is filling the *syringe*, not a *dump*. (C) The woman might be a *nurse*, but she is not *making her rounds*, or seeing patients, in this picture.

15. (B) The man has a newspaper under his right arm. (A) The man is carrying an umbrella because it is raining, so it is obviously not a *sunny day. (C)* The *umbrella* is open in the picture, the man is using it, he is not *putting it away.* (D) This option is incorrect because the man is *wearing* a coat. He is not *taking it off.*

16. (D) There are lots of people sitting at tables in the square. (A) There are a lot of people in the picture and most of the tables are *full*, not *empty.* (B) The picture shows people *walking,* or *standing,* in the square, not *running through.* (C) There is a *crowd,* but there are no *police* and there is no need to control it.

17. (B) The people in the picture are helping to *build a house.* (A) The people are carrying something that looks like *wood,* but they are not *cutting trees down* in the picture. (C) The people on the ground have pieces of wood in their hands. (D) There are no *windows* visible in the picture.

18. (B) The picture shows that the ship in the *foreground* is *smaller* than the ship in the *background.* (A) The ship may be a *cruise ship,* but there is nothing to indicate it *is leaving the harbor.* (C) No sailors can be seen on board *either* ship, so this option is incorrect. (D) The *ships,* not the *shops,* are next to the dock.

19. (A) All of the *gates,* or entryways, are closed. (B) The picture shows *gates,* not *wooden doors.* (C) This entrance *may* be guarded at night, but it is daytime in this picture, so we have no way of knowing. (D) *Enclosed* sounds like *closed,* and could be easily confused. The road in this picture is too wide to be a *passage.*

20. (A) *Both* of the women have hair which is quite *short* and *wavy,* or curly. (B) *Both* women are wearing *jewelry.* The woman who is sitting down is wearing a necklace and the other woman is wearing a watch. (C) One of the women is standing, but next to a *desk,* not *on a stage.* (D) Both of the women are *smiling.* They are not *unhappy.*

PART II

21. (B) According to the schedule, the charter bus leaves at 6 p.m. (A) *Bus* is repeated. *Left* is the past tense of *leave,* but the words are used with different meanings. (C) *Six* is repeated, but the question refers to *time*, not *quantity.*

22. (C) The appointment *was* at nine, but there is no problem. We can guess that the speaker has arrived late to the appointment. (A) This is an attractive option because *no* is a common answer to a tag question. However, *appointment* and *point* are confused because they have the same root, but different meanings. (B) *Appointment* sounds similar to *meant it* and could be easily confused.

23. (A) The lamps are *so popular* they sold out immediately. (B) *Popular* is used in both the question and the option, and *item* sounds like *I am.* However, the question is not about a person. (C) *I* is a common response to a question with *you,* but the question is not about literally finding something.

24. (C) The respondent has never noticed how much the

gas tank holds. (A) *Much* and *hold* are both repeated, but the option does not answer the question. (B) *Tank* is repeated, but the question remains unanswered.

25. (B) The respondent would consider leasing a car *if* the company paid for it. The TOEIC often has qualified responses like this one. Rather than a simple *yes* or *no,* you learn the speaker's conditional response. (A) *Lease* is repeated, but the option does not answer the question. (C) *Consider* and *considerate* may be confused because they have the same root, but their meanings are different.

26. (C) The respondent did help to renovate the store, by hanging the wallpaper. (A) *They* is a logical response to a question with *them. Store* is used in both the question and the option, but with different meanings. (B) *Store* is repeated, but this option does not answer the question.

27. (C) The loudspeaker would be tested outside, but it is *raining* so it cannot be. (A) *Test* is repeated in the question and the option, but the option refers to a *written* test. Also *outside* and *inside* might be confused. (B) *Loudspeaker* sounds similar to *speak to her* and could be confused.

28. (B) The respondent knows which paper to buy because it is written on the order form. (A) This option confuses *by* with *buy.* (C) *Paper* is repeated, but this option would answer *when?*

29. (C) The respondent was present for *part* of the sales meeting. (A) This option would be a logical answer to a question about a *future* sales meeting. The question refers to a *past* meeting. (B) *Meeting* is repeated, but the answer refers to the *future* and the meeting has already happened.

30. (B) Demand falls off suddenly because of a drop in sales during the Autumn. (A) *Demands* and *sudden* are both used in the option, but with different meanings so it does not answer the question. (C) *So suddenly* can be associated with not giving somebody any notice. However, this option does not answer the question.

31. (C) The respondent is not altogether comfortable. In particular, he would prefer a *lower monthly payment.* (A) *Comfortable* is often associated with the fit of clothing, but shoes are not being asked about. (B) *Comfortable* is associated with *relaxing,* but *this arrangement* would be answered by *it*, not *they.*

32. (C) The glue is in the drawer. The speaker implies the answer *Yes, I have glue* by giving its location. (A) *To do* sounds like *glue,* but this option does not answer the question. (B) *No* is a logical reply to a *do?* question and the verb *have* is repeated. The reference to a color is because *glue* might be confused with *blue.* However, this option does not answer the question.

33. (B) The position has been offered and turned down. Mrs. Dano was not interested. (A) *Lying down* is a physical position, but the *position* referred to in the question relates to a job. (C) *Offer* is repeated, but the question refers to Mrs. Dano, not the respondent.

34. (A) The item is already being shown *at cost*, so there could be no lower price range. *At cost* refers to the price that the store paid to acquire the item. (B) *Show* is used in both the question and the option, but with different meanings. The question is not concerned with a theater performance. (C) *Lower range* is repeated, but the question remains unanswered.

35. (C) She has just been promoted to art director. (A) *Art* is used in both the question and the option, but the option refers to a man's work (*his*) rather than a woman's. (B) *Director* is used in the question and *direct* in the option. However, the pronoun changes from *she* to *he*, and the question is about *art* not *musicals*.

36. (B) Now that she has passed the bar, she is able to start practising law. The *bar* refers to an examination for becoming a lawyer. (A) *No* is a logical response to *did you know?* and *know* and *no* sound alike. However, a bar which sells drinks is inferred in the option, not a legal examination. (C) This option confuses the sounds of *pass the ball* with *pass the bar*, so it is incorrect.

37. (A) They will speak with hospital personnel tonight when they meet. (B) *Spoke* is used and *hospital* is repeated. However, this option does not answer the question. (C) This option confuses the words *hospital* and *hospitable*, but the question is not about staying in an inn.

38. (A) The *exposure* that the media would bring is the reason they should be invited. (B) *Media* sounds like *middle*, and *invited* is repeated, but *management* is not the topic of the question. (C) *Invited* could be associated with *go together*. However, the topic is the media.

39. (C) It *is* the Taj Mahal, and the respondent finds it *remarkable*. (A) This option does not answer the question. (B) *It's* is a logical response to the tag, *isn't it?* However, being *comfortable* is not relevant.

40. (A) The department's performance was so good that the speaker is recommending bonuses for the *whole team*. (B) *Performance* is associated with *show* and *intermission*. However, this option is incorrect. (C) *Thinking* is repeated, but the option does not answer the question.

41. (B) There is no reason to have someone else look at it, as the respondent trusts this person's judgment. (A) *Look at it* might be confused with *see it*, but this is not an appropriate response to the question. (C) *Looking* and *someone* are repeated, but the question is not answered correctly.

42. (C) If they ordered a six-month supply, they would probably get a discount. (A) *Six-month* might be confused with *six-man*. (B) *Supply* is used in both the question and the option, but the contexts are different.

43. (A) The marketing department has *already* been notified. The speaker just finished talking to them on the phone. (B) *Marketing* and *market* might be confused. (C) *Notify* is used in the question and *notified* in the option, but the police are not the topic.

44. (B) A translating service may be found on *Hilton Street*. (A) *Service* is repeated, but the option does not answer the question. (C) *I found* is a logical response to *where can I find?* but clothes are not the topic.

45. (C) An office will be opening in either Hong Kong or Japan. (A) *Open* is repeated, but the office has not yet been opened, so it cannot be *kept open*. (B) *Hong Kong* is a *port* city. However, this option confuses the words *office* and *officers*.

46. (A) The new engine is more efficient because it uses less fuel. (B) *Efficient* is associated with *on time*, but nobody's arrival is being asked about. (C) *Engine* is used in the question and the option, and *old* is the opposite of *new*. However, this option does not answer the question.

47. (C) A membership application can be applied for over the phone if you have a major credit card. (A) *Membership* is associated with *price*, but cost is not being asked about. (B) This option might cause confusion because *membership* and *ship* have the same root, and *remember which ship* sounds like *membership*, but boats are not the topic of the question.

48. (B) The return-trip reservations have *already* been made, or taken care of, according to what the speaker knows. (A) *Trip* is repeated, however the question implies the trip is in the *future* whereas this option refers to a *past* trip. (C) *Return* is used in both the question and the option, and *you* is a logical answer to a question with *who's?* However, this is not the correct option.

49. (A) The respondent bought more books than he should have. (B) *Reference books* are associated with a *library*, but you do not *buy* books in a library. (C) *Bookstore* is associated with buying books, and *spent* is associated with *buy*. However, the question is about spending *money*, not *time*.

50. (C) The writing style does look familiar, but the respondent cannot place, or *identify*, it. (A) This option confuses the sounds of *writing style* and *ride side-saddle*. (B) *Knew immediately* is a logical response to *don't you recognize?* However, this option does not answer the question.

PART III

51. (C) *Car*, *shop*, *mechanic*, and *wrong* are all associated with a *broken down automobile*. (A) *Shop* is associated with *buying*, but mechanics do not work on *bicycles*. (B) *Wrong with it* and *doctor* may be associated, but there is nothing else to indicate this. (D) *Shop* and *store* have the same meaning, but they are not discussing when it opens.

52. (B) The man cannot get a dog because his *wife* does not like them. (A) This option confuses the sounds of *beagle* (a type of dog) and *bagels* (a type of food). (C) The sounds of *shelf* and *myself* could be confused, but this option is not relevant to the question. (D) *He already has one* does answer the question, but according to this dialog, he does not.

53. (C) The *supermarket* closed down yesterday. (A) In the option, *street* is only mentioned in connection with the location of the supermarket. Also streets do not usually *close down*. (B) *Store* is repeated, but there is no mention of a *hardware store* in the dialog. (D) *Groceries* is mentioned in the dialog, but the *grocery store* has not closed down.

54. (B) *Couch* means *sofa*. (A) and (C) *Coffee table* and *desk* are mentioned in the dialog, but neither are new. (D) There is no mention of a bed in the dialog.

55. (C) John is still at his old job. This question may be confusing because the dialog uses the present progressive, *John is leaving the company*, to refer to the near future. He is not likely to be physically walking out of the company door as they speak. (A) John intends to *find* a new job, but he does not have one yet. (B) While *school* might be reason to leave one's job, there is no mention of this in the dialog. (D) John may be *between jobs* after he has left his old job, but at the moment he is still at his old job.

56. (A) The man has been *on a diet* for several months. (B) *Sickness* may explain why a person has lost weight, but it is not the reason in this dialog. (C) *Exercise* may explain why a person has lost weight, but it is not the reason in this dialog. The *woman* says she will try to exercise more. (D) He has been on a diet for several months, so he does know how he lost weight.

57. (B) Because the man is ordering food, we know that he is in a *restaurant*. (A) *School* may be associated with the subject of *French*, but *French* in the dialog refers to food. (C) *French* and *France* are related, but *French* in the dialog refers to food. (D) There is no mention of a *bank*.

58. (C) Betty thinks that the *dry cleaners* can get the ink stain out. (A) *Ballpoint pens* are associated with *leaks*, but Betty does not suggest he uses one. (B) *This weekend* is when the man has an important meeting, so he is unlikely to take time off then. (D) She does not suggest the important meeting be cancelled.

59. (D) The man needs a *pen* because his ran out of ink. (A) *Pencils* are related to *pens*, but this is not what he is asking for. (B) *Check* is repeated in both the dialog and the option, but with different meanings. (C) His pen *ran out* of ink, he does not need to *run an errand*.

60. (C) The woman was in Beijing for *six weeks*. (A) *Weeks* is mentioned, but she was there longer than just a *week*. (B) This option confuses *two* with *too*. (D) The woman was *supposed* to be in Beijing for a *couple of* (two) *months*, but in the end only stayed for *six weeks*.

61. (C) Susan's aunt is calling on the *telephone*. *Call back* indicates a phone call. (A) If she's on the phone and if Susan can call her back, she cannot be *in the room*. (B) *In the shower* is *Susan's* location, not the aunt's. (D) There is no mention of the *television*.

62. (C) The man cannot work out which cable belongs to which machine. He cannot *tell the cables apart*. (A) *Keyboard*, *printer*, *cable*, and *print out* are all associated with *computers*, but there is no mention of anything being *wrong* with the computer. (B) The man wants to *print* a report, but he does not say it is *late*. (D) *Phone* and *fax* are repeated in both the dialog and the option, and the woman once had her *phone and fax cables mixed up*, but that is not the current problem.

63. (B) The woman might go to Boston *this year*. (A) *Next week* is not mentioned. (C) *Autumn* means *Fall*, but this is mentioned by the *man*. (D) *Year* is mentioned in the dialog, but not *next year*.

64. (C) The woman thinks that *Mr. Dupont* got the job. (A) *Mr.* and *Mrs.* might be confused, but *Mrs. Dupont* is not mentioned. (B) *Carol* is mentioned in the dialog as somebody else who went for the job. (D) One of the speakers is a woman, but she did not get the job and we do not know if she applied for it.

65. (D) We know that they're in an *office*, because Rebecca just *stepped out of the office*. (A) *Copy machines* may be associated with *computers*, but there is no reference to the *computer lab*. (B) A *library* may have a *copy machine*, but these speakers refer to an office. (C) *Jam* may be associated with a *cafeteria*, but *jam* in the dialog refers to the paper being *stuck*.

66. (B) *Wallpaper, shelving,* and *kitchen and bathroom accessories* would all be found in a *home improvement store.* (A) *Kitchen accessories* are available in this store, but this is not a kitchen store because *bathroom accessories* and *wallpaper* are also available. (C) There is no *reference* to paint, and this store sells a variety of things, not just paint. (D) *Kitchen and bathroom accessories* may be found in a *plumbing store,* but not *wallpaper* and *shelving.*

67. (D) The man wants to choose a *cheaper* sweater, so he must think that this one is *too expensive.* (A) The man says he *likes* the color. (B) The man says it *fits well.* (C) The *quality* of the sweater is not mentioned.

68. (A) The speakers are playing to break the *tie.* This means the game was a *draw,* nobody won. (B) *Michelle* is the man's opponent, but she did not beat him. (C) *Rain* may be a likely reason for a rematch, but not in this case. (D) They played for *three hours,* but this is not mentioned as a reason for playing again.

69. (C) They are waiting for a table so they can eat a *meal.* (A) They have to wait in the *bar* for their table, so they may have a *drink,* but this is not what they are waiting for. (B) *Bar* could be confused with *car,* but there is nothing else to suggest they are waiting for a taxi. (D) These people have made a *reservation,* but it is for a *table,* not a flight.

70. (D) The man says his house is getting *cramped.* He wants to *make space* by building an *add-on.* (A) The woman describes the man's neighborhood as *great* and the man agrees, so he is unlikely to want to be moving. (B) The man has *already* started his own business. (C) The man *already* has a garage, but he may build *above* it.

71. (A) *Press five* refers to pushing an *elevator* button. (B) There is no mention of a *cafeteria.* (C) *Five* may be associated with a *golf course,* but this is not where they are. (D) *Law firm* is associated with *court,* but this option is incorrect.

72. (C) The woman is going to bed which suggests she is at home. She is going to miss the *show* and she asks the man to *tape* it for her. It must be a *TV show.* (A) A *play* is a *show,* but you cannot normally *record* one. (B) This option confuses the sounds of *new set* and *upset.* (D) *Computer games* are not mentioned.

73. (C) The woman offers to *put away the dishes.* (A) *Kitchens* and *dishes* are associated with *counters,* but this is not what the woman offers to do. (B) *Clean* is repeated in both the dialog and the option, but the *bathroom* is not mentioned in the dialog. (D) *Tables* are associated with *dishes,* but there is no mention of *clearing* one.

74. (B) The woman is expecting a *promotion,* because her boss told her she is *next in line* for one. (A) *Promotions* are associated with *jobs,* but the woman is not getting a *new job.* (C) *Promotion* and *higher* are associated. *Raise* and *higher* are associated. However, there is no mention of changing offices. (D) She has spoken to the boss *already,* she does not say she is going to have a meeting with him.

75. (D) *Tests, passing, failing* and *course* are all associated with *students.* (A) There is no mention of *designers.* (B) *Teachers* and *tests* are a logical connection, but teachers do not usually *take* tests. (C) Scientists *perform* tests, or experiments. It is not this type of test which is under discussion.

76. (B) The woman has realized that *sales are seriously down,* which at worst might lead to *bankruptcy court.* Therefore, the finances are *in bad shape.* (A) The man *went over* the reports, but there is no mention that any are *missing.* (C) *Immediately* means *right away. Go back* can mean *turn around.* However, this option is incorrect. (D) *Bank* and *bankruptcy* can be associated, and *court* is associated with *suing.* However, there is no mention that the bank is actually suing them.

77. (B) *Station, show,* and *listen* are associated with the *radio.* (A) This option confuses the verb *watch* which can be associated with a *show,* with the *watch* you can tell the time with. (C) *TVs* have *stations,* but you do not only *listen* to them. (D) *Fair* is repeated in both the dialog and the option, but with different meanings.

78. (B) *Candles* and *cake* are associated with a *birthday party,* and the woman says she does not know *how old* the person is. (A), (C) and (D) These options all refer to parties where a cake might be eaten, but *age* and *candles* would not be relevant at these parties.

79. (D) *Song, group* and *music* are all associated with a *rock group.* (A) *TV shows* are not mentioned. (B) *Movie stars* are not mentioned. (C) A song can *play,* but these speakers are not talking about a play you go to see.

80. (C) The woman is going to the *store,* and the man asks her to get, or buy, several items. (A) *Orange juice, cereal, milk* and *bread* are all associated with *breakfast,* but it is the *man* who wants these things. (B) *Orange juice* and *milk* might *go* in a *refrigerator,* but the *refrigerator* is not mentioned. (D) The *man* says what he needs, the *woman* isn't going to.

PART IV

81. (B) The speaker is announcing the *closing* of the offices for the long weekend. (A) Staff are asked to *leave* the monthly reports, but there is no reason to think they are being *printed out* right now. (C) The staff is being addressed, and *long* is repeated in both the announcement and the option. However, there is no suggestion that they are having a *long meeting*. (D) The *treasurer* is mentioned in the announcement, but we do not know what he or she is doing right now.

82. (D) Providing clients with *ads* for *TV, newspapers* and *magazines* is an indication of an *ad agency. Ad* is short for *advertisement.* (A) *TV* is mentioned in relation to ads, but the announcement is not taking place in a *TV station.* (B) *Financial* is related to *monthly reports* and *treasurer's desk,* but it is not a *financial company.* (C) *Newspaper* is mentioned in relation to ads, but the announcement is not taking place in a *newspaper office.*

83. (C) Staff may have to do some *overtime* in the coming week. *Overtime* means *working long hours.* (A) There is no mention of any TVs having to be repaired. (B) *Client* and *newspaper* are mentioned in the announcement, but it is the *ads* which are required. (D) It is the *Magazine ads* which need to be ready.

84. (B) The report is about the relationship between a *drug,* the *XR2 channel blocker,* and an *increased risk of breast cancer.* (A) The drug is *for* high blood pressure, but there is no mention of how to *detect* it. (C) The drug is *for* heart disease, but there is no mention of a *new treatment.* (D) The drug is referred to as *calcium channel blockers,* but there is no mention of the *nutritional need* for calcium.

85. (C) The report advises that women *continue taking the drug,* because the *potential merits may outweigh the risks.* (A) *Drug* and *twice* are both repeated in the report and the option, but there is no advice given about how often to take the drug. (B) Women over 65 are referred to in the report, but there are no recommendations given for other drugs. (D) The drug is referred to as *calcium channel blockers,* but women are not being advised to increase their *intake* of calcium.

86. (A) Women who took the drug ran *twice the risk* of developing breast cancer. (B) *Blood pressure* is repeated in both the report and the option, but there is no mention of it *increasing.* (C) *Outweigh* may seem to relate to putting on *extra weight,* but this is not the case. (D) *Increased* is repeated in both the report and the option, and *blood pressure* is associated with *stress.* However, there is no mention of *stress.*

87. (C) There was a *delay* in the *Paris airport* which affected Mr. Gupta's plane. (A) Mr. Gupta's flight *originated* from New Delhi, but we do not know if there were *take-off problems* there. (B) Mr. Gupta is *about to* give a talk, but we do not know if he had an *earlier engagement.* (D) There are *upcoming trade fairs* in India, but Mr. Gupta has not just been to one.

88. (D) Mr. Gupta will talk about the contribution of the trade fairs to India's *industrial prominence.* (A) *Fair* is repeated in both the report and the option, but with different meanings. There is no mention of a *court.* (B) India's economy *is* healthy, the dialog refers to its industrial prominence. (C) Leaders uniting behind India is not the message.

89. (C) Repair work on the *Biltmore Turnpike* is being completed. (A) Plans for the city are described, but these do not appear to be nearly finished. (B) *Shirley May* is a former *town councilwoman,* but no report is being made by the *town council* itself. (D) The *park* and the *construction of the boathouse* are at the *funding* stage.

90. (C) The notice says that an *all-volunteer commission* is working on plans for the park. (A) Shirley May is a *former town councilwoman,* but the *town council* is not involved. (B) *Park officials* are not involved. (D) *Parking* is mentioned, but there is no reference to *Highway authorities.*

91. (D) The park is referred to as a *Mystic Waterfront Park,* so *water* is its theme. (A) The park may *have* a botanical garden, but this is not mentioned. (B) *Parking* is referred to, but a *car park* is not the focus. (C) It is not a *zoological park.*

92. (A) Comptor's *first representative office in Spain* was opened in *March of last year.* (B) Another office is being opened in Barcelona now. (C) *Representative* is repeated in both the notice and the option, but there is no mention of the *Trade Council.* (D) Comptor is the *world's largest manufacturer* now. It does not say when they became this.

93. (C) *Comserve* is one of two *authorized distributors* for *Comptor.* (A) They will be *sponsoring* computer training, but they are not a *training institute.* (B) There is no mention of a *partnership.* (D) They will be *sponsoring* educational programs, but they are not a *research corporation.*

94. (C) *Future manufacturing* may be done in *Milan,* in Italy. (A), (B) and (D) These options are mentioned in the notice. However, none is mentioned as a possible future location for manufacturing.

95. (B) Because advice is being given about finding an apartment when a company relocates, we can assume that the listeners are *employees* of the *company.* (A) *Real estate offices* are mentioned as a source of information, but *agents* are not being addressed. (C) *Apartments* are mentioned in the talk, but *apartment managers* are not being addressed. (D) There is no reason to think that *entrepreneurs* are being spoken to.

96. (C) The speaker advises calling *real estate offices* for their *listings* of apartments. (A) Listeners are advised to *look at* ads in the local newspaper, not *place* them. (B) *Friends* and *business associates* are mentioned as possible sources of information. (D) *Kansas City* is where they are going, but they are not advised to move to its *outskirts.*

97. (B) *Tips* are associated with *assistance*. (A) *Cars* are only mentioned in relation to finding them in the classified ads. (C) They are advised to *contact* real estate offices, but *real estate* is not being directly *sold*. (D) They are advised to *look at* classified ads but these are not being *explained*.

98. (B) The advertisement promotes *Russian massage therapy*. (A) The method is called *Russian Sports Massage*, but there is no mention of a *sporting event*. (C) *Pharmaceutical drugs* are mentioned, but this advertisement is not for a new one. (D) *Physical therapists* are mentioned as having PhDs, but *educational techniques* are not discussed.

99. (A) Compared to the *drug-approach* of the rest of the world, Russia focused on the art of *natural healing*. (B) *Hundreds*, but not *all* Russian medical doctors were *trained* in massage. (C) The success of the massage therapy may *imply* more outpatient clinics, but this is not mentioned in the ad. (D) Physical therapists are mentioned as having PhDs in physical therapy, but we do not know if they have done *more* research in this field than others in the world at large.

100. (B) *Lymph activity* is not mentioned in the ad. (A), (C) and (D) These options are all specifically named as being affected by *Russian Sports Massage*.

PART V

101. (A) *To make headway* means *to make progress*.
(B) and (D) *Had* is followed by the past participle in the past perfect tense; *took* and *went* are the simple past forms.
(C) *Had* is illogical in this context.

102. (A) *Options* is the plural noun form. (B) *Opts* is the third person singular form of the verb. (C) *Optional* is an adjective. (D) *Opting* is the gerund form.

103. (D) *Season* refers to one part of the year.
(A) and (B) Both *era* and *epoch* refer to longer periods of time, usually many years. (C) *Course* does not refer to a period of time.

104. (B) *For the sake of* means *in order to help or achieve*.
(A), (C) and (D) *In, to* and *at* are incorrect prepositions.

105. (D) *Only* is an adjective that emphasizes uniqueness.
(A) *Alone* is not used as an adjective preceding a noun.
(B) *Single* is a synonym of *only;* however it is not used in this context. (C) *Lonely* is an adjective, but it means *without companions* or *isolated*.

106. (C) The verb *suggests* indicates a possibility.
(A) *States* refers to spoken or written words. (B) *Tells* could be used in this context, but only with an object.
(D) A person, not an object, *advises* another person.

107. (B) *Them* is the object pronoun for *they*. (A) *Their* is the possessive pronoun. (C) *They* is the subject pronoun.
(D) *Theirs* is a stand-alone pronoun indicating possession.

108. (A) The third person singular of the present tense, *mentions*, fits the context. (B) *Mentioning* is the gerund form and would leave the sentence without a main verb.
(C) and (D) *Has been mentioned* and *is being mentioned* are passive forms and are illogical.

109. (D) *Supplier* is the person who supplies materials or goods. (A) *Supplicant* is a person who begs, and is illogical.
(B) *Supporter* is a person who supports a political party, team, etc.; it does not fit the context. (C) *Suppressor* is someone who withholds information and is also illogical in this context.

110. (C) *To rise above* means *to overcome* or *to be capable of dealing with*. (A) The preposition *over* is not used with *rise*. (B) *Rise up* would not be followed by an object.
(D) *Rise on* is not a possible combination.

111. (D) *Unintelligible*, meaning *impossible to understand*, is the adjective form which follows the verb *is*.
(A) *Unintelligibly* is the adverb form. (B) *Unintelligibility* is the noun form. (C) *Unintelligent* is also an adjective form, but means *not intelligent*.

112. (B) *Many* is used with plural, count nouns. (A) *Much* is used with non-count nouns. (C) *Any* is used with the negative; as in *'there isn't any fruit.'* (D) *Less* is used with comparisons.

113. (C) Industry is singular and therefore the singular form of the present perfect, *has evolved*, is used. (A) *Evolution* is a noun, and in this sentence a verb is needed. (B) *Are evolving* is the plural form of the present progressive.
(D) *Have evolved* is the plural form of the present perfect.

114. (C) The sentence is in the past and the verb *to wear* is used in the progressive form, so the past progressive, *was wearing*, is correct. (A) *Was being worn* is the passive voice, and in this sentence the active is required. (B) *Will have worn* is the future perfect and does not follow the past tense form, *noticed*. (D) *Wearing* needs to be preceded by the correct form of the verb *to be,* in order to form the progressive tense.

115. (A) *Vacate* is a synonym of *leave*. (B) The apartment is left in good condition by someone else when you *move in*.
(C) You would not normally *escape from* an apartment.
(D) *Go out* is illogical in this context.

116. (C) *Out of order* is used to describe a machine or device that does not work, or is broken.
(A), (B) and (D) The sentence could be logically completed with *is not operating, performing* or *functioning again*, but not with the noun forms.

117. (A) *Liable* is a synonym of *responsible*. (B) The company could be *guilty of* something. (C) *Obligated* needs to be followed by an infinitive such as *to pay for* or by the preposition *to* plus an object. (D) The company might be *susceptible to* something.

118. (C) The conjunction *because* introduces a clause that explains the first clause. (A) *So* would introduce a clause referring back to the subject (I) of the first clause.
(B) If *which* is used, the pronoun *they* would not be used as it would be redundant. (D) *But* introduces a contradictory clause.

119. (C) *With* is the correct preposition to follow *luck*.
(A) and (B) *Throughout* and *among* are incorrect prepositions to use in this context. (D) *On behalf of* is followed by a person.

120. (D) *Out of court* is an idiom, meaning *without going to court*. (A) The noun *courthouse* refers to the physical building. (B) *Courting* is a gerund, meaning *dating*.
(C) *Courts* is the plural noun.

121. (C) *Prior to* is a synonym for *before* and is followed by a gerund. (A) *Ahead of* is generally followed by a noun, not a gerund. (B) *Beforehand* follows a verb or phrase.
(D) *Previously* is followed by a form of the past tense.

122. (A) *From ... to ...* is used to refer to a range of numbers. (B), (C) and (D) These prepositions would not be used in this context.

123. (A) *Enticed* means *to tempt or persuade*. (B) A person *teases* someone. (C) *Illustrated* is followed by *to*. (D) The sentence could read *... attracted him to the position*.

124. (C) *Helped out* is a separable two-word verb. *Each other* indicates that one trainee helped another, etc. (A) *One another* could be used, but not *another*. (B) *The other* is singular; however, the plural is needed. (D) *Other* needs to be followed by a noun.

125. (B) The *human resources* department in a company deals with matters involving employees. (A) *Resource* is the singular form of the noun. (C) *Resourcing* is the gerund. (D) *Resourceful* is an adjective.

126. (B) *Passing* is a gerund and is used as the subject of the sentence. (A) *Passes* is the third person, singular form of the verb. (C) *Pass* is the base form of the verb. (D) *Passed* is the past participle form.

127. (D) When you *pay attention to* something, you *observe it closely*. (A), (B) and (C) You do not pay *observation*, *notice* or *time* to something.

128. (A) The noun *information* follows the definite article. (B) *Information* is a non-count noun and the plural ending *-s* is not used. (C) *Informative* is the adjective form. (D) *Inform* is the base form of the verb.

129. (C) The base form of the verb, *do*, follows *would*. (A) The past participle, *done,* would need the correct form of the verb *have* in order to form the perfect tense. (B) The base form of the verb *to be* is needed before *able to do*. (D) The gerund *doing* does not follow *would*.

130. (B) *Former* is an adjective referring to an earlier time. (A) *Precedent* is a noun and is not used to modify *competitors*. (C) *Last* is illogical in this context. (D) *Sooner* is a comparative form, but no comparison is indicated in the sentence.

131. (A) In this case, *had* begins the sentence and forms part of the past perfect tense. (B) *Since* is used as a conjunction and would need to be followed by the subject (*he*) plus *had*. (C) If *should* is used, the following clause would need to refer to future time. (D) In order to use *were*, *become* would need to be omitted.

132. (D) *Delivering* is parallel with *making,* the other object of the verb *responsible for*. (A) *Delivered* is the past participle. (B) *Delivers* is the third person singular form of the verb. (C) *Deliverer* is a noun and refers to a person.

133. (B) The preposition *against* indicates that there is contact between objects. (A) The preposition *with* indicates that the objects moved together. (C) *Away* is an adverb that could be used with the preposition *from*, but would not be logical in this context. (D) *Crash behind the waves* is illogical.

134. (C) *Restoration* is a noun meaning *repairing something to its former condition*. (A) *Reinforcement* means *making something stronger* and is illogical in this context. (B) *Fabrication* means *invention*. (D) The gerund form *furbishing* is not followed by the preposition *of*.

135. (C) *Disaster* means a *great misfortune*. (A) *Disgust* is used to describe a feeling, not an event. (B) *Discord* means *disagreement*, which is not the appropriate word choice. (D) *Disclosure* means *to reveal or discover something*.

136. (A) *An air of expectation* is used to describe a mood in the room. (B) *A stillness of expectation* is not a possible combination. (C) *A moment of expectation* defines a specific time period. (D) *A scent of expectation* would describe a smell.

137. (D) *Taking* is the gerund form and used as the subject of the sentence. (A) The base form of the verb, *take*, is not used as a noun with an article. (B) *Taken* is the past participle. (C) *Take* is the base form of the verb.

138. (B) The two-word verb *chalked up* means to attribute something to something else. (A), (C) and (D) *Chalk* does not form a two-word verb with the prepositions *out, on* or *for*.

139. (C) An *impasse* is an inescapable situation or a standstill, and in this sentence, neither party could do anything. (A) *Impairment* is the spoiling of something. (B) An *impedance* is an obstruction. (D) *Implosion* is a collapse inward and is not used in this context.

140. (C) *Ravaged* is the past participle and is used with the form of the verb *to be*, to form the passive voice. (A) *Ravage* is the base form of the verb. (B) *Ravaging* is the gerund form of the verb. (D) *Ravages* is the third person, singular form of the verb.

PART VI

141. (A) *Even though* is needed in this context, to form a conjunction. (B) *Never* is an adverb modifying the verb in the past perfect, *had seen*. (C) *Identified* is the past tense form of the verb. (D) *Off the plane* is a prepositional phrase indicating direction.

142. (C) The subject of the sentence is *the shareholders*; therefore the pronoun *they* is redundant. (A) The preposition *for* introduces the phrase. (B) The adjective *uninterrupted* describes the noun *years*. (D) *Quarterly*, meaning *every three months*, is an adjective that describes the frequency of the checks.

143. (C) The superlative form, *best*, must follow the definite article in this sentence. (A) *We* is the subject of the sentence, followed by the past tense form of the verb, *tested*. (B) The past tense form of the verb, *seemed*, is followed by the infinitive. (D) *For our purposes* is a prepositional phrase.

144. (B) The past progressive requires the verb *to be*, in this case *were declining*. (A) The past tense form of the verb, *reported*, is used, followed by the relative pronoun, *that*. (C) *Before* is used as a conjunction to join the two clauses. (D) *Was reduced* is the passive voice.

145. (C) *Than* indicates a comparison and therefore *more* should precede *difficult*. (A) *Found* is the past tense form of *find*. (B) The preposition *at* indicates location. (D) The adjective *previous* indicates which *years*.

146. (A) The relative pronoun *that* introduces an effect clause and therefore *so* must be used in the cause clause. (B) *The employees* indicates who and is followed by the past tense form of the verb *to be*. (C) *Master* is the base form of the verb and follows *were able to*. (D) *A matter of days* indicates the time period.

147. (B) The infinitive is formed with *to* plus the base form of the verb *remind*; *reminding* on its own would also be possible. (A) *Was written* is the passive voice in the past tense. (C) *To bring* is the infinitive form, following the verb *remind*. (D) The *negotiating table* is a formal meeting to discuss wages, etc.

148. (D) The present tense is used to express future meaning after the preposition *before*; in this case the passive voice, *it is signed*, should be used. (A) The preposition *to* precedes the pronoun *me*. (B) The modal *would* is followed by the base form of the verb *to like*. (C) The infinitive form *to review* is used after *like*.

149. (C) The past participle form *are related to* should be used. (A) *Is being done* is the passive voice in the present continuous tense. (B) *How* introduces the noun clause; *the many* is part of the subject of the noun clause. (D) *They've* is the contraction for *they have* and forms the present perfect tense with *evolved*.

150. (D) A person is *interested in* something; a thing is *interesting*. (A) *As* is used as a preposition and precedes the object of the phrase *a sponsor*. (B) *Balcony* is used as an adjective to describe the location of the *tickets*. (C) *More* is used to qualify the adjectives *unusual* and *interesting*.

151. (B) The *safari*, is a trip, not a place, so *went on* is required. (A) The comparative form, *earlier*, is used to indicate a time frame. (C) The adjective, *exciting*, follows the verb *to be*. (D) *The least* is the superlative form and follows the infinitive *to say*.

152. (B) The passive voice is formed by the appropriate form of *to be* plus the past participle: *is required*. (A) *Generally* is an adverb indicating how often. (C) The modal, *can*, is followed by the base form of the verb. (D) *One* is a pronoun that refers back to *account*.

153. (B) *Glue* is a non-count noun and uses *much* not *many* as a modifier. (A) The gerund *understanding* is used along with the negative indicator, *not*. (C) *Applied* is the past tense form of the verb. (D) *Extraordinary* is an adjective describing *amount*.

154. (B) The past participle of *drive* is *driven; drove* is the simple past tense. (A) The adjective *noticeable* describes *decline*. (C) *To renovate* is the infinitive. (D) *Entire* is an adjective, describing the extent of *the downtown area*.

155. (D) When used as an adjective, the plural *-s* ending is not used: *twenty dollar bill*. (A) The conjunction *even though* begins the sentence and is followed by the subject, *we*, and the past tense verb, *asked*. (B) *Was* is the past tense form of the verb *to be*. (C) *Be able to* is followed by the base form, *cash*.

156. (A) The gerund, *understanding*, and not the past participle, *understood*, should follow the negative *not*. (B) *Involved* is describing *risks*: and is a reduced form of *that were involved*. (C) *Entire* is an adjective describing the amount of the *inheritance*. (D) An investment is made *in* the stock market.

157. (D) The preposition *about* should be used. (A) The verb *to try* is followed by the infinitive *to convince*. (B) *Had* is the past tense form of the verb. (C) *Certain* is an adjective, modifying *charm*.

158. (A) The gerund form *facing* is needed. (B) A person experiences *dissatisfaction with* something or someone. (C) *The legislative body* is the organization that passes laws. (D) *To formulate* is the infinitive.

159. (C) The conjunction *but*, not *then*, is needed. (A) *Not only* indicates that more than one thing will be mentioned. (B) *Them* is the object pronoun form of *they*. (D) *To give* is the infinitive form, which follows the verb *forget*.

160. (B) The verb *made* is in the past tense, therefore *forget* should also be in the past tense. (A) The preposition *despite* introduces the phrase. (C) *When* is used as a conjunction. (D) The preposition *for* is correct.

PART VII

161. (D) The first paragraph lists four categories for *the use of cattle in today's world*. (A) *The number of cattle in various countries* is not mentioned. (B) *The use of cattle in developed countries* is mentioned, but it is only part of the article. (C) Some of the uses mentioned involve *agriculture*, but not all.

162. (D) In *Ethiopia*, cattle help farmers by pulling plows and carts. (A) In *Sudan*, cattle are used as pack animals. (B) In *Oklahoma*, cattle are used in the rodeo. (C) In *Spain*, cattle are used in bullfights.

163. (A) The first sentence mentions *the materials needed for the upcoming deadline*. (B) Authors' materials are being collected, but they are not mentioned as being *invited to the conference*. (C) A *postponement* is not mentioned. (D) *Photo specifications* are mentioned, but they have not changed.

164. (C) The second paragraph says that *authors will send in their shots, which have to meet certain ... requirements*. (A) *Book covers* will be presented at the conference. (B) *Technical requirements*, not *technical terminology* is mentioned. (D) Authors will send their photos, not *come in to have their pictures taken*.

165. (C) New authors often send in photos that *don't meet certain specifications.* (A) The photos are *perfectly good*, but they do not meet the technical requirements. (B) The specifications for the photos (such as *black and white*) are not mentioned. (D) *The length of time* is not mentioned.

166. (D) The agreement came about because of *a ban on all wood exports from Vietnam.* (A) Only part of the *capital is available now*, the rest will be raised over five years. (B) The period to raise the capital is *five years.* (C) *Relations between the companies* is not mentioned.

167. (B) There is a ban on exports from *Vietnam.* (A) One of the companies is from *Myanmar.* (C) One of the companies is from *Laos.* (D) The third company is from *Malaysia.*

168. (C) *Timber Master* will contribute 65%. (A) *The May Flower Trading Company* will contribute the balance, or 35%. (B) There is no mention that *the Kuala Lumpur government* will contribute money. (D) *Laos Lumber* is one of the participating companies.

169. (B) *Manufacturing* or *production* will be transferred to Mexico. (A) and (C) *Research and development* and *administration* take place in Edinburgh. (D) *A joint venture* is being considered with Germany.

170. (D) The last sentence of the first paragraph mentions *... reasons for reducing operating costs.* (A) There is no mention that the *old factory was run down.* (B) *The Edinburgh factory* is being used as an administrative headquarters and for research and development. (C) *Research and development* is in Edinburgh.

171. (A) The first sentence indicates that the purpose is *to confirm ... and to thank you.* (B) Ramona invited Winfried to *take part in the Pusan Project.* (C) The ideas for the *ad campaign* will be discussed at the meeting. (D) *An Intex 5000* was purchased, but it is not the purpose of the letter.

172. (C) A *marketing executive* deals with ad campaigns and sales. (A) There is no indication that Winfried is *an office manager.* (B) A computer was purchased, but Winfried is not a *technician.* (D) There is no mention of an embassy or an *ambassador.*

173. (D) The writer proposes meeting in *London.* (A) Winfried will be in *East Grinstead*, but suggests having the meeting in London. (B) Ramona is located in *Bristol.* (C) The ad campaign is in *Brunei.*

174. (C) Julie's experience with ads will be helpful for *the Pusan Project.* (A) *She could advise* on ads, not on *the Intex 5000 Computer.* (B) There is no mention that Julie is *familiar with the competitors.* (D) There is no mention that Julie *could work out the travel itinerary.*

175. (D) The topic of the meeting was suggestion boxes, which represent *a new system.* (A) There was *a meeting* but it is not the topic of the report. (B) *Better morale* will be a result of the new system. (C) *Production* is not mentioned.

176. (A) The report says that *... employee's suggestions would not only save money ...* (B) *Complaints* are not mentioned. (C) Department heads will be involved in the new system, so it will not *take some of the burden off them.* (D) The *finance department* will approve the suggestions.

177. (C) *Forms for the suggestions are to be kept inside the box.* (A) Forms will be passed on to *department heads.* (B) Department heads will pass on suggestions to *the plant manager.* (D) *The director of finance* is not mentioned.

178. (D) The plant manager, when necessary, will gather or *compile data.* (A) The plant manager may review some, not all, *suggestions with the employees (where necessary).* (B) There is no mention of who will issue the *bonus check.* (C) Not all suggestions *will be routed through the finance department.*

179. (D) Employees should *clearly state which situation they are trying to improve ...* (A) *Troublesome coworkers* are not mentioned. (B) *The duration of the problem* might be included if it is pertinent. (C) *The bonus* is commensurate with the savings to the company.

180. (B) The latest, *state-of-the-art equipment* will be installed. (A) *Water is getting polluted* in the river. (C) *A dam* is not mentioned. (D) *An alarm system* is not mentioned.

181. (C) The *color* of the water will be rust. (A) During the entire period, *water pressure* will be diminished. (B) The water will be *rusty in color not in taste.* (D) There is no mention of smell, or *odor.*

182. (A) The Yushu Water Department is *issuing brochures explaining the process.* (B) There is no mention that anyone is *working overtime.* (C) The water will remain *potable.* (D) There is no mention of any *tours.*

183. (D) *Runners at any ability level are encouraged to join.* (A) The run is for *Alzheimer's.* (B) Participants will *raise money for the cause.* (C) *A T-shirt* is given to all participants.

184. (A) Runners and walkers collect *pledges*, or *ask people to promise donations.* (B) *$25* is not mentioned. (C) Participants receive *T-shirts.* (D) The funds will go to *the Alzheimer's Foundation.*

185. (B) Children under 12 can register for only *$5.* (A) No one pays *$0.* (C) Early registration is *$15.* (D) After December 1, registration is *$20.*

186. (B) Registration includes a *one-of-a-kind T-shirt.* (A) They receive a running pack, not *running gear.* (C) The money is used for *research for Alzheimer's.* (D) *Enrollment in the Alzheimer's Foundation* is not mentioned.

187. (D) A *full refund on all unmailed issues* is given if you cancel. (A) The *trial issue* is yours, no matter what you decide. (B) There is no mention of returning *unwanted issues.* (C) There is no mention of whether you *will receive air mails* if you cancel.

188. (A) A trial issue would be intended for *first-time* *subscribers.* (B) Air miles are mentioned, but not *pilots.* (C) *Lawyers* are not mentioned. (D) *Credit card users* may subscribe, but they are not the only group.

189. (A) The 1000 air miles will be credited *upon receipt of full payment.* (B) You have to *accept the trial issue*, but you must also pay. (C) A *new subscriber* who pays in full will receive the air miles. (D) There is no mention of a *subscription renewal.*

190. (B) The person arrives in Hawaii on 3/11 and leaves on 3/13. (A) According to the itinerary, the person does not spend *one night* anywhere. (C) The person spends *four nights* in Hong Kong. (D) According to the itinerary, the person does not spend *six nights* anywhere.

191. (A) The person starts in *Atlanta.* (B) The person travels from Atlanta to *L.A.* (C) The person travels to *Hawaii* after L.A. (D) The person's final stop is in *Hong Kong.*

192. (B) The first part of his trip is by *rail.* (A) He uses a *limousine service* in Hong Kong; however, he takes the train in Atlanta. (C) He arrives at all of his destinations in the afternoon. (D) The class is not indicated.

193. (C) The questions in the memo concern *hiring practices.* (A) There is no mention of a *wage increase.* (B) He indicates what he has asked *Judy to do*; but that is not why he sent the memo. (D) The *working conditions* are comparable to those elsewhere in the industry.

194. (A) *Personnel turnover* indicates that employees do not stay for very long. (B) Their *pay* is comparable to competitors. (C) *Overtime* is not mentioned. (D) They have looked into *working conditions*, but there is no indication that employees are *dissatisfied.*

195. (A) John Rankine thinks they may *be hiring the wrong people.* (B), (C) and (D). These business practices were not mentioned as reasons a worker would leave the company.

196. (B) Shirley is concerned with *personnel turnover*, or *employees quitting.* (A) *Wages*, since they are comparable with the competition, should not be her concern. (C) The memo does not indicate that the *competition* is her concern. (D) The memo does not mention *promotions.*

197. (B) The first sentence indicates the main idea is *who owns Antarctica.* (A) Some *conditions* are mentioned, but they do not represent the main idea. (C) More than *seven nations* are mentioned, but not *the ownership settlements.* (D) *The South Pole* is not mentioned.

198. (A) The third paragraph states that ... *it is possible that Polynesian navigators reached Antarctica earlier.* (B) and (C) *An American* and *a Russian were the first to actually reach the mainland.* (D) Cook's was the first recorded approach, but ... *it is possible that Polynesian navigators reached Antarctica earlier.*

199. (D) The Russian and an American were the first to *land on the mainland itself.* (A) There was no *native population in Antarctica.* (B) The important factor is not *that the Russian and the American traveled together*, rather that they were the first to reach the mainland. (C) There is *mineral wealth*, but there is no indication that the Russian found it.

200. (D) Nations cannot exploit *the fossil fuels and minerals.* (A) There was never a *native population.* (B) *10% of the earth's entire land surface is in Antarctica*, but there is no indication that the *land is arable.* (C) A *whale population* is not mentioned.

Answer Sheets

Answer Sheet Practice Test 1

Listening Comprehension

Part I

	A	B	C	D
1	A	B	C	D
2	A	B	C	D
3	A	B	C	D
4	A	B	C	D
5	A	B	C	D
6	A	B	C	D
7	A	B	C	D
8	A	B	C	D
9	A	B	C	D
10	A	B	C	D
11	A	B	C	D
12	A	B	C	D
13	A	B	C	D
14	A	B	C	D
15	A	B	C	D
16	A	B	C	D
17	A	B	C	D
18	A	B	C	D
19	A	B	C	D
20	A	B	C	D

Part II

	A	B	C
21	A	B	C
22	A	B	C
23	A	B	C
24	A	B	C
25	A	B	C
26	A	B	C
27	A	B	C
28	A	B	C
29	A	B	C
30	A	B	C
31	A	B	C
32	A	B	C
33	A	B	C
34	A	B	C
35	A	B	C
36	A	B	C
37	A	B	C
38	A	B	C
39	A	B	C
40	A	B	C
41	A	B	C
42	A	B	C
43	A	B	C
44	A	B	C
45	A	B	C
46	A	B	C
47	A	B	C
48	A	B	C
49	A	B	C
50	A	B	C

Part III

	A	B	C	D
51	A	B	C	D
52	A	B	C	D
53	A	B	C	D
54	A	B	C	D
55	A	B	C	D
56	A	B	C	D
57	A	B	C	D
58	A	B	C	D
59	A	B	C	D
60	A	B	C	D
61	A	B	C	D
62	A	B	C	D
63	A	B	C	D
64	A	B	C	D
65	A	B	C	D
66	A	B	C	D
67	A	B	C	D
68	A	B	C	D
69	A	B	C	D
70	A	B	C	D
71	A	B	C	D
72	A	B	C	D
73	A	B	C	D
74	A	B	C	D
75	A	B	C	D
76	A	B	C	D
77	A	B	C	D
78	A	B	C	D
79	A	B	C	D
80	A	B	C	D

Part IV

	A	B	C	D
81	A	B	C	D
82	A	B	C	D
83	A	B	C	D
84	A	B	C	D
85	A	B	C	D
86	A	B	C	D
87	A	B	C	D
88	A	B	C	D
89	A	B	C	D
90	A	B	C	D
91	A	B	C	D
92	A	B	C	D
93	A	B	C	D
94	A	B	C	D
95	A	B	C	D
96	A	B	C	D
97	A	B	C	D
98	A	B	C	D
99	A	B	C	D
100	A	B	C	D

Reading

Part V

101	A	B	C	D	121	A	B	C	D
102	A	B	C	D	122	A	B	C	D
103	A	B	C	D	123	A	B	C	D
104	A	B	C	D	124	A	B	C	D
105	A	B	C	D	125	A	B	C	D
106	A	B	C	D	126	A	B	C	D
107	A	B	C	D	127	A	B	C	D
108	A	B	C	D	128	A	B	C	D
109	A	B	C	D	129	A	B	C	D
110	A	B	C	D	130	A	B	C	D
111	A	B	C	D	131	A	B	C	D
112	A	B	C	D	132	A	B	C	D
113	A	B	C	D	133	A	B	C	D
114	A	B	C	D	134	A	B	C	D
115	A	B	C	D	135	A	B	C	D
116	A	B	C	D	136	A	B	C	D
117	A	B	C	D	137	A	B	C	D
118	A	B	C	D	138	A	B	C	D
119	A	B	C	D	139	A	B	C	D
120	A	B	C	D	140	A	B	C	D

Part VI

	A	B	C	D
141	A	B	C	D
142	A	B	C	D
143	A	B	C	D
144	A	B	C	D
145	A	B	C	D
146	A	B	C	D
147	A	B	C	D
148	A	B	C	D
149	A	B	C	D
150	A	B	C	D
151	A	B	C	D
152	A	B	C	D
153	A	B	C	D
154	A	B	C	D
155	A	B	C	D
156	A	B	C	D
157	A	B	C	D
158	A	B	C	D
159	A	B	C	D
160	A	B	C	D

Part VII

	A	B	C	D		A	B	C	D
161	A	B	C	D	181	A	B	C	D
162	A	B	C	D	182	A	B	C	D
163	A	B	C	D	183	A	B	C	D
164	A	B	C	D	184	A	B	C	D
165	A	B	C	D	185	A	B	C	D
166	A	B	C	D	186	A	B	C	D
167	A	B	C	D	187	A	B	C	D
168	A	B	C	D	188	A	B	C	D
169	A	B	C	D	189	A	B	C	D
170	A	B	C	D	190	A	B	C	D
171	A	B	C	D	191	A	B	C	D
172	A	B	C	D	192	A	B	C	D
173	A	B	C	D	193	A	B	C	D
174	A	B	C	D	194	A	B	C	D
175	A	B	C	D	195	A	B	C	D
176	A	B	C	D	196	A	B	C	D
177	A	B	C	D	197	A	B	C	D
178	A	B	C	D	198	A	B	C	D
179	A	B	C	D	199	A	B	C	D
180	A	B	C	D	200	A	B	C	D

Answer Sheet Practice Test 2

Listening Comprehension

Part I

1	A	B	C	D
2	A	B	C	D
3	A	B	C	D
4	A	B	C	D
5	A	B	C	D
6	A	B	C	D
7	A	B	C	D
8	A	B	C	D
9	A	B	C	D
10	A	B	C	D
11	A	B	C	D
12	A	B	C	D
13	A	B	C	D
14	A	B	C	D
15	A	B	C	D
16	A	B	C	D
17	A	B	C	D
18	A	B	C	D
19	A	B	C	D
20	A	B	C	D

Part II

21	A	B	C
22	A	B	C
23	A	B	C
24	A	B	C
25	A	B	C
26	A	B	C
27	A	B	C
28	A	B	C
29	A	B	C
30	A	B	C
31	A	B	C
32	A	B	C
33	A	B	C
34	A	B	C
35	A	B	C
36	A	B	C
37	A	B	C
38	A	B	C
39	A	B	C
40	A	B	C
41	A	B	C
42	A	B	C
43	A	B	C
44	A	B	C
45	A	B	C
46	A	B	C
47	A	B	C
48	A	B	C
49	A	B	C
50	A	B	C

Part III

51	A	B	C	D
52	A	B	C	D
53	A	B	C	D
54	A	B	C	D
55	A	B	C	D
56	A	B	C	D
57	A	B	C	D
58	A	B	C	D
59	A	B	C	D
60	A	B	C	D
61	A	B	C	D
62	A	B	C	D
63	A	B	C	D
64	A	B	C	D
65	A	B	C	D
66	A	B	C	D
67	A	B	C	D
68	A	B	C	D
69	A	B	C	D
70	A	B	C	D
71	A	B	C	D
72	A	B	C	D
73	A	B	C	D
74	A	B	C	D
75	A	B	C	D
76	A	B	C	D
77	A	B	C	D
78	A	B	C	D
79	A	B	C	D
80	A	B	C	D

Part IV

81	A	B	C	D
82	A	B	C	D
83	A	B	C	D
84	A	B	C	D
85	A	B	C	D
86	A	B	C	D
87	A	B	C	D
88	A	B	C	D
89	A	B	C	D
90	A	B	C	D
91	A	B	C	D
92	A	B	C	D
93	A	B	C	D
94	A	B	C	D
95	A	B	C	D
96	A	B	C	D
97	A	B	C	D
98	A	B	C	D
99	A	B	C	D
100	A	B	C	D

Reading

Part V

101	A	B	C	D	121	A	B	C	D
102	A	B	C	D	122	A	B	C	D
103	A	B	C	D	123	A	B	C	D
104	A	B	C	D	124	A	B	C	D
105	A	B	C	D	125	A	B	C	D
106	A	B	C	D	126	A	B	C	D
107	A	B	C	D	127	A	B	C	D
108	A	B	C	D	128	A	B	C	D
109	A	B	C	D	129	A	B	C	D
110	A	B	C	D	130	A	B	C	D
111	A	B	C	D	131	A	B	C	D
112	A	B	C	D	132	A	B	C	D
113	A	B	C	D	133	A	B	C	D
114	A	B	C	D	134	A	B	C	D
115	A	B	C	D	135	A	B	C	D
116	A	B	C	D	136	A	B	C	D
117	A	B	C	D	137	A	B	C	D
118	A	B	C	D	138	A	B	C	D
119	A	B	C	D	139	A	B	C	D
120	A	B	C	D	140	A	B	C	D

Part VI

141	A	B	C	D
142	A	B	C	D
143	A	B	C	D
144	A	B	C	D
145	A	B	C	D
146	A	B	C	D
147	A	B	C	D
148	A	B	C	D
149	A	B	C	D
150	A	B	C	D
151	A	B	C	D
152	A	B	C	D
153	A	B	C	D
154	A	B	C	D
155	A	B	C	D
156	A	B	C	D
157	A	B	C	D
158	A	B	C	D
159	A	B	C	D
160	A	B	C	D

Part VII

161	A	B	C	D	181	A	B	C	D
162	A	B	C	D	182	A	B	C	D
163	A	B	C	D	183	A	B	C	D
164	A	B	C	D	184	A	B	C	D
165	A	B	C	D	185	A	B	C	D
166	A	B	C	D	186	A	B	C	D
167	A	B	C	D	187	A	B	C	D
168	A	B	C	D	188	A	B	C	D
169	A	B	C	D	189	A	B	C	D
170	A	B	C	D	190	A	B	C	D
171	A	B	C	D	191	A	B	C	D
172	A	B	C	D	192	A	B	C	D
173	A	B	C	D	193	A	B	C	D
174	A	B	C	D	194	A	B	C	D
175	A	B	C	D	195	A	B	C	D
176	A	B	C	D	196	A	B	C	D
177	A	B	C	D	197	A	B	C	D
178	A	B	C	D	198	A	B	C	D
179	A	B	C	D	199	A	B	C	D
180	A	B	C	D	200	A	B	C	D

Answer Sheet Practice Test 3

Listening Comprehension

Part I				
1	A	B	C	D
2	A	B	C	D
3	A	B	C	D
4	A	B	C	D
5	A	B	C	D
6	A	B	C	D
7	A	B	C	D
8	A	B	C	D
9	A	B	C	D
10	A	B	C	D
11	A	B	C	D
12	A	B	C	D
13	A	B	C	D
14	A	B	C	D
15	A	B	C	D
16	A	B	C	D
17	A	B	C	D
18	A	B	C	D
19	A	B	C	D
20	A	B	C	D

Part II			
21	A	B	C
22	A	B	C
23	A	B	C
24	A	B	C
25	A	B	C
26	A	B	C
27	A	B	C
28	A	B	C
29	A	B	C
30	A	B	C
31	A	B	C
32	A	B	C
33	A	B	C
34	A	B	C
35	A	B	C
36	A	B	C
37	A	B	C
38	A	B	C
39	A	B	C
40	A	B	C
41	A	B	C
42	A	B	C
43	A	B	C
44	A	B	C
45	A	B	C
46	A	B	C
47	A	B	C
48	A	B	C
49	A	B	C
50	A	B	C

Part III				
51	A	B	C	D
52	A	B	C	D
53	A	B	C	D
54	A	B	C	D
55	A	B	C	D
56	A	B	C	D
57	A	B	C	D
58	A	B	C	D
59	A	B	C	D
60	A	B	C	D
61	A	B	C	D
62	A	B	C	D
63	A	B	C	D
64	A	B	C	D
65	A	B	C	D
66	A	B	C	D
67	A	B	C	D
68	A	B	C	D
69	A	B	C	D
70	A	B	C	D
71	A	B	C	D
72	A	B	C	D
73	A	B	C	D
74	A	B	C	D
75	A	B	C	D
76	A	B	C	D
77	A	B	C	D
78	A	B	C	D
79	A	B	C	D
80	A	B	C	D

Part IV				
81	A	B	C	D
82	A	B	C	D
83	A	B	C	D
84	A	B	C	D
85	A	B	C	D
86	A	B	C	D
87	A	B	C	D
88	A	B	C	D
89	A	B	C	D
90	A	B	C	D
91	A	B	C	D
92	A	B	C	D
93	A	B	C	D
94	A	B	C	D
95	A	B	C	D
96	A	B	C	D
97	A	B	C	D
98	A	B	C	D
99	A	B	C	D
100	A	B	C	D

Reading

Part V									
101	A	B	C	D	121	A	B	C	D
102	A	B	C	D	122	A	B	C	D
103	A	B	C	D	123	A	B	C	D
104	A	B	C	D	124	A	B	C	D
105	A	B	C	D	125	A	B	C	D
106	A	B	C	D	126	A	B	C	D
107	A	B	C	D	127	A	B	C	D
108	A	B	C	D	128	A	B	C	D
109	A	B	C	D	129	A	B	C	D
110	A	B	C	D	130	A	B	C	D
111	A	B	C	D	131	A	B	C	D
112	A	B	C	D	132	A	B	C	D
113	A	B	C	D	133	A	B	C	D
114	A	B	C	D	134	A	B	C	D
115	A	B	C	D	135	A	B	C	D
116	A	B	C	D	136	A	B	C	D
117	A	B	C	D	137	A	B	C	D
118	A	B	C	D	138	A	B	C	D
119	A	B	C	D	139	A	B	C	D
120	A	B	C	D	140	A	B	C	D

Part VI				
141	A	B	C	D
142	A	B	C	D
143	A	B	C	D
144	A	B	C	D
145	A	B	C	D
146	A	B	C	D
147	A	B	C	D
148	A	B	C	D
149	A	B	C	D
150	A	B	C	D
151	A	B	C	D
152	A	B	C	D
153	A	B	C	D
154	A	B	C	D
155	A	B	C	D
156	A	B	C	D
157	A	B	C	D
158	A	B	C	D
159	A	B	C	D
160	A	B	C	D

Part VII									
161	A	B	C	D	181	A	B	C	D
162	A	B	C	D	182	A	B	C	D
163	A	B	C	D	183	A	B	C	D
164	A	B	C	D	184	A	B	C	D
165	A	B	C	D	185	A	B	C	D
166	A	B	C	D	186	A	B	C	D
167	A	B	C	D	187	A	B	C	D
168	A	B	C	D	188	A	B	C	D
169	A	B	C	D	189	A	B	C	D
170	A	B	C	D	190	A	B	C	D
171	A	B	C	D	191	A	B	C	D
172	A	B	C	D	192	A	B	C	D
173	A	B	C	D	193	A	B	C	D
174	A	B	C	D	194	A	B	C	D
175	A	B	C	D	195	A	B	C	D
176	A	B	C	D	196	A	B	C	D
177	A	B	C	D	197	A	B	C	D
178	A	B	C	D	198	A	B	C	D
179	A	B	C	D	199	A	B	C	D
180	A	B	C	D	200	A	B	C	D

Answer Sheet Practice Test 4

Listening Comprehension

Part I

1	A	B	C	D
2	A	B	C	D
3	A	B	C	D
4	A	B	C	D
5	A	B	C	D
6	A	B	C	D
7	A	B	C	D
8	A	B	C	D
9	A	B	C	D
10	A	B	C	D
11	A	B	C	D
12	A	B	C	D
13	A	B	C	D
14	A	B	C	D
15	A	B	C	D
16	A	B	C	D
17	A	B	C	D
18	A	B	C	D
19	A	B	C	D
20	A	B	C	D

Part II

21	A	B	C
22	A	B	C
23	A	B	C
24	A	B	C
25	A	B	C
26	A	B	C
27	A	B	C
28	A	B	C
29	A	B	C
30	A	B	C
31	A	B	C
32	A	B	C
33	A	B	C
34	A	B	C
35	A	B	C
36	A	B	C
37	A	B	C
38	A	B	C
39	A	B	C
40	A	B	C
41	A	B	C
42	A	B	C
43	A	B	C
44	A	B	C
45	A	B	C
46	A	B	C
47	A	B	C
48	A	B	C
49	A	B	C
50	A	B	C

Part III

51	A	B	C	D
52	A	B	C	D
53	A	B	C	D
54	A	B	C	D
55	A	B	C	D
56	A	B	C	D
57	A	B	C	D
58	A	B	C	D
59	A	B	C	D
60	A	B	C	D
61	A	B	C	D
62	A	B	C	D
63	A	B	C	D
64	A	B	C	D
65	A	B	C	D
66	A	B	C	D
67	A	B	C	D
68	A	B	C	D
69	A	B	C	D
70	A	B	C	D
71	A	B	C	D
72	A	B	C	D
73	A	B	C	D
74	A	B	C	D
75	A	B	C	D
76	A	B	C	D
77	A	B	C	D
78	A	B	C	D
79	A	B	C	D
80	A	B	C	D

Part IV

81	A	B	C	D
82	A	B	C	D
83	A	B	C	D
84	A	B	C	D
85	A	B	C	D
86	A	B	C	D
87	A	B	C	D
88	A	B	C	D
89	A	B	C	D
90	A	B	C	D
91	A	B	C	D
92	A	B	C	D
93	A	B	C	D
94	A	B	C	D
95	A	B	C	D
96	A	B	C	D
97	A	B	C	D
98	A	B	C	D
99	A	B	C	D
100	A	B	C	D

Reading

Part V

101	A	B	C	D	121	A	B	C	D
102	A	B	C	D	122	A	B	C	D
103	A	B	C	D	123	A	B	C	D
104	A	B	C	D	124	A	B	C	D
105	A	B	C	D	125	A	B	C	D
106	A	B	C	D	126	A	B	C	D
107	A	B	C	D	127	A	B	C	D
108	A	B	C	D	128	A	B	C	D
109	A	B	C	D	129	A	B	C	D
110	A	B	C	D	130	A	B	C	D
111	A	B	C	D	131	A	B	C	D
112	A	B	C	D	132	A	B	C	D
113	A	B	C	D	133	A	B	C	D
114	A	B	C	D	134	A	B	C	D
115	A	B	C	D	135	A	B	C	D
116	A	B	C	D	136	A	B	C	D
117	A	B	C	D	137	A	B	C	D
118	A	B	C	D	138	A	B	C	D
119	A	B	C	D	139	A	B	C	D
120	A	B	C	D	140	A	B	C	D

Part VI

141	A	B	C	D
142	A	B	C	D
143	A	B	C	D
144	A	B	C	D
145	A	B	C	D
146	A	B	C	D
147	A	B	C	D
148	A	B	C	D
149	A	B	C	D
150	A	B	C	D
151	A	B	C	D
152	A	B	C	D
153	A	B	C	D
154	A	B	C	D
155	A	B	C	D
156	A	B	C	D
157	A	B	C	D
158	A	B	C	D
159	A	B	C	D
160	A	B	C	D

Part VII

161	A	B	C	D	181	A	B	C	D
162	A	B	C	D	182	A	B	C	D
163	A	B	C	D	183	A	B	C	D
164	A	B	C	D	184	A	B	C	D
165	A	B	C	D	185	A	B	C	D
166	A	B	C	D	186	A	B	C	D
167	A	B	C	D	187	A	B	C	D
168	A	B	C	D	188	A	B	C	D
169	A	B	C	D	189	A	B	C	D
170	A	B	C	D	190	A	B	C	D
171	A	B	C	D	191	A	B	C	D
172	A	B	C	D	192	A	B	C	D
173	A	B	C	D	193	A	B	C	D
174	A	B	C	D	194	A	B	C	D
175	A	B	C	D	195	A	B	C	D
176	A	B	C	D	196	A	B	C	D
177	A	B	C	D	197	A	B	C	D
178	A	B	C	D	198	A	B	C	D
179	A	B	C	D	199	A	B	C	D
180	A	B	C	D	200	A	B	C	D